ENTREPRENEURIAL
MANAGEMENT

Other books in The McGraw-Hill Executive MBA Series:

FINANCE AND ACCOUNTING FOR NONFINANCIAL MANAGERS
  by Samuel C. Weaver and J. Fred Weston
CORPORATE STRATEGY
  by John L. Colley, Jr., Jacqueline L. Doyle, and Robert D. Hardie
MANAGERIAL LEADERSHIP
  by Peter A. Topping
MERGERS AND ACQUISITIONS
  by J. Fred Weston and Samuel C. Weaver
SALES MANAGEMENT
  by Robert J. Calvin
STRATEGIC MARKETING MANAGEMENT
  by Mark E. Parry

ENTREPRENEURIAL MANAGEMENT

THE McGRAW-HILL EXECUTIVE MBA SERIES

ROBERT J. CALVIN

McGraw-Hill

New York   San Francisco   Washington, D.C.   Auckland   Bogotá
Caracas   Lisbon   London   Madrid   Mexico City   Milan
Montreal   New Delhi   San Juan   Singapore
Sydney   Tokyo   Toronto

Library of Congress Cataloging-in-Publication Data

Calvin, Robert J.
    Entrepreneurial management / by Robert J. Calvin.
        p.cm.
    ISBN 0-07-138200-3
    1. New business enterprises—Management.   I. Title.
HD62.5.C345   2002
658.4'21—dc21   2001044982
                                         CIP

McGraw-Hill

A Division of The **McGraw·Hill** Companies

1 2 3 4 5 6 7 8 9 0   DOC/DOC   0 9 8 7 6 5 4 3 2

ISBN 0-07-138200-3

Printed and bound by R. R. Donnelley & Sons Company.

McGraw-Hill books are available at special discounts to use as premiums and sales Promotions, or for use in corporate training programs. For more information, please write to the Director of Special Sales, Professional Publishing, McGraw-Hill, Two Penn Plaza, New York, NY 10121-2298. Or contact your local bookstore.

This book was printed on recycled, acid-free paper containing a minimum of 50% recycled, de-inked fiber.

In memory of my father,
Joseph K. Calvin;
my mother,
Pauline H. Calvin;
and my daughter,
Amy E. Calvin

I would like to acknowledge with grateful thanks my wife Jane, for her patience; my daughter Susan, for her support; and my associate Lynne Sinton, for her suggestions. I am also grateful to my editor Kelli Christiansen, who functioned as intellectual partner for both of my McGraw-Hill Executive MBA Series books, *Entrepreneurial Management* and *Sales Management*.

CONTENTS

INTRODUCTION

THE PROVEN FORMULA
FOR SUCCESS

North America, Asia, and Western Europe have been undergoing an entrepreneurial renaissance. We are moving from being nations of managers to becoming nations of owners. Until 1990, bigger was better, but since 1990, smaller has been smarter. Until 1990, North America's economic engine of growth centered in the Fortune 1000 firms. Since 1990, the Fortune 1000 have been declining in total employment because of downsizing, right-sizing, and reengineering.

The Commerce Department and the Small Business Administration estimated that in the year 2000, two million U.S. firms employed more than 25 people, but only 15,000 companies employed over 500 people. Those firms employing fewer than 500 people accounted for 40 percent of the gross domestic product, 50 percent of the workforce, and over 50 percent of all new jobs. From 1990 to 2000, firms employing fewer than 500 people created 19 million new jobs, while firms employing over 500 people lost 3.7 million jobs.

The Small Business Administration defines a small business as any nonfarm enterprise with over $10,000 of annual income and under 500 employees. In addition to the two million firms employing 25 to 500 people, the SBA's Office of Advocacy estimates there are another four million firms employing under 25 people, and yet another 12 million self-employed individuals. There are more small business owners and managers than union members. These small businesses provide customers for, and are suppliers to, the 15,000 firms that employ over 500 people.

That is the good news. The bad news is that 60 percent of all new businesses fail within their first two years and 70 percent fail within the first five years of their existence. Of those that continue, many remain in holding patterns, moving sideways, trapping their founder's investments and careers. In the year 2000 the Commerce Department reported that one million new employer firms were formed.

1

This book contains the knowledge, information, and lessons to make you not only one of the 30 to 40 percent who survive but one of the even smaller percentage who succeed. Defining entrepreneurial success depends on your expectations and goals. This book attempts to bridge the old and new economy with a proven strategic and tactical formula for entrepreneurial success.

This book contains the quantitative and qualitative knowledge, concepts, approaches, strategy, tactics, and philosophy to increase the entrepreneur's probability of success and reduce the risk of failure. Many entrepreneurs understand these issues but still fail, or don't reach their full potential, because they can't implement and execute their plan. Successful entrepreneurs must be able to translate their ideas into action.

ENTREPRENEURIAL REWARDS AND RISKS

Being an entrepreneur or small business manager satisfies our personal needs for freedom, flexibility, variety, creativity, responsibility, control, and authority. The entrepreneur can reap the fruits of his or her labor. Moreover, entrepreneurial ventures have many rewards for all employees, not just the entrepreneur. Start-ups, early-stage, and growth-stage firms have many advantages compared to working for larger companies. Generally, larger businesses are more oppressive, more political, have more organizational levels, and lack personal freedom. Employees don't control their destiny or see the fruits of their labor, because most decisions are made by groups. In an entrepreneurial situation the employee has number-one billing, not the organization.

Entrepreneurial opportunities represent a wish list of what most people want in a career. However, as noted, although the advantages and rewards are high, so are the risks. This book contains the quantitative and qualitative knowledge, concepts, approaches, strategy, tactics, and philosophy to allow you to reap the advantages and avoid the disadvantages, by reducing the risks.

If the approach in this book sometimes sounds pessimistic it is only to bring a touch of reality to the very seductive and addictive goal of being an entrepreneur.

STRENGTHS AND WEAKNESSES OF ENTREPRENEURIAL VENTURES

Entrepreneurs often complain about the new enterprise's weaknesses rather than leverage its strengths. For a new venture to succeed it must either have a competitive advantage in operational excellence, like

AOL or Dell; new product or service innovation, such as Cisco or Intel have; or customer intimacy, as does Southwest Airlines. To achieve these competitive advantages requires the entrepreneur to leverage a new enterprise's strengths in speed, size, flexibility, personal service, information technology, and "first- or last-mover advantage." Entrepreneurs must also understand how to compensate for a new enterprise's weaknesses or critical risks, such as limited human and financial resources and lack of diversification.

Speed allows smaller businesses to make decisions quickly and take action sooner than their larger competitors. Smaller firms don't have the organizational layers of bureaucracy to navigate when introducing new products or changing customer policies or internal procedures. Larger firms resemble elephants, with an overabundance of strategy. Smaller entrepreneurial enterprises resemble gazelles, with the emphasis on tactics and speedy implementation. To capitalize on this advantage, entrepreneurs need to create horizontal organizations and empower people at all levels to make appropriate decisions.

Size allows entrepreneurs to profitably target market segments, niches, too small for larger competitors. A smaller business can create positive cash flow; earnings before interest, taxes, depreciation, and amortization (EBITDA); as well as pretax margins and earnings before income taxes (EBIT), with revenues equal to 10 percent of a 10-million-dollar market. Larger firms need economies of scale. A larger, more established business with greater fixed costs could not be cash-flow positive in such a small market. Such a business would require 10 percent of a hundred-million-dollar market.

Flexibility allows entrepreneurial firms to better serve the customer by customizing products and services to reflect different market segment needs. Customized personal service creates customer intimacy, which becomes a competitive advantage. A smaller firm can customize products and services to better meet customer needs, such as private labels for retailers, longer store hours on weekends for consumers, less expensive Internet routers for midsized telephone companies, or forming customer or user groups. An entrepreneurial enterprise must understand and leverage these core competencies.

Part of the entrepreneur's strategy should involve both using information technology to level the playing field and possibly realizing a last-mover advantage. Information technology (IT) has become the great equalizer between smaller and larger businesses. Smaller entrepreneurial firms must budget for the newest hardware and software in accounting, human resources, operations, supply chain management, customer relationship management, and sales management. As costs decrease and capacity increases, information technology and communication networks allow smaller firms to act like larger ones, meet customer demands for information and service, and lower human resource costs.

Whether you manufacture sweaters, distribute imported gift-ware, provide cost-reduction software to hospitals, or have a business-to-business e-commerce exchange for packaging materials, you can learn from your predecessors' successes and failures. Who are the competitive leaders in your market segment and industry and why? Did previous companies fail because of poor quality, improper location, lack of reliable suppliers, a weak sales organization, inoperable technology, or long, complex sales cycles? First-movers have the advantage of more brand recognition, critical mass, and larger customer bases. Last-movers have the advantage of more current technology, which is often better and less costly; an existing, more established market, which is less expensive to reach; and knowledge of who and what has previously succeeded or failed. Many entrepreneurs complain about not being a first-mover, but fail to realize there is a last-mover advantage. Siebel did not invent sales force automation or customer relationship management. Many firms that preceded it failed in the early 1990s. However, Siebel implemented its later-mover advantage to capture over 50 percent of the customer relationship management market by 2000. Siebel understood the entrepreneurial proven formula for success.

Entrepreneurs must also understand how to compensate for a new enterprise's weaknesses or critical risks, such as limited human and financial resources and lack of product, service, or customer diversification. Limited human resources means that most small business managers wear many hats. For example, the controller also manages the office and supervises information technology; the sales manager also supervises marketing, advertising, and new-product development; the operations manager also supervises research and development.

The candidate profile for hiring a new enterprise manager should reflect experience, skills, knowledge, and personal characteristics that allow him or her to work in more than one function. Once hired, these managers require cross-training in other related functions they will supervise. Some entrepreneurial firms have managers periodically rotate positions. For example, the controller and sales manager might switch positions the last Friday of each month.

Limited human resources often make succession planning difficult, if not impossible. Successful entrepreneurs create plans for replacing key managers who leave or become ill. Who else in the organization can do each manager's job? Where, outside the organization, would you look for a replacement?

Entrepreneurs must also understand that limited financial resources means that a major bad debt, bad hire, bad lease, or weak product introduction could put the new firm in financial distress. Credit, recruitment, leases, and the introduction of new products or services involve necessary risks. Entrepreneurs must match these risks to their resources. For example, carefully monitoring of all accounts receivable over a certain dollar amount ($25,000) and/or over a certain aging period (60 days) helps to limit these credit risks.

To compensate for both limited human and financial resources, you should sequence hiring, rather than rush it. Don't hire more than one person at a time. Have some confirmation on the success of the last hire before you recruit the next manager. Using proper hiring techniques will lower the risk of a bad hire and increase the probability of recruiting the best person. Even in a five-person entrepreneurial start up, proper hiring techniques require everyone to have a job description (a list of anticipated duties), every position to have a candidate profile (who we are looking for), and every candidate to undergo reference checks and probing interview questions.

Lack of diversification creates another entrepreneurial risk. Most entrepreneurial early-stage enterprises depend heavily on a few products and a limited number of customers. The loss of a major customer, the failure of a product or service, and changes in the market dynamics and competitive landscape can quickly lead to financial distress. Entrepreneurs should search for ways to diversify the income stream, such as distributing another firm's products or services or using channel partners to represent their firm in related markets. Entrepreneurs need to focus their limited resources, but they also need a strategy to balance this by creating some diversification.

An investment research firm in Chicago publishes and hand delivers a daily hard copy newsletter for Treasury bond traders on the futures exchange. By 1995 this niche had created a very profitable million-dollar business. But in the late 1990s the exchange went from floor trading to electronic trading, and because of reduced Treasury bond offerings, volume declined dramatically. The research firm's subscription income dropped by half.

In the year 2000 this investment research firm explored starting a similar letter for the Financial Times Stock Exchange in London, offering a commodities trading investment letter in Chicago, doing private-label investment publications for large brokerage firms, offering their T-bond letter on-line, and hiring a salesperson. However, the owners can't decide where to focus or diversify, what strategy is most important, and feel locked in to their present products and markets by legacy issues related to their computers and software. This firm represents an example of the need to manage today but think about tomorrow. It represents an example of the small business dilemma between diversification and focus and the need to make decisions and take action.

FOCUSING RESOURCES AND CUSTOMIZING THE OFFERING

Successful entrepreneurs understand the importance of targeting, differentiation, and market segmentation. Chapter 4 deals in detail with differentiation, segmentation, targeting, and customizing the offering. The proven formula for success starts with targeting customers and market segments, which forces early-stage firms to customize products or services to the customers' and segments' needs and thus to differentiate themselves. Without clearly differentiating the offering, entrepreneurs will not receive financing or market acceptance.

As stated, early-stage entrepreneurial enterprises have limited human and financial resources. Therefore, they cannot be all things to all people and survive commercially in the new millennium's global markets. Entrepreneurs must target customers and market segments where their firm has an easily definable, quantifiable competitive advantage. Once targeted, the ability to differentiate, to create customer switching costs and competitor barriers to entry, separate success from failure. Targeting creates a dilemma because of the new venture's dependence on only a few customers.

However, the proven formula for success and the marketing funnel begin with understanding how to accurately determine target customers, market segments, buying center issues, buyer behavior, and customer needs. Early-stage companies with clearly defined, easy-to-reach customers have a lower risk of failure. Because many entrepreneurs have developed and innovated the products or services being sold, they focus on the product or service, not the customer. Successful entrepreneurs realize their firms don't sell products or services but rather solve customer problems and meet customer needs with the quantifiable features and benefits of these products or services.

Targeting decisions are made early in a firm's history without much experience and evidence. Often the first 10 customers, or the first 5 repeat customers, who may arrive quite by chance, are thought to be the target. Entrepreneurs must continually test targeting decisions, admit mistakes, and take corrective action. Perpetuating this type of a mistake is wasteful, sometimes fatal.

Target customers, target markets, and market segments are determined by:

1. Dollars of present and potential revenue and income over time
2. The cost to sell and serve
3. The probability of success

Once market segments are identified, the key is customizing your offering for each segment. For a regional telco, government agencies might be most interested in privacy and security, large businesses in data transmission, and midsized firms in long-distance voice service. Once target customers are identified, you must organize your sales force to effectively and efficiently sell and service them. Chapter 4 discusses this subject further.

SUCCESSFULLY DEALING WITH CHANGE

Entrepreneurs are agents of change who take advantage of change, manage change, and change people's behavior. Entrepreneurs are innovators who see every problem as an opportunity. Change occurred quickly in the 1990s. In the new millennium, however, it will proceed at a blistering speed because of new products and technologies, and new competitors, customers, strategies, regulations, processes, and market shifts. Business is a dynamic process; the future, a moving target. Entrepreneurs organize and harvest this dynamic process, this moving target, and this changing landscape. Entrepreneurs who can continually "unlearn" the past, overcome legacy issues, anticipate and manage change (especially changes they have no control over), survive, and succeed. For example, entrepreneurs who can successfully navigate changing exchange rates, interest rates, power costs, government regulations, overseas competitors, inflation, natural disasters, and terrorist attacks have a higher probability of surviving and succeeding.

As start-ups, early-, and growth-stage firms mature, they encounter key inflection points, unanticipated changes from outside their company over which management has no control. For example, the price of random access memory semiconductors drops by half as exports flood domestic markets; demand for optical switching equipment drops by half as telecom funding for expansion dries up; energy costs double, significantly lowering a firm's margins; or people stop flying due to safety concerns. Entrepreneurs who can successfully manage these inevitable critical changes succeed and actually improve their market share.

Many new enterprises are formed to take advantage of change but then incorporate their own legacy issues, which prevent them from keeping up with change. Successful entrepreneurs create a culture that continually unlearns the past and reinvents the future. For example, AOL, Intel, ebay, and Citibank have continually reinvented themselves through mergers, new products or services, new markets, and new management techniques. While others perished or struggled, they unlearned the past and became today's giants.

A COST-EFFICIENT, EFFECTIVE SALES ORGANIZATION AND MARKETING APPROACH

The proven formula for success demands the entrepreneur target customers, differentiate products and services, segment markets, manage change, and create an efficient, effective marketing and sales strategy to reach these target customers at a cost which represents a proper percent of the sales dollar. Chapters 5 and 6 deal with these issues in detail. Many new entrepreneurial enterprises fail because the founders do not understand or cannot properly execute sales management and marketing strategies and tactics. These areas, along with proper financing, represent the major problems and opportunities for entrepreneurs and the major uses of their time.

Early-stage firms with limited resources need an understanding of how to turn their universe of targeted customers from suspects to prospects (marketing) and then the steps to transform a high percent of prospects into customers (sales). Entrepreneurs who can shorten long sales cycles, improve closing ratios, find strategic partners to help with the sales process, and make their own salespeople profitable sooner, increase their probability of survival and success. In longer sales cycles with many steps between customer search and purchase, smaller firms are at a competitive disadvantage to larger ones, because longer, more complex sales cycles require greater sales and marketing resources. Similarly, products or services with shorter life cycles, for example, one year versus three years, again, place smaller, younger firms at a competitive disadvantage to larger, more matured ones, because shorter life cycles require greater resources for continual new product development.

PRICING TO MAXIMIZE DOLLARS OF INCOME OVER TIME

Many early-stage entrepreneurial firms fail from underpricing; few, from overpricing. The proven formula for entrepreneurial success involves pricing products or services at what the market will bear based on competitive advantage in features, benefits, and image; and type of customer and product. This simple equation determines a firm's pricing power. Chapter 7 deals with proper pricing techniques in detail.

Most entrepreneurs fail to realize that proper pricing can help to internally fund their business and reduce the need for expensive outside equity financing. Many entrepreneurs don't realize that price is part of the product or service image. Both commercial and consumer customers equate a higher price with quality. Combine these pricing misconceptions with a lack of information on each product's or service's costs, and the result becomes prices that do not maximize dollars of income over time.

Proper pricing requires entrepreneurs to quantify their product or service value-added customer proposition. How will the product or service increase customer revenues, decrease customer costs, reduce working capital or capital expenditures? Does the price reflect this? Can you develop customer spreadsheets to demonstrate this value-added proposition? How much will your hospital software reduce the cost per patient day, increase revenues from HMOs, allow faster turnover of supplies or reduce investments in MRI equipment? Does the software reduce alternative costs of collecting these data manually?

Are your products or services better, the same, or inferior to the competition in features, benefits, and image? Can you prove it? If better or the same, can you command a premium price? If inferior, can you command the same price? The answers to these questions depend on the type of service or product sold and the type of customer. Leaders and early adapters, consumers, and businesses that desire the best and the newest represent customers willing to pay a premium price for a competitive advantage, especially if it can be quantified. Often these are larger, more successful corporations and wealthy individuals. Heterogeneous products or services, which are easy to differentiate, command a premium price for a competitive advantage. Furniture, computers, software, consulting, automobiles, and apparel represent heterogeneous products or services.

Many early-stage firms fail to understand the fixed and variable costs associated with each product or product line. This key control point is necessary to understand each product or service's dollars and percentage of contribution margin after manufacturing or operation costs. Entrepreneurs must price at what the market will bear to maximize dollars of contribution margin over time. However, we manage what we measure, and the contribution margin for each product or service or product/service group represents a key metric for judging success. The contribution margin by product or product line can be easily accessed by properly coding and sorting cost and revenue data.

The proven formula for success also requires understanding the differences between list and transactional prices and then how to merchandise your prices. This means understanding pocket pricing or the waterfall of discounts between list and net price. In determining dollars of contribution margin by product or customer, entrepreneurs must analyze net, not gross, prices (that is, prices after freight allowances, terms, promotions, advertising, and other discounts).

Merchandising prices and differential pricing means offering products or services at different prices depending on quantity, functions, market segments, and bundling, all of which make these prices more difficult to compare. Often this involves customizing prices for different business-to-business or business-to-consumer market segments. For example, the cost of an airline ticket depends on length and days of stay, hours of departure, advance purchase, and type of service. The cost of overnight delivery service depends on delivery time, destination, and type of pickup. This makes price comparisons more difficult as does bundling airline tickets with car rentals or software with hardware.

PROPER FINANCING

The proven formula for success demands that entrepreneurs properly plan and manage the financing of their enterprises. Too much money, too soon, can be expensive in terms of equity ownership. Too little money, too late, can put the new enterprise in financial distress, create a competitive disadvantage because of missed opportunities, and divert management's energy to a continual search for capital. Chapter 2 deals with proper financing in detail.

To properly manage financing, the entrepreneur must analyze the amount of money required over the next five years, the sources, and for equity funding the rounds involved. Looking at financing on a five-month rather than a five-year basis results in irreversible problems.

Debt financing, which has different risks, rewards, and costs of capital than equity financing, must be considered. Banks, asset-based lenders, leasing firms, government agencies, mezzanine investors, suppliers, landlords, and customers can provide debt financing for early-stage firms. Where possible, debt generally proves cheaper than equity, because there is no ownership dilution, and interest payments are tax deductible.

Most new enterprises will rely heavily on equity financing raised from different sources in different rounds. Round one generally involves friends, family, founders, and government agencies. Round two generally involves value-added private investors, sometimes called angels, who have had previous successful experience as entrepreneurs and early-stage investors. Round three involves venture capitalists and strategic partners. Strategic partners differ from financial investors because their own business may benefit from the investment. Intel, Compaq, Dell, Cisco, Staples, and Home Depot all invest in start-ups whose products or services have synergies with their own. In 2001, Intel had more committed early-stage investments than any other venture firm. Round four involves an initial public offering or private placement.

The success of each round of financing depends on properly executing the previous rounds. Investment bankers doing an IPO look for prestigious venture capitalists who have previously backed the firm now going public. If angel investors are given too many rights or their investment places too high a value on the new enterprise, venture capitalists may not want to be part of the following round.

Obtaining financing can consume the entrepreneur, diluting his or her efforts to manage the business. To prevent this, for each round of financing you should target investors as you would customers. You will save time and increase the probability of success by approaching investors who have a knowledge of your industry, adequate funds, and experience in early- or latter-round investing. Also research potential investor's past investments and what they look for. This allows you to customize a presentation for different investor types and different groups.

Look for lead investors who can attract others with common exit goals, industry knowledge, proximity to your location, and expertise in areas where you have weaknesses or needs. Many equity investors, including venture capitalists, have a five-year time horizon, which may or may not match yours. Can the investors help with recruiting, sales, or product development? Do you want a passive or active investor?

PROPER FINANCIAL CONTROLS

Although an entrepreneurial firm may have products or services that meet a need in the marketplace, it may fail for lack of proper financial controls. Many firms fail to plan and control expenses relative to revenues or disbursements relative to receipts. Chapter 3 deals with proper financial controls in detail.

Manage the parts and you manage the whole. Someone in the early-stage entrepreneurial firm should be responsible for preparing and monitoring financial controls. This person could be part-time. We manage what we monitor, and the entrepreneur must decide the key control points for his or her business. This will vary by industry and size.

However, the minimum financial controls for any entrepreneurial venture include:

- A sales forecast by month, customer, territory, and product line prepared by salespeople, channel partners, and possibly customers.
- Monitoring contribution margins by product or service, customer, and territory.
- Monitoring labor- and capacity-utilization rates.
- Line-item monthly expense budgets prepared by department managers.
- Monthly cash flow projections. Cash is king in a small business.
- Capital expenditure budgets.

- Balance sheet ratios.
- Accounts receivable aging by customer in descending order of dollar importance.
- An available for sale inventory report by stock-keeping unit (SKU). This report shows quantity on hand plus quantity on order from suppliers or in process, less unfilled customer orders.

In addition, entrepreneurs should put in place certain nonfinancial controls.These include:

- Customer and employee satisfaction surveys
- Quality control checks
- Purchasing efficiency checks
- Employee productivity monitoring

LEVERAGING INFORMATION TECHNOLOGY

As mentioned earlier, information technology is the great equalizer between smaller and larger businesses. The proven formula for success involves selecting and implementing technology which makes your entrepreneurial firm look larger and act competitively. Technology allows the smaller firm to seamlessly integrate with larger customers, prospects, and suppliers. Technology allows the smaller firm to reduce head counts, better utilize fixed assets, compress time, and improve employee morale. Customers, suppliers, and employees respect entrepreneurial firms with good systems and information technology, because they create a good image.

As costs have decreased and capacity has increased, good systems and information technology no longer represent a competitive edge for the entrepreneur or small business, but merely table stakes to stay competitive. Information technology and systems include not only software and computers but the Internet, e-mail, integrated digital telephone systems, cellular telephones, faxes, photocopy machines, and personal digital assistants (PDAs). Entrepreneurs and small business managers use information technology for sales and marketing, Web pages, databases, customer service, accounting, spreadsheets, communications, word processing, human resources, decision making, manufacturing, and inventory management. Banks and investors evaluate information technology systems as part of their due diligence.

Most experts suggest the entrepreneur or small business manager select the necessary software before buying the necessary hardware. Software can be sorted into the following groups: business productivity, communications and networking, graphics and design, development and programming, Internet/intranet, and utilities. Each group contains the following types of programs.

Business Productivity

- Accounting/financial
- Business plan/legal
- Computer-based training programs
- Contact manager/ organizer
- Database
- Marketing
- Optical character recognition

- Office suite
- Desktop operating system
- Personal digital assistant

- Project management

- Spreadsheet
- Voice recognition
- Word processing

Communication and Networking

- Connectivity
- E-mail
- Fax
- Groupware

- Network utilities
- Operating system network
- Remote access
- Video conferencing

Graphics and Design

- CAD/CAM
- Clip art/fonts
- Design and illustration

- Multimedia
- Presentations

Development and Programming

- Database
- Programming language

- Programming suites

Internet/Intranet

- HTML authoring
- Web browser

- Web graphics and animation
- Web server and firewall

Utilities

- Antivirus
- Backup
- Conversion
- Drive

- Enhancement utilities
- Security
- Utility suites

To guide them through this multitude of choices entrepreneurs need to develop a comprehensive technology plan to reflect the needs of both the business and the customer. The entrepreneur or small business manager needs a three-year plan for integrating technology to add more value to or to transform his or her business.

The plan should first define the problem, needs, or opportunities by answering these questions:

- What types of technology does your company need?
- Have you clearly defined the business issues you will be addressing with technology?
- What do you want the technology to accomplish?
- How do you want technology to better serve your customers and your company?
- What is important to end users?
- How many customers and employees do you anticipate having in each of the next five years?
- What are the compatibility issues? (Some technologies are geared at companies of a specific size. So, also consider any compatibility issues with existing technology owned by your firm, your customers, and your suppliers.)

Next, determine the technology, software, hardware, and communication equipment necessary to satisfy the needs, solve the problems, and take advantage of the opportunities defined above. On-line research and shopping makes it easier to discover what types of technology can best benefit your organization. Useful Web sites include:

- www.zdnet.com
- www.buyerzone.com
- www.inc.com
- www.smallbiz.com
- www.symantec.com

Also, network with other small-business people and entrepreneurs to get practical reviews of specific software programs and specific hardware configurations.

In choosing software, hardware, and communication systems, consider how much technology is required. For instance, can you choose one technology application to satisfy multiple needs and solve multiple problems? Buy enough capacity to handle anticipated growth but don't buy features which employees don't find helpful. Remember, the more complex the technology, the more training, installation, and maintenance will cost. More is not necessarily better. A highly equipped program may not boost productivity if employees find it difficult to use or it requires extensive training.

In purchasing hardware, buy enough power and speed to run your business applications. Because marginal costs are low, buy more power and speed than you currently need to reflect future applications. Buy hardware with expansion capabilities in memory and speed to extend its useful life, but avoid buying more than you will require. Whatever you choose make sure it integrates with your total present system and future plans.

In the new millennium entrepreneurs have a last-mover advantage because through application service providers (ASPs) you can receive the benefits of technology without actually owning it. ASPs host technology applications for businesses, typically charging a monthly service fee.

Don't forget security issues, especially when using the Internet. Also, consider whether you want to allow for access to your technology solutions from remote locations.

If the small business or new enterprise already owns some equipment or has some employees, customers, and suppliers, use a questionnaire to survey their needs. Form a technology committee to discuss these issues, and then choose, develop, implement, and manage the resulting systems. For a start-up or early-stage firm, the committee should include the entrepreneur, his or her accountant, key managers, if any, and an outside technology consultant with small business and industry-specific experience. For a small business or growth-stage firm, also include the head of each department—sales, marketing, operations, development, human resources, and so on. This creates better decisions and builds consensus and buy-in for actual use.

Entrepreneurs and small business owners must develop a technology budget to determine the financial resources necessary to purchase or lease required software, hardware, and communications equipment. Be sure to include the costs of training personnel on use, plus installation and maintenance costs. Prepare budgets for two or three years into the future, the useful life of most technology. For future years consider upgrading existing technology rather than replacing it

In choosing custom hardware, software, and communications equipment, develop relationships with competing vendors, or value-added retailers (VARs). Share your firm's needs, plans, and budget as outlined above. Ask each vendor to submit a proposal or bid that includes total costs and return-on-investment calculations. This will establish baselines for comparing one vendor to another.

Use these proposals to set performance standards and metrics by which to measure the effectiveness of your automation program. Be sure to ask each vendor for a free trial.

Also, ask each vendor, or VAR, for industry references from firms that use the proposed systems and for the name of a key person to call. You might also ask for one reference who did not buy and one who bought but was not satisfied.

Software can be purchased boxed in retail stores, downloaded from the vendor's Web site using electronic software distribution (ESD), leased through ASPs or custom designed by a consultant or VAR. Consultants and VARs not only custom design applications but help you with installation and training.

For a small business, the greatest cost of information technology lies not in the initial price, but in installation, training, maintenance, upgrades, troubleshooting, and lost time due to system failures and lack of user training. A good support and upgrade strategy will help minimize these costs. Also, on-line tutorials, self-paced manuals, and training videos prove helpful.

In the past, many small businesses have dismissed enterprise resource planning (ERP) solutions because of cost and complexity. ERP systems allow for centralized data that can be seamlessly accessed by many departments in an organization. However, scaled-down, less costly versions are now available through ASPs, which means small businesses can bypass much of the time-consuming installation process. As early-stage firms mature to their growth stage, the entrepreneur should consider ERP.

Entrepreneurs and small business owners have limited human and financial resources and therefore a high risk and cost of failure. Electronic disasters could put early- and growth-stage firms and small businesses in financial distress. Therefore, you must anticipate critical technology risks, create contingency plans, and take appropriate action. Always back up valuable data and have an alternative plan in case the system crashes or the facility loses power.

Many computers include jaz or zip drives, which can back up data from floppy or hard disks quickly and easily. Most disk management programs include backup features, which automatically make copies (to tape or disks) at a predetermined time. Entrepreneurs and small business owners should also make arrangements for a backup computer system in case the computer goes down and an auxiliary power system in case of a power outage. The costs of such backup are a small fraction of the costs involved in the alternative.

Entrepreneurs should include computer-integrated phone systems in their overall technology plan. Such systems can identify which customer is calling and then download all pertinent customer information on the recipient's computer monitor. Such information makes start-ups seem much larger, impresses customers, enhances the firm's image, saves time, makes employees feel important, and reduces the head count.

LEVERAGING LIMITED HUMAN RESOURCES

As mentioned earlier, start-ups, early-, and growth-stage entrepreneurial ventures have limited financial and human resources. Therefore, managers must be selected and trained to multitask. One person may have responsibility for all customer-related functions and another for all operation-related functions. Succession planning, although necessary, becomes more difficult. To solve these types of problems, the entrepreneur or small business manager must use outside contract services, advisory boards, part-time and retired employees, hire the best, compensate properly, train people well, use nonmonetary motivation and performance evaluations, delegate and communicate effectively, and leverage human resources with information technology.

The proven formula for success involves leveraging limited human and financial resources. For example, most entrepreneurial ventures lack at least one critical management function, such as a controller or a sales manager. An outside accounting firm, a part-time employee, a channel partner, or a retired person could perform these functions.

Virtual and horizontal organizations allow early-stage enterprises to reduce head count and related supervision by using outside experts. The entrepreneur should analyze each function in his or her start-up, early-, or growth-stage business to decide which functions must be done internally and which can be contracted to outside services. A five-person Midwest firm, with five million dollars of annual revenue in the streaming video distance learning field, contracts out-selling to a consulting firm that has a related service, uses university professors for content, and an independent production firm to produce the videos. This firm uses summer interns from a local university to do customer satisfaction surveys, and part-time retired people staff their administrative office.

Entrepreneurs also leverage human resources by creating outside advisory councils of customers and peers. The founder of a Web site that sells flowers on-line to businesses asks her largest customers to attend a once-a-month, 30-minute teleconference on how to better serve present accounts and open new ones. She also pays her lawyer, accountant, and several small local business owners to meet once a quarter and advise her on matters from group health insurance to training.

This same entrepreneur has an inside advisory board of key personnel from each department, who advise her on lowering costs, better serving customers, and keeping all employees satisfied. Members of the employee committee meet each month and rotate each year.

Most entrepreneurs have little experience or training in hiring staff and this perpetuates recruiting mistakes. They hire in a hurry, they hire the best of a bad bunch, they oversell the position, and they hire nonthreatening, easy-to-manage people who reflect their own image, often friends. First-rate entrepreneurs hire first-rate people. Second-rate entrepreneurs hire third-rate people. Hiring the best represents one of the most important tasks for an entrepreneur, because mediocre people produce mediocre results. The entrepreneur's job involves getting work done through other people.

Proper hiring involves many steps that act as filters, eliminating the bad hire and increasing the probability of hiring the best. Proper hiring involves job descriptions, candidate profiles, proper sourcing, reference checking, probing interview questions, credit and drug checking, and skill and personality testing.

Leveraging human resources means training the people you hire. Pay people more than they are worth, and then use training to make them worth more than what you pay them. Successful entrepreneurs have a training checklist for each position, whether the firm involves 5, 25, or 100 employees. The training checklist is a list of topics, skills, knowledge, and techniques necessary for each employee's success in their particular position. Employees receive the necessary training on-the-job and at outside seminars.

Similarly, successful entrepreneurs periodically evaluate all employees on results and the skills, knowledge, activities, and personal characteristics that drive those results. Each employee is evaluated by his or her manager and together they agree on next quarter's goals and objectives. Regardless of an organization's size, employees have a need and a right to know what is expected of them, whether those expectations are being met, and, if not, the corrective action. Performance evaluations force entrepreneurs and small business managers to communicate with and delegate to their people.

The proven formula for success includes leveraging human resources through appropriate performance-based and deferred compensation. Entrepreneurs structure employee compensation so that half is performance-based and of that half, at least one-third is deferred. This helps cash flow, financially rewards people for achieving goals, and improves retention. However, an employee's total compensation should reflect the complexity of the job, market rates, and the person's capabilities, skills, knowledge, and experience.

In a start-up, early-, or growth-stage firm, half of an employee's performance pay is based on the company's results that year and the remaining portion is paid the following year based on certain job-related metrics. Company results might include revenues, profit, and cash flow growth in absolute dollars and as a percentage of sales, while individual metrics might include productivity, quality issues, customer satisfaction, and appropriate results. In addition, all employees from sales to manufacturing, from secretary to executive, should receive stock options that vest in two to three years.

In creating compensation programs involving deferred compensation, performance pay, and stock options, be sure to consult a knowledgeable attorney and an accountant. Decisions on compensation and options that meet entrepreneurial needs for a start-up may lock your firm into undesirable situations for later-stage growth.

In start-ups, early- and growth-stage firms, and small businesses, nonmonetary motivation proves very important. Assuming your firm has a compensation system that rewards positive individual action and results, you need to add programs for individual and group recognition, programs to make people feel useful, important, and worthwhile, and programs to give employees a feeling of belonging. You must personally provide strong leadership. Successful entrepreneurs and small business managers realize that different sparks light different people's fires, and you need a different blend of recognition, usefulness, belonging, and leadership for each employee. You also must realize that because the entrepreneur, owner, or small business manager has a tremendous impact on each employee's motivation, your actions and words can turn employees on or off for days.

Some entrepreneurs, owners, and small business managers have high needs for authority and control and so often don't trust the people they employ. As a result, proper tasks are not delegated and everyone's productivity suffers.

Also, many entrepreneurs, owners, and small business managers communicate well with investors, bankers, and customers, but not so well with fellow employees. Leveraging human resources requires using performance evaluations, sales forecasts, business and strategic plans, and expense budgets to improve communication and delegation. This prevents silos and forces people to cooperate.

Human resources must also be leveraged by using information technology, as discussed previously.

OPERATIONAL EXCELLENCE

Operational excellence separates success from failure for new ventures and represents an important element in the proven formula for success. This includes consistently providing customers with the promised product or service at the quality level that creates customer satisfaction. This includes providing the product or service at a cost that produces appropriate margins. Entrepreneurs must remember the adage "sales are made on the street, but profits are made from operations." Operational excellence supports marketing goals and assures that dollars will stick to the cash register. Operational excellence involves choosing the correct vendors, equipment, processes, employees, location, and facilities, plus properly managing quality, quantity, pricing, and timing.

Entrepreneurs should use their last-mover advantage and freedom from legacy issues to implement total quality management (TQM). TQM sets predetermined standards based on customer satisfaction for all elements of the business and then creates processes to eliminate problems that interfere with meeting those standards. TQM continually removes the obstacles to achieving zero defects.

In creating operational excellence look at each step in the processes between first customer contact, delivery of the product or service, and after-delivery expectations. What can you do to lower costs, plus increase customer and employee satisfaction at each step? If your new enterprise manufactures a product, analyze the purchasing function. If your small business supplies a service, analyze the hiring process. Use your analysis to set performance and cost standards. For example, does your firm have the best prices from the right suppliers and are you using economical order quantities for just-in-time delivery?

Operational excellence often depends on state-of-the-art equipment and facilities. As a start-up or early-stage firm you have an opportunity to evaluate and purchase the best.

ALTERING EXISTING PRODUCTS TO MEET UNFILLED NEEDS IN SPECIALIZED MARKETS

Sixty percent of all new businesses fail within the first two years of their existence and 80 percent of all new products or services fail. Yet, new products or services often represent the basis for starting a new business and once started are the fastest way for a new enterprise to increase revenues, market share, earnings, cash flow, return on investment, and net present value. Successful new product or service introduction represents an important ingredient in the proven formula for success. Customers and employees prefer firms that successfully develop new products or services. Your firm's image and your employees' morale benefit from the development of new ideas.

New product or services fail from lack of customer demand or when competitors with greater resources exploit your successful idea. Heads you lose, tails you don't win. The high failure rate created by this paradox often keeps smaller firms from investing in new products or services. The solution to this dilemma is discussed in Chapter 9 and involves a model/methodology that increases the probability of success and reduces the risk of failure of a new product or service.

In its simplest form the model/methodology involves innovating rather than inventing. Altering existing products to meet unfilled needs in specialized markets by:

- Changing packaging
- Using color identification to create inexpensive branding
- Offering unusual sizing
- Offering unusual guarantees
- Combining or bundling existing products or services
- Unbundling or offering modules of existing products or services
- Licensing technology, products, or trademarks from others
- Cobranding with customers or suppliers
- Adopting ideas from overseas or related markets
- Reviving an old idea
- Developing new markets and uses for existing products or services

Often these new product or service innovations involve little risk and small investment, but they have low barriers to entry and low customer switching costs, which invite competition.

Successful entrepreneurs continually search for new ideas from customers, competitors, employees, salespeople, trade shows, conferences, trade publications, and the Internet. To reduce the risk of failure, we search for unfilled customer needs or competitive weaknesses; we search for legacies where customers require innovation from suppliers, but suppliers have vested interests that prohibit change. For example, dentist's require patient chairs with more positions or hand tools with greater speed and flexibility. The dental industry giants have large investments in capital equipment to produce the existing chairs and tools, which prohibit change. The entrepreneur seizes this opportunity by finding a foreign firm to manufacture the new designs and several large U.S distributors to sell it.

But how does the ant protect itself from the gorilla's competitive response when barriers to entry and customer switching costs are low? It may be possible to file patents and to apply for copyrights and trademarks to establish intellectual property rights, but expensive to defend them. The entrepreneur always wants to create a portfolio of intellectual property rights to protect himself or herself against competition and increase the firm's market value for investor financing. As suggested previously, niche markets, where your smaller enterprise can be profitable but a larger one cannot, offer the best protection against competitors with greater resources.

As previously mentioned, a smaller enterprise is at a competitive disadvantage in markets where products or services have shorter lives and longer sales cycles. Such markets require greater resources for constant new product or service development and greater resources for the many steps involved between customer search and purchase. Consider this before developing the new product or service.

Most entrepreneurs don't analyze a new product's return on investment or lifetime value before they start investing. Doing so is part of the model/methodology and will reduce the risk of failure and increase the probability of success. Chapter 9 discusses this and other steps for reducing risk, such as inexpensive market research and test marketing. The Internet, phone interviews, focus groups, and direct-mail surveys can inexpensively determine a new product's or service's salability and scalability. Test marketing can determine and measure actual customer response, reorders, and suggested product or service alterations. All this research will help you properly screen, modify, and even name the new product or service.

Many entrepreneurs and small business managers neglect or fail at new product or service development because they lack the resources to create a demand for or to presell them. The proven formula for success involves using inexpensive promotional techniques, such as trade shows, trade publication advertising, seminars and workshops, informationals, permission e-mail, direct mail, third-party catalogs, press releases, and statement stuffers, to advertise new and existing products or services. Then, it suggests asking your suppliers, channel partners, and (if appropriate) retail customers, to share in the cost of these promotional efforts.

BUSINESS AND MARKETING PLANS

Planning makes good things happen (bad things happen by themselves). The proven formula for success includes a well thought-out business plan and a well thought-out marketing plan. In their business plans most entrepreneurs overestimate the market size, their share, growth rates, and future company revenues. Most entrepreneurs underestimate present and potential competition, competitive responses, and critical risks. Most entrepreneurs don't present best- and worst-case financial scenarios, sensitivity analysis, valid market research, or proper financial assumptions. A well thought-out business plan not only helps you raise capital but becomes your strategic plan for running the business. However, be careful of the previously described tragic flaws.

If a business plan is used to raise equity financing, make sure it quickly states the opportunity, accurately describes the market potential, identifies both competitive weaknesses and strengths, relates to industry norms, forecasts working capital needs, and states possible exit strategies. Investors evaluate management based on training, experience, and the sophistication of the business plan.

A well thought-out marketing plan not only analyzes past, present, and future markets, competitors, target customers, and your sales organization, but it becomes your operating plan for efficiently and effectively reaching these markets. Business plans and marketing plans help entrepreneurs search for opportunities and add value.

Chapter 1 describes how to write an effective business or strategic plan and what to include. Every business plan should contain at least the following topics:

- Management duties, organization, compensation, and background
- Past, present, and future customers
- Past, present, and future markets and market segments
- Past, present, and future competitors
- Past, present, and future products and services
- Channels of distribution
- Sales organization
- Marketing, advertising, promotion
- Human resource issues
- Information technology issues
- Operations and/or manufacturing
- Past, present, and future financial statements and cash flow
- Critical risks and contingency plans
- A mission statement
- Short history
- Timetable of events
- An executive summary

AVOIDING THE GROWTH BUSTERS

The proven formula for success involves:

- Using target marketing to focus resources
- Using market segmentation to differentiate and customize the offering
- Successfully dealing with change
- Having a cost-efficient, effective sales organization and marketing approach

- Pricing to maximize dollars of income over time
- Using proper financing
- Maintaining proper financial controls
- Leveraging technology
- Leveraging human resources
- Ensuring operational excellence
- Altering existing products to meet unfilled needs in specialized markets
- Following business and marketing plans

For entrepreneurs and small business managers to increase their probability of success and reduce their risk of failure, they must understand not only the proven formula for success but the growth busters. *Growth busters* are personal characteristics, styles, and business models that inhibit or prevent success:

- Management's inability to act, implement, and execute
- Creating legacies that block change
- Allowing silos that block effective communications and prevent seamless service to customers
- Lack of focus
- Concentrating on tactics without understanding strategy
- Not delegating
- Long, complex sales cycles
- Short product or service life cycles

Management's Inability to Act, Implement, and Execute.

Entrepreneurial success requires being right 60 percent of the time, but knowing that you are wrong 75 percent of the time and taking corrective action. For entrepreneurs, analysis is simple but action is essential. If you have "analysis paralysis" or a high fear of failure, think twice about a career in new enterprise.

Business is a dynamic process, the future a moving target, the landscape continues to change, and so early-stage entrepreneurial managers must continually act, make decisions, and take risks. When the founder or president of a new or small enterprise cannot or does not act, it proves contagious and spreads to other managers. Chronic inertia and corporate paralysis set in. In the changing landscape of a small business, managerial excellence relies on the ability to successfully execute and implement strategy and tactics. Knowledge is only power if we use it.

I have spent hours with the heads of second-generation family-owned businesses planning the detailed strategy and tactics to introduce new products, change sales force compensation, or alter human resources. A year later nothing has changed because the person in control has prevented others from taking action. In the late 1990s many e-commerce firms had excellent business models for bringing buyers and sellers together in a specific industry and had obtained appropriate financing. Those that survived executed and implemented the model. The dot coms that could not translate ideas into action became dot bombs.

Entrepreneurs must look at alternative solutions to problems and alternative means to capitalize on opportunities and then choose the best alternative based on risks versus rewards. For example, the risk in raising prices 5 percent is that unit volume might decline. The reward of raising prices 5 percent is that the dollars of contribution margin will increase. The entrepreneur needs a process, model, or methodology to think this through. For instance, if unit sales decline 30 percent, will that totally offset the dollars of margin increase generated from a 5 percent higher price? The risk of unit volume declining 30 percent when prices increase 5 percent depends on whether the product is easy to differentiate, the degree of customer switching costs, the type of customer, and the product's or service's competitive advantages. Entrepreneurs that consider the rewards and risks of alternative decisions like this one find it easier to act, implement, and execute.

Creating Legacies That Block Change

Successful entrepreneurs take advantage of opportunities created by competitors' complacencies that generate legacy issues. In the 1990s, on-line brokerage firms flourished because their larger, more established competitors had large investments in research staffs and customer advisers that initially prevented them from offering on-line services and potentially created channel conflicts. Successful entrepreneurs and small business managers create their own legacies, which again create opportunities for competitors. An established bathroom-remodeling firm sold exclusively through company-owned stores. This was industry tradition. A new competitor started franchising a similar product or service directly to plumbers, carpenters, and contractors. Franchising allowed the start-up to reduce fixed costs in leases and payroll and put more resources into direct mail, cable TV, and e-mail marketing. Within three years the start-up became the industry leader, while the established firm which hung on to the legacy of retail outlets wondered why its market share continued to decline.

Allowing Silos That Block Effective Communications

As new enterprises mature and evolve, employees draw their lines in the sand and stake out their turf. Because new enterprises represent greater career risks, employees become very territorial. Bad attitudes can develop, such as "that is not my job" and "this is not my fault."

On the other hand, regardless of new or old economy or company size, customers seek seamless service from all company representatives. All company employees must "sing the same song." Customers demand that backroom functions, such as billing, coordinate with sales and that service people, designers, and engineers understand customer issues. Customers, whether businesses or consumers, consider this the table stakes necessary to play in their markets. Therefore, internal employee turf battles must end. The customers' positive faith in and image of a start-up or small business is destroyed when one department or person will not take total responsibility for a customer's problems or concerns.

To prevent this, make teamwork part of the candidate profile and job description. Discuss it in prehiring interviews and make seamless service and silo prevention part of the training program. As mentioned previously, do cross-training by having key people work one day a month in other departments. Have an 800 number and a Web site for customer feedback on good and bad experiences. Then, every quarter do customer satisfaction surveys.

A Minneapolis cellular phone company that provides important digital and voice services to subscribers found that the digital service and voice staffs continually aggravated customers by blaming the other department for problems. Management then merged the two departments but found there were technical problems. Finally, management separated the departments but cross-trained and rotated people every other month between digital and voice, which finally eliminated the problems.

Often, lack of communication creates silos. Often, communication is worse in a small enterprise than in a large one. In the small enterprise people think everyone knows what is on the other person's mind, but they often neglect to communicate it. Good communication does not depend on the number of people involved, but on the proper skills, techniques, commitment, concern, and sensitivity of those people.

For example, a sweater company based in Hickory, North Carolina, terminated the Florida salesperson but continued to pay her because sales did not notify payroll. The same company built excess inventory because sales did not effectively communicate a product deletion to manufacturing. Poor communications can exist between two individuals or between two departments within a business.

A regional telephone start-up did surveys of potential customers for 100 buildings to determine which buildings to wire for broadband service. Marketing personnel performed these surveys, but did not properly communicate the information to engineering. As a result engineering spent several hundred thousand dollars wiring buildings without enough potential to justify the cost, which eroded scarce human and financial resources.

As you can see, poor communication in early-stage businesses represents a waste of precious energy, time, financial, and human resources. Smaller enterprises can improve communication techniques by training their people in proper listening skills and the use of feedback. Smaller enterprises also can improve communication processes through performance evaluations, forecasts, budgets, and planning.

Managing people in an entrepreneurial environment means using communication to not only explain but persuade and change them. After all, we spend 70 to 80 percent of our working hours communicating. For a new enterprise, good communication starts at the top, which influences people at all levels, and can represent a competitive advantage. However, entrepreneurs often communicate better with customers and investors than with employees and associates.

Communication is a transfer of ideas and information, an attempt to become understood. To communicate effectively, entrepreneurs must understand the skills, techniques, sensitivities, and human dynamics involved. These include feedback, perception, initiation of action through commands and persuasion, organization and clarity of expression, simplicity, the role of personal prejudice and of informal or unconscious communication, listening skills, and result measurement.

All communication involves four parts—a sender, a receiver, a message, and feedback. The sender and receiver do not establish a commonness of meaning until the sender receives feedback that his or her message was received in its intended form. Also, even though entrepreneurs have strong belief systems, they must convey messages with a sensitivity for the receiver's perception. In other words, since you cannot mass produce communication, you must tailor it to each person's value system. Also, because communication means not only explaining but persuading and changing, to communicate effectively with each person, you must understand how they use and filter information, how they make decisions.

Regular performance evaluations, quarterly plans and objectives, expense budgets, and sales forecasts force the people in a smaller enterprise to periodically have meaningful dialogues about their jobs and the business. Weekly reports, which compare actual results and activities to plan and budget with a narrative on variances, continue this dialogue.

Communication platforms include well-planned meetings of appropriate people with agendas and time frames, e-mail, teleconferencing, and an efficient reporting system (hard copy or on-line). However, remember that information is not necessarily communication.

Lack of Focus

Because new enterprises have limited human and financial resources, they must stay focused on key strategic issues. Offering too broad a product line spreads human resources thin and increases necessary working capital for inventory. Not focusing on key market segments or customers has the same result. As previously mentioned, focusing to leverage key resources versus diversification to lessen dependence on a few key customers, products, or markets represents a continual dilemma for smaller businesses.

Concentrating on Tactics, Forgetting Strategy

Strategy creates structure and drives tactics. Not having a strategy encourages lack of focus and becomes a growth buster for many new enterprises. A software consulting firm, which targeted customers that employ between 50 and 500 people in the greater Minneapolis area, offered services from PC programming to mainframe networking. Full-time staff became difficult to recruit and retain, necessitating that many staff members be independent contractors. The strategy for obtaining new customers was word of mouth.

Because the software firm had stagnant revenues and falling profits, the founder decided to focus her firm on Internet operations for business-to-business firms. E-mail marketing was used to produce leads, and a new salesperson was hired. Revenues and margins started to expand and full-time employee recruiting and retention improved. As this description illustrates, managing today involves tactics but thinking about tomorrow requires strategy.

By 2001 the software firm felt too dependent on Internet-related businesses because that market growth had slowed and the founder decided to add another countercyclical specialty, health care. The business remained focused but less dependent on one application.

Lack of strategy, not pursuing strategy, not building structure and tactics around strategies are common growth busters for entrepreneurs. Some entrepreneurs are visionaries but most are myopic. Think about what you want the house to look like before you build it. Once built, step out on the balcony occasionally to see what surrounds you. The finished house and the blueprint represent strategy. The tools to build the house, hammers and saws, represent the tactics. Business and marketing plans can help you create strategy and the tactics necessary to implement them. Entrepreneurs must manage everyday survival with many tactical decisions but also plan strategy so they will have a business next year.

An ornamental flower seed firm sold to consumers through independent garden centers, independent hardware retailers, and midsized grocery stores. Annual sales approached $5,000,000. Independent sales representatives sold and serviced the thousands of retail customers.

The company president and owner saw the consumer ornamental flower seed market shifting toward mass merchants and made a strategic decision to pursue this market segment. However, he did not change and align tactics to reflect strategy. The mass merchants wanted to be sold by management, not independent reps; they demanded next-day delivery and weekly stock counting at all their branches. The president's wise change in strategy failed because he had not aligned the corporate structure and tactics with the new strategy. It took two years to hire and train major account managers, staff a customer service center, contract with a reliable independent stock-taking service, and develop programs to control inventory levels during the peak March to June selling season.

Not Delegating

Entrepreneurs dislike delegating important tasks to others, and this creates yet another growth buster, another obstacle to the proven formula for success. Entrepreneurs have a strong need to control and often don't trust associates. These traits lead them to careers as entrepreneurs but impede the progress of their new enterprises.

Successful entrepreneurs know how to hire the best, skillfully train them, and then motivate them to full potential, full productivity. Ultimately, the entrepreneur's success depends on the success of his or her employees and the ability to get work done through these people. Although the founder, president, entrepreneur might do a task better than someone else, he or she can only do so much. Decide what functions represent the key control points for the business, decide what tasks only you can do, then prioritize the rest and start delegating to the appropriate people. If your subordinates do the job only 80 percent as well as you could, the enterprise still wins. Reason tells the entrepreneur to delegate. There is only one of me and five other qualified people, but emotion says hang on to all you can control.

For example, the founder of a bakery supply firm knows she must sell major accounts, the founder of a consumer electronics firm knows he must manage product development, and the president of a tier-two auto supplier knows he must manage manufacturing and procurement. These entrepreneurs delegate other functions to their employees and associates.

Performance evaluations, expense budgets, sales forecasts, and marketing and business plans create better communication and force managers, including the entrepreneur, to delegate. In order to hold people responsible for their results, activities, goals, and plans, you must delegate work, decisions, responsibility, and authority to the proper level.

Another worthwhile exercise that encourages the entrepreneur to delegate involves reviewing an organization chart and listing key decisions each manager is responsible for. Include the president, who might be the founder and entrepreneur, plus all the managers reporting to him or her and all those reporting to the managers. This might include five people or a hundred. Have a meeting to discuss possible changes. This exercise visually shows which decision-making authority resides with the incorrect person and clarifies the proper decision-making authority at all levels.

Long, Complex Sales Cycles

As previously alluded to, another growth buster for early-stage enterprises occurs when the product or service sold involves a long, complex sales cycle with many steps between customer search and purchase. A North Dakota miniature transformer firm with annual revenues of ten million dollars sold its products to electrical utilities, computer firms, communication equipment manufacturers, and telephone companies. The sales cycle/marketing funnel involved calling design engineers to identify upcoming projects; meeting with design, manufacturing, and purchasing managers to qualify needs; producing a prototype; submitting samples for a trial; running a beta test; meeting with upper management; and, finally, submitting a quote. This process required seven months and considerable expense, which larger, more established competitors could better afford. In addition, this smaller competitor only won 20 percent of its final bids. Knowing that the competitor who can shorten the sales cycle generally wins the order, this smaller firm planned, tracked, and budgeted each step in the sales cycle. The firm asked salespeople for monthly status reports, stating the probability of moving from one step to the next and giving details on visits to key decision makers and the probability of ultimately receiving a production order. This resulted in fewer bids and more projects being aborted in midprocess. The company discovered that this long process also proved expensive for the customers/prospects. By offering financial incentives, lower prices to qualified prospects in exchange for a shorter, less complex purchasing cycle, the transformer firm created a faster, less expensive sales cycle for itself.

Short Product or Service Life Cycles

Another growth buster for early-stage enterprises occurs when the product or service sold involves a short life cycle and small lifetime value. Smaller enterprises don't have the financial or human resources to deal with constant product or service turnover. The key is finding a way to extend the life cycle and lifetime value of your products or services.

This can be accomplished by selling the same product or service to a different or new market segment or even to an overseas market, possibly a Third World country. Also, product life can be lengthened through enhancements and line extensions. A New York City women's sportswear firm with seven million dollars of annual sales introduces new products each season for department and better specialty stores in major metropolitan areas. The next season the same designs are sold to the chain stores and the following season to the mass merchants. Finally, the same sportswear style is exported to Mexico and sold in rural U.S. markets through mail-order catalogs and small retailers. This small sportswear distributor could not support new styles that lasted for only one season, but it can support a new style that has a lifetime value of four seasons.

This same sportswear firm does seasonal enhancements and extensions of its fashion products by adding a new color or an extra pocket or a different waistline. These line extensions create a newer look at a smaller cost.

THE OLD ECONOMY VERSUS THE NEW ECONOMY

The Internet, e-commerce, telco, and biotech are not silver bullets but very complex business models where many more businesses fail than succeed. Many differences separate clicks from bricks, voice from data, and genomics from traditional pharmaceutical firms. The following are some issues that differ from the old to the new economy: speed to market; scalability; critical mass; viral marketing; fixed versus variable costs; marginal revenues versus marginal expenses; break-even points; customer switching costs; database sales; first- versus last-mover advantage; pricing; compression of time, space, and material; strategic partners; competitors becoming customers and vice versa; and barriers to entry. However, as we move into the new millennium, we are finding that the proven formula for success for new economy and old economy start-ups has more similarities than differences. Every week executives successfully move from old economy firms to new economy firms and back again. Every week another old economy retailer or manufacturer announces a new economy subsidiary. Every week we read articles where new economy companies utilize old economy techniques and skills. Successful companies use the best techniques and have the best people from both cultures. The business models are merging, and the proven formula for success and avoiding growth busters applies to both worlds.

USING THE PROPER DECISION-MAKING MODEL, METHODOLOGY, AND METRICS

The proven formula for success requires entrepreneurs to understand the decision-making process involved in solving problems and taking advantage of opportunities. In its simplest form, this model or methodology involves understanding:

- What is and is not the problem; that is, clearly defining the problem or opportunity.
- What is causing the problem. Some causes are obvious, others more subtle. When we understand the cause, problems become easier to solve.
- Alternative solutions. There is always more than one solution, and identifying realistic alternatives helps to define both the problem and the cause.
- How using quantitative and qualitative data to measure the risk and reward of each alternative solution helps us choose the best one.
- How to make decisions with limited information and insufficient time by relying on a more strategic focus.
- The absolute importance of implementation and execution of the decision. This involves creating a plan of action and a time frame with tactical and strategic goals and objectives.
- The performance standards or metrics necessary to measure the decision's results. Were you right or wrong?
- If you chose the wrong alternative or implemented the wrong action plan, admitting mistakes and taking corrective action.

Decisions become easier to make and more accurate when we have a model. As mentioned earlier, entrepreneurs constantly make decisions. Success involves not only being right 60 percent of the time but knowing that we are wrong 75 percent of the time and taking corrective action. Entrepreneurs who understand this equation find decision making much easier.

Have you ever solved a problem only to find out it was the wrong one? Small business managers and entrepreneurs have strong emotional ties to their firms. This causes them to not fully understand or define the problem, which may result in their confusing a problem's cause with the problem itself and then not looking at *all* alternatives.

A regional Long Island health-care provider had 40 percent annual turnover of its caregivers and declining revenues in several markets. Management decided the problem was compensation, including fringe benefits. Actually, compensation was one possible cause of turnover.

Management changed compensation but never defined the problem correctly as declining revenues and caregiver turnover. Therefore, revenues continued to decline, turnover remained at 40 percent, expenses rose, profits and market share declined.

Eighteen months later, the founder, entrepreneur, and president realized he had solved the wrong problem. He then correctly identified the twin problems or opportunities as caregiver turnover and declining revenues in the two largest markets. He and his staff then set a time frame and metrics for measuring the success of any corrective action: At the end of 12 and 24 months, quarterly turnover must decrease to 20 and 10 percent, respectively; quarterly revenues must increase by 10 percent over the previous year; the number of clients under care must increase by 7 percent over the previous year; customer satisfaction must not decline; the number of new referral sources must increase.

Management then looked at possible causes of each problem. The possible causes of turnover included hiring techniques, training, compensation, and motivation. Caregivers were asked to fill out a climate survey questionnaire dealing with these issues. The possible causes of revenue decreases included competition, service, pricing, the sales organization, Medicare reimbursement policies, and demographic changes. Referral sources, present and past clients, and prospects were surveyed. Based on the quantitative and qualitative data, management determined that the most likely cause of high turnover and falling revenues was poor caregiver training, which caused job and customer dissatisfaction. The risks of putting more resources into training were cost-related; the rewards could result in reduced turnover and revenue growth.

Possibly more caregiver and customer input were necessary, but time limited the number of respondents. The training decision reinforced one of the firm's strategic goals.

Management created a training checklist for caregivers, a universe of topics necessary for success. Topics included medical and psychological patient issues, plus equipment knowledge, nutrition, medicine, etiquette, family issues, and general health care. Each new and existing caregiver had a quarterly development plan based on the training checklist. Training included initial classroom work, reading assignments, and then field coaching at the patient's residence. Finally, every quarter tests were given to caregivers on these subjects.

By the end of one year turnover had decreased from 40 percent to 25 percent and at the end of two years to 12 percent, almost meeting the previously set performance standards. At the end of one and two years, revenues, customer satisfaction, number of patients, referrals, and customer satisfaction all improved dramatically.

This decision-making process, model, and methodology can help entrepreneurial organizations make better decisions. The decision-making process, the model, and methodology, represent an important tool for the proven formula of success.

ENTREPRENEURS' MAJOR MISTAKES AND WEAKNESSES

- Improperly balancing diversification with focus.
- The inability to anticipate and deal with change.
- Failing to create a cost-efficient, effective sales organization and marketing approach.
- Not pricing to maximize dollars of income over time.
- Lack of appropriate financial controls.
- Product rather than market or customer orientation.
- Not realistically understanding competitive advantages and disadvantages.
- Not planning financing as a continual long-term process.
- Substituting analyses for action and information for knowledge.
- Tolerating silos which prevent seamless service to customers and effective communication within the organization.
- Choosing markets with long complex sales cycles, or short product or service lives, or both.
- Concentrating on tactics, forgetting strategy.

QUESTIONS AND EXERCISES

1. What is your new enterprise's strategy for dealing with and leveraging limited human and financial resources?
2. What changes in the business landscape does your new enterprise or smaller firm take advantage of?
3. List the past, present, and future changes from outside your company, the key inflection points over which management had or has no control.
4. How is your entrepreneurial firm leveraging technology to level the playing field?
5. What is your enterprise's strategy for creating operational excellence?
6. List the action your firm is taking to avoid the growth busters.

PART ONE

FINANCE AND CONTROL

CHAPTER 1

Writing a Business Plan or a Strategic Plan

Three strategic alternatives exist for you to become an entrepreneur or small business manager. Each strategic alternative has different risks, merits, and rewards as well as different advantages and disadvantages. You may choose to start a new business by (1) developing and introducing a new product or service; (2) buying an existing business, managing it, and possibly someday selling it; (3) cloning an existing business model, possibly by franchising someone else's idea.

To achieve any of these goals, the entrepreneur or manager must understand target marketing, differentiation, and market segmentation. That person must have created a cost-efficient, effective sales organization and marketing approach, with proper pricing. In addition, the new enterprise must leverage its human resources and have established proper financial controls.

Whatever strategic alternative is chosen, the entrepreneur must receive financing for the enterprise, either debt or equity. These different means of financing involve different risks and rewards, different costs of capital, different advantages and disadvantages, and different expected returns.

To help navigate this journey and obtain proper financing, the entrepreneur and small-business person needs a well-thought-out business plan or strategic plan. Although closely related, business plans usually concentrate on the future, while strategic plans examine the past, present, and future. Start-ups and early-stage businesses rely on business plans, while more mature latter-stage businesses use strategic plans. Strategic plans often deal with broad goals or objectives for longer periods of time, while business plans deal with tactics to accomplish those goals over shorter periods of time. These broad categories also include marketing and financial plans, which deal with more specific subjects.

Planning makes good things happen—bad things happen by themselves. We've learned that 60 percent of all small businesses fail within the first two years of their existence. Planning helps entrepreneurs survive. However, the best business or strategic plans will fail if not properly implemented. Many entrepreneurs and small business-people can write excellent business plans. The challenge is to effectively implement them.

Whether you call your plan a *business, strategic, marketing,* or *financial plan,* is not important. However, entrepreneurs and small business managers do need to alter these plans depending on the use. If you are looking for equity funding, the plan should emphasize scalability, differentiation, management, merits, risks, and exit value. If you are looking for debt financing, the plan becomes a selling piece emphasizing reliable, predictable cash flow, liquid collateral, competitive advantages, quality customers, and competent management. As an important, powerful management tool, the plan helps the entrepreneur or manager search for opportunities to add value and acts as a standard against which to measure actual results. As such the plan needs frequent updating.

Properly prepared and thought-out business plans require time and organization. Consider hiring a summer intern to help you with this and consider going off-site with your management team to prepare it. Be sure to have trusted business advisers read and critique the plan. Did they quickly grasp the essence of the proposal? Were they excited by what they read? Regardless of feedback, however, the entrepreneur must realize that he or she has final responsibility for the plan. You must own it, use it, and continually revise it to reflect the changing landscape.

Business plans act as a filter for start-ups. The plan forces the entrepreneur to think through competitive forces, product differentiation, expenses, potential revenue, and critical risks. As a filter the plan may flash a stop sign to the entrepreneur indicating the risk is not worth the reward, thus saving human and financial resources. Many entrepreneurs decide to abort or significantly change their start-up after writing the business plan, because the process of preparing a plan points out so many deficiencies. For example, you might discover a smaller market with less growth than you anticipated or possibly more competitors. Or the filter may flash a green light to the entrepreneur indicating what it will take to succeed, and the necessary steps between start and exit. In a global economy sweat equity alone, without a plan, will not lead to success. Your plan is a necessary step in the management of your business.

In a new enterprise, a business plan is a living document which needs to be updated frequently and which can function as a benchmark or guide for employees at all levels. Yet, less than 10 percent of new enterprises have formal business plans, and many smaller enterprises that have business plans don't use them to monitor results and actions. Often the business plan is prepared for financing but then forgotten. In those cases, entrepreneurs are flying blind in a snowstorm.

THE PLAN'S TOPICS

A business plan should set future goals and objectives as well as list the strategy, tactics, action, human resources, and financial resources to reach those goals. It should put this in a time frame and state the critical risks that might prevent the business from reaching these goals. Most business plans lack realism by overestimating markets, market share, and sales and underestimating present and potential competition and expenses.

Business or strategic plans should include pertinent information on:

- Management
- Customers
- Markets
- Competitors
- Products or services
- Distribution channels
- Sales organization
- Marketing
- Operations

- Human resources
- Information technology
- Financial statements and forecasts
- Critical risks and contingency plans
- Time table of events
- Short history
- Mission statement
- Executive summary

Let's look at each of the topics that should be covered in the plan.

MANAGEMENT

A business plan used to raise equity and debt financing should accurately state management's previous industry and entrepreneurial experience. Whereas a successful background in cell phones or semiconductors at Motorola shows domain knowledge, which is important for a start-up in these industries, it does not reflect actual start-up experience leveraging limited human and financial resources. The plan should emphasize management's ability to effectively implement the business plan and deal with unanticipated changes. You should note any management weaknesses, possibly the need for a controller or credit manager, and how or when you plan to handle this. Can missing needs be filled by part-time help or outside consultants?

State each management member's areas of responsibility, whether it is product development, sales, or recruiting, and how that person's experience will help him or her perform those duties. Be sure to list your board members, attorney, accountant, and advisers. State why you chose them and how they bring value to the enterprise. Perhaps a board member creates credibility with the medical profession or an adviser provides extensive experience in sales management. The proper attorney was chosen for her expertise in start-up and early-stage financing. The choice of board members, lawyers, accountants, and advisers communicate important corporate images to outsiders.

In preparing a business or strategic plan used for internal purposes, also include each management member's résumé and job description as exhibits. This will force you to prepare a list of each manager's duties. Discuss the management team's evolution; for example, who left and why, on what dates did present managers arrive? Discuss each management member's strengths and weaknesses and necessary training or development; for example, the founder and CEO understands the technology but cannot read a financial statement.

Discuss critical risks as to which manager may leave and discuss specific management individuals you plan to hire in the future. Should managers leave or become ill, what is the succession plan, who has the skills and knowledge to temporarily step in? These topics force entrepreneurs to address these important issues.

Include an organization chart showing who reports to whom and what the chart will look like in six months and in two years. What sources will be used to fill the empty boxes? Today, management includes two people but in two years it may include six. The organization chart may be a traditional one, an entirely horizontal organization or a circle with the founder at the center. Planning makes good things happen.

If the business plan is to be used for raising funds, state management's present fixed compensation and the members' deferred performance compensation as compared to that in their last job. In start-ups and early-stage businesses, investors want assurances that management's fixed compensation is less than members' received in their previous job and that their performance pay is more than what they received in their previous job.

The business plan should include information on key managers' investment in the firm, and present dollar ownership and options. Investors want managers to have incentives that maximize exit values plus down risks if the venture fails.

CUSTOMERS AND PROSPECTS

A business plan used to raise equity and debt financing should list the top customers of the present business and the top prospects for future business. What percentage of your total revenues and income do they represent? Why do they or will they buy your product or service? What percentage of their business do you have or hope to have? If appropriate, state customer turnover or retention rates. For future prospects, what is the timing for and probability of receiving their business? How many customers does the organization presently serve and how many do you plan to have in six months, two years, and five years? Decide the characteristics of a target account. What criteria are used to define A, B, and C accounts—dollars of revenue and income, cost to sell and serve, probability of success, or all three? Give specific examples of A, B, and C accounts.

In preparing a business or strategic plan used for internal purposes, also include a list of all your present customers and prospects, not just the top ones. If appropriate, rank the top customers today, the percentage of total revenue each represents versus the top customers for the past several years and who you forecast the top customers to be in the next several years. In other words, create a moving picture of customers and prospects rather than a snapshot in time. Business is a dynamic process, the future a moving target.

Your business plan should answer the following questions: Why has and will the customer mix change? Does this reflect new products or services, changing competitors, different distribution channels, or a more efficient sales force? What customer needs does the product or service satisfy? What customer problems does it solve? Are these changing and evolving? Can you quantify how the product or service reduces customers' costs, increases revenues, or lowers working capital needs?

In your internal business or strategic plan discuss how customers use the product or service and whether this has or will change. For example, initially the software you sell was used by marketing people to track direct-mail responses. Now your software is used by salespeople for contact management.

Your business plan should answer the following questions: How long is the order and sales cycle? For example, are miniature transformers purchased every month or every year? Is the purchasing decision made by a design engineer, a purchasing agent, or both? Does it take one visit or many visits to obtain an order? What are the steps from search to purchase in the sales cycle? Does buyer behavior reflect a one-time or first-time purchase, a repetitive modified rebuy process, a new product or service purchase, or a commodity purchase?

How can your enterprise add value by better serving the customer in the future? For example, let's say that presently you analyze or sequence genome. Possibly you should also perform annotation or an explanation and create a Web site for customer service. Maybe your salespeople should perform more consultative selling.

Include a list of previous customers who no longer use your product or service. Who did they replace you with and why? Have you attempted to reactivate these accounts?

Depending on your business's growth stage, you will have varying amounts of data on customers and prospects. Your salespeople, along with their customer files and profiles, represent the best source of information. However, the Internet, credit reports, trade associations, trade publications and trade shows also provide excellent customer and prospect information. The competitor with the best customer knowledge generally receives a generous portion of that customer's business.

MARKETS

Market size and growth rates address a firm's scalability or opportunity. It is easier to be a hero in a growing market than a declining one. As mentioned previously, most new enterprises and small businesses overstate the market size, their potential share of this market, and the resulting revenues.

A business plan should list the markets and market segments addressed by your firm in dollars and units. For example, the larger markets might be compact discs and consumer electronics, but your segments might include accessories and handheld devices sold at retail. Include data on size and growth of key markets and market segments. Do not base growth in your market or segment on growth in an unrelated market or segment.

Realistically choose market drivers that create growth and appropriate comparable markets for your product or service that reflect growth. For example, growth in the total sales of software may not be related closely to growth in a market segment such as medical software. Sales of neckware may not relate to a market for bow ties. A sea of market data is available on-line and in hard copy from government agencies by Standard Industrial Code (SIC), from trade publications, and trade associations, as well as from annual corporate reports and consultants' reports. Obtain appropriate market data for each segment for the past five years and project this into the future. Consider hiring a graduate student part-time to help you obtain the data. Sources for this data are listed in Chapter 4.

For more detailed information or for markets on which little data exist, the entrepreneur may conduct his or her own customer focus groups or original research. You could hire a consultant to help with the project and possibly share the cost with a potential investor.

Besides defining market segments and targets by traditional industry breakdowns, look at segmentation and targeting based on present and potential dollars of revenue and income, the cost to sell and service, and the probability of success. For example, do mass merchants or specialty stores represent your target markets for imported leather bags? Do utilities, railroads, or airlines represent your best opportunity to sell telephone equipment? How can your product, equipment, or services be customized for each market segment? Other means of segmenting markets are discussed in Chapter 4.

State the key driver for each market or market segment. Is it newly discovered cases of prostate cancer or interest rates? Use micro- and macrodrivers such as changes in interest rates, demographics, technology, or hospital admissions.

As discussed later in this chapter, your sales forecast will be driven by market size, unit and dollar growth, and expected market share. Investors and lenders will evaluate future returns and cash flow based on sales and profit forecasts and the validity of the market data they are based on. Accurate market data help create accurate financial projections on which investors and lenders base decisions, on which the entrepreneur bases his or her planning, and against which the entrepreneur or small business manager measures actual results. The business plan summarizes these market data.

A business or strategic plan should include a discussion of present and potential strategic partners who can help the new- or early-stage enterprise make or sell its products or services. For example, the radioactive seed firm for the treatment of prostate cancer has a strategic partnership with an exclusive distributor for reaching one market segment and with an exclusive source of radioactive material for all its manufacturing needs.

Many new enterprises and small businesses overlook the export market, which may be several times the domestic opportunity. Your business or strategic plan should discuss overseas opportunities in Europe, Asia, NAFTA, and third-world countries. For example, your cutting fluid chemicals or portable reading lights may represent a mature product in North American but a growth market in Central and South America.

Similarly, are there overlooked domestic niche markets for your product or service, such as the premium market, direct-mail catalogs, or government procurement centers? For example, many large postal centers contain a cafeteria where you may be able to market your firm's frozen dough. Besides selling golf shirts to retailers, why not sell through corporate gift and premium distributors?

The business plan should contain a discussion about government regulations in each of your firm's market segments. For example, home health-care providers must meet certain government guidelines. The radioactive seed firm has regulatory issues with the Federal Drug Administration, IDNS, Department of Transportation, and the Nuclear Regulatory Commission.

As you can see, the business or strategic plan makes the small-business person and entrepreneur take a hard look at many parts of the present or proposed business.

COMPETITION

As mentioned, most new enterprises and small businesses underestimate their present and potential competition. A business or strategic plan should realistically list present competitors' ranked by importance and market share for the past five years, plus present and potential competitors ranked by importance and market share for the next three years. Who are the leaders and why? A business or strategic plan should also include a competitive grid listing competitors across the top and competitive issues down the left-hand side. How do customers choose between one competitor and another: breadth of line, capacity, lifetime value, bandwidth, relationships, return on investment, value-added services, or price? How does your company compare to competition, ants and gorillas, on each competitive issue? Which competitive issues are table stakes, and which differentiators? Can you quantify benefits and competitive advantages in dollars? What market segments and target customers do the firm's competitive advantages point it toward? Which competitors have recently left or entered the market and why? Which competitors in your market or a comparable one have been successful using your proposed approach or model? Can your enterprise benchmark their process and success? Which competitors in your market or a comparable one have failed using your approach or model and why? What will your firm do differently to avoid such a failure?

Professional investors are wary of entrepreneurs who do not fully understand their competitors, market dynamics, and customer characteristics, or who underestimate competition and overestimate markets. The business plan allows you an opportunity to demonstrate what you know and how you plan to translate that into action. Again, the business plan forces the entrepreneur and small business owner to think strategically about the business.

For the entrepreneur, small business manager, investor, and lender an accurate assessment of competition helps evaluate an enterprise's future scalability, probability of success, revenue, and profit potential. A realistic assessment of past, present, and future competition also strategically identifies target markets where you are strong and competition is weak.

In analyzing potential competitors, consider barriers to entry by answering these questions: Do barriers to entry exist in the uniqueness of a product or service or in the marketing of it? Can your firm overcome barriers to entry in market segments not presently sold by wrapping a service around the product? Might successful firms in related markets decide to enter your segment?

Be sure to consider potential entrants from overseas markets such as China or Mexico, which might have a competitive advantage in labor or raw material costs. For example, should China or Brazil receive new trade status, would that affect the market for women's handbags?

In analyzing competition, your business or strategic plan must discuss present and potential prices by answering these questions. For example, does your waste hauling company charge based on cost plus or what the market will bear? Can you raise prices or use different prices for different market segments? The business plan forces you to reconsider pricing every six months. Does your pricing maximize dollars of income over time based on competitive advantages in features, benefits, and image, type of product, and type of customer? How much pricing power exists for your enterprise? How sensitive is unit volume to price today and will that change in three years when certain patents expire? Professional investors become concerned when after justifying your product's or service's superior features and benefits, you suggest underpricing competition. An accurate and realistic assessment of these pricing issues influences future profits and cash flow. These pricing issues are discussed in Chapter 7.

In preparing its business plan, one early-stage commercial security device firm discovered that without a company-run monitoring and maintenance service, the company was at a tremendous competitive disadvantage. They also discovered that with a leasing program the company could create long-term barriers to entry. By preparing a business plan management discovered their most serious competitors were not ADT or Wells Fargo but other newly funded start-ups. Management also discovered the most profitable commercial market was retail stores located in low-income areas. A properly prepared and updated business plan can help entrepreneurs look at alternatives, measure risks and rewards, make decisions, and take action.

PRODUCTS OR SERVICES OFFERED

Business plan topics overlap and intersect each other in many areas. A discussion of products or services will certainly allude to previous material covered in sections on customers, markets, and competition. Here, again, as with customers, markets, and competition, the business or strategic plan looks not only at the present and future but at the past.

What customer needs does the product or service satisfy? Could it satisfy other needs? For example, a compact disc scratch removal device, which has been sold through music stores, also satisfies a need for removing scratches on CD-ROMs, which have different channels of distribution, such as computer stores.

In discussing your product or service, describe not only the features, but also how they benefit the customer. For example, with business-to-business (B2B) exchanges, benefits can be quantified in terms of increased dollars of revenues, reduced dollars of expenses, or lower working capital and capital expenditure needs. For example, the compact disc device removes scratches so that consumers don't have to replace their damaged CDs. It saves consumers the cost of a replacement.

Assuming the business has a history, the plan ranks products or services in terms of not only present dollars of revenue and income and percentage of total company sales but for past and future periods. What are, have, and will be the top sellers and why? For example, in 2000 a Chicago firm's top revenue and income-producing distance learning class was an e-commerce boot camp; in 2001, the top class involved strategy; and in 2002, the owner projects it will concern sales management. The topics reflect client needs in a changing business environment.

Past, present, and future products or services should be ranked not only by dollars of annual sales, and percentage of total company revenues, but also by dollars of annual margin, income, or profit. This analysis can be done by product or service or product line. Which products or services generate the greatest sales dollars and which the greatest profit dollars? What factors drive sales, what influences profits, and are they changing?

Most new enterprises lack diversification in products, customers, and markets. Entrepreneurs and small-business people continually debate the merits and risks of focus versus diversification. Writing a business or strategic plan gives you an opportunity to consider product enhancements and line extensions, plus other areas in which to develop new products or services and cultivate new customers. For example, a prostate cancer seed firm might logically enter the market for treating breast cancer. A one-day bathroom remodeling firm might consider kitchen remodeling. A reform math textbook firm might consider entering the social studies area. Be sure to state the costs and potential returns involved in developing new products or services.

In the section on products or services, you certainly want to discuss specific future opportunities. For example, this year a distributor plans to offer a new imported line of coated paper from France, a transformer manufacturer plans to develop a miniature transformer, or a communications firm plans to offer a new teleconferencing service. Next year these same three firms, respectively, plan to distribute a new line of low-cost paper for copying machines, develop a high-capacity transformer for utility firms, and offer a wireless teleconferencing service.

For a new enterprise, the business plan should discuss what development work at what costs are necessary to transform any present prototypes or working models into final products or service ready for the marketplace. What costs are necessary for the development of new products or services over the next three years?

If appropriate, you might want to include dependence on a few products or services and customer or market concentration in the section on critical risks. Other, more macro critical risks, alluded to previously, might include established competitors and talented but unproven management.

Although repetitive, you might want to do a competitive grid for each individual product or service or product line. Do competitors and customers differ for different products or services? If so, why?

Include a paragraph or two on intellectual property issues. Do you have or will you apply for patents, copyrights, and trademarks? What is the cost to defend them and the probability of success? Do present or potential competitors have patents, copyrights, and trademarks? When do your present patents and trademarks expire?

If the business plan is being used to raise equity or debt financing, you should include a complete description of the products or services and possibly attach product literature. How technical is the product or service and is the related technology changing? Where are the products or services in their life cycle: growth or maturity? Remember, since professional investors look for easily differentiated products or services, your business plan must emphasize this.

Although pricing was discussed under competition, each product's or service's transactional pricing, pricing zone, and rationale for pricing should be discussed in this part of the plan as well. Is there an opportunity to raise prices in the future? Does your firm have any power to maintain present pricing? As the product or service matures and barriers to entry decrease, will new competitors force lower prices?

How customers measure and define quality represents an important business plan topic, along with your ability to maintain these quality standards. Can you consistently knit sweaters that maintain their shape, color, fit, and sizing after numerous cleanings or washings? Can your e-commerce Web site handle thousands of visitors on a 24/7 basis? The answers to such questions should be included in your business plan.

CHANNEL CHOICE

In addition to information about management, customers, markets, competition, and products, a business or strategic plan should discuss past, present, and future channel choices. For example, imagine that your new enterprise presently uses channel partners, independent sales representatives, to sell reform math textbooks. These channel partners represent a variable cost, 100 percent performance pay, and have excellent contacts at school boards. However, in two years you plan to start replacing these independent representatives with full-time salespeople, because new products will require a longer sales cycle and more consultative selling. Such strategic issues should be included in your business plan. Business is a dynamic process and the future is a moving target.

Channel choice might include a description of the retailers you sell through or how you support salespeople with telemarketing, e-mail, electronic data interchange (EDI), or a Web site. In this section the entrepreneur or small business manager examines more efficient ways to reach the gatekeeper and end user. For example, presently, an emission control firm uses full-time direct salespeople to call on original equipment manufacturers. The business plan discusses adding distributors to sell replacement parts in the after-markets.

Early-stage enterprises often initially choose distribution channels with variable or low costs, which are not appropriate as the enterprise matures. Therefore, each year, use the business plan to analyze whether your distribution channels need adjusting to reflect your business's growth and the changing marketplace.

SALES FORCE

Business is a dynamic process and the future is a moving target. Business or strategic plans help you deal with change and avoid legacy issues. The sales organization must change to reflect changing markets, customers, competition, and products. An annual business or strategic plan analyzes the number of salespeople, their revenues, profits, organization, deployment, and productivity.

For example, each year an early-stage national limousine service based in Los Angeles, which takes reservations over the Internet, analyzes its sales force, which calls on large corporations and travel agents. After subtracting from the salesperson's revenues their compensation, benefits, expenses, and contract drivers' fees, management determines how many gross margin dollars each salesperson contributes to company profits. Based on each salesperson's gross margin dollars, call rate or capacity versus the territory's number of present and potential A, B, and C accounts, present and potential revenue and income; the firm's management decides whether to adjust territory boundaries or hire more salespeople. The limousine service business plan also states their two-year goal of changing the sales force from territories organized by geography alone to a hybrid organized by type customer, one for travel agents and one for large corporations. All this is presented in the annual business plan.

Some criteria you might use to measure sales force or salesperson productivity include:

Average calls per week per salesperson
Frequency of calls on A accounts
Hours per week per salesperson in front of customers
Revenues per salesperson per call or per customer
Closing ratios
Number of active accounts
Product mix
Average order size
Average cost of a call

Business plans used to raise equity and debt funds must clearly describe and rationalize the number and type of salespeople and channel partners needed over the next several years. These business plans must discuss what type compensation, fixed versus performance pay, will be used and why. As products or services mature and move from new system sales to a modified rebuy, maybe the business plan should suggest shifting to a greater or lesser portion of performance pay. Business plans force the entrepreneur to think ahead, plan, and set goals. A well-prepared business plan gives investors and banks confidence in management and the business model.

Business plans used to raise equity financing and debt should discuss how often customers are seen, the number of customers each salesperson has, how salesperson productivity is measured, buyer behavior, and buying center issues. Again, these subjects overlap with other topics in your business plan.

Similarly, business plans used to raise equity and debt financing must describe who is responsible for sales management, that person's qualifications, and how he or she plans to hire, train, compensate, organize, motivate, and evaluate the sales force. A weak sales manager or no sales manager increases the risk of failure and decreases the probability of success. If your start-up or early-stage venture has no sales manager, state this, but also state when such a person will be hired and how the function will be handled in the interim.

The business plan should include data on and rank each salesperson by sales, income, productivity, market share, number of customers, product mix, growth rate, and percentage of total company revenue. It should also identify the number-one salesperson in each category and indicate the reason.

The business or strategic plan should discuss programs for training salespeople in product, customer, and competitor knowledge and in selling skills. Will this involve sales meetings and field coaching? A business plan should discuss not only possibly expanding the sales organization but also necessary replacements and improvements.

Your business plan should also identify what percentage of each revenue dollar goes for selling expenses. In the future will it grow or decrease in dollars and as a percentage of revenues?

MARKETING

Your business plan should outline advertising and promotional activities plus associated costs. Under marketing you might also discuss new product or service development and pricing issues. Here again, you can see overlap in topics and how you have a choice of where and when to discuss various topics.

How do you plan to presell or create a demand for your product or service and what will it cost? Possibly, in year one of an early-stage firm you will exhibit at trade shows and advertise in trade publications plus send press releases to appropriate magazines and newspapers. In year two the company will hold user and prospect workshops and seminars, plus engage in telesales prospecting and e-mail advertising. You will ask suppliers to help pay for all these expenses.

Most early-stage firms are unknown to their customers, prospects, and markets. Investors look for creative, low-cost marketing, advertising, and promotion that create necessary awareness. Entrepreneurs must realize that as the business matures, different advertising and promotion becomes more efficient. For example, a two-day bathroom remodeling firm based in Tampa began by advertising on cable television but within two years migrated to home improvement fairs instead of cable.

OPERATIONS

Sales are made on the street, but profits are made from operations. In today's highly competitive global markets, the entrepreneur must not only have an effective, efficient means of reaching the marketplace and customers, but must also be the low-cost producer or low-cost service provider in his or her price range. The business plan helps the entrepreneur to plan for this and the investor to understands this.

Whether a service business or a product manufacturer, capacity issues require constant attention in business plans. For example, as a contract service provider for computer programming or maintenance, your success depends on the firm's ability to attract and retain qualified people. In a highly competitive environment, where the demand for qualified technicians far outstrips the supply, how will you attract and retain the best?

For example, as a supplier of bedding plants to mass merchants, your capacity is limited by the acres under glass in your greenhouses. As a supplier of high-speed semiconductors for cellular phones, your capacity is limited by fabricating machines. The business plan projects unit growth of 20 percent, but using these projections shows you would run out of manufacturing capacity to supply growth in year three. Can you contract out manufacturing, import product, or must you construct more greenhouses and buy more fabricating equipment? If more equipment must be purchased or more greenhouses constructed, what will it cost, and how can this be financed with debt, equity, or internally generated cash flow? What return can you expect from these capital expenditures? All these questions must be addressed in the business plan and will be of interest to the entrepreneur, investor, or lender. The answers to these questions will create future standards against which to measure actual results.

If a manufacturing enterprise, the business or strategic plan must address not only issues of machine, facility, and labor capacity, but also issues of equipment speed, versatility, age, and technology. As a start-up, your competitive advantage might lie in being able to purchase the latest and best generation of equipment. As a latter-stage business, last-generation equipment and facilities might represent a competitive disadvantage, which requires capital expenditures to regain a competitive edge.

Investors and lending institutions will express interest in a business's information technology systems. Are they adequate, or what is required to make them adequate? Information technology is the great equalizer for new and smaller enterprises, leveling the playing field with larger businesses. Appropriate computers, communication systems, and software allow new enterprises and smaller firms to efficiently interact with larger suppliers and customers and reduce labor costs. By continually updating the proper information technology and communication systems, smaller enterprises can double revenues without doubling the head count. Your business plan should describe the present uses of computers, communication systems, and software, plus plans to update the equipment, systems, and programs in future years.

Next, your business plan should analyze human resource issues. Include an organization chart and head count by department for the last three years, this year, and the next three years. How many salespeople, engineers, machine operators, clericals, microbiologists, programmers, carpenters, installers, warehouse people, service people, or truck drivers will be required in future years? What will their duties be and what skills, knowledge, experience and personal characteristics are required? How will you recruit, train, compensate, organize, motivate, and evaluate this growing number of employees or contractors? Who will manage the human resource functions and who will have direct responsibility for the people in each department? In three years, assuming certain growth rates, will you hire full-time people to replace outside contract services? Will you need a controller or systems person and how will all these human resource issues impact costs including direct compensation, fringe benefits, and support expenses? A business plan that answers these questions helps the entrepreneur plan and set standards against which to measure future results.

Why did you choose the present location of your business: proximity to employees, customers, or suppliers? Might that change in future years, requiring the firm to move?

For a start-up, when and how will you acquire the necessary facilities, equipment, and people? What are the associated costs and how will they be financed?

In planning operations consider the cost per unit of providing your product or service (productivity) and alternative means of doing this. An urban parcel delivery service estimates the cost of a same-day delivery at $8, but plans to lower this to $7 by giving delivery people cellular phones. A genomics firm estimates the present cost of sequencing at 10 cents per genome, but plans to reduce it 30 percent through better utilization of equipment. Can cycle times be reduced through the use of total quality management? Your business plan should contain information on operating costs in absolute dollars, the cost per unit, and ideas for reducing both. These issues influence profits and cash flow and will be of interest to investors and lenders.

A business plan should discuss opportunities for make versus buy. What operations are more cost efficient and critical to keep inside versus to contract out? The business plan exercise forces entrepreneurs and small businesspeople to consider these issues. For example, a genomics firm may contract out sequencing to a low-cost provider, but maintain internal control over annotation or interpretation of the sequencing. A compact disc scratch-removal device firm might farm out plastic injection molding of parts but maintain control over final assembly. A distance learning firm might maintain control over content but allow other firms to distribute its programs. You might consider contracting out the field sales force by using independent reps or distributors. You might consider contracting out administrative functions such as payroll, accounting, human resources, or information technology to firms that specialize in these services. Alternative costs represent part of the decision, but control over proprietary material and key processes for customer satisfaction represent equally important aspects. As companies grow and change over time, these make-versus-buy decisions must be rethought.

If operations involve or might involve employees who belong to unions, the business or strategic plan must address the key issues such as wages, benefits, work rules, contract dates, and pensions. Entrepreneurs must plan for this and investors or lenders must understand it.

Also, government regulations related to operations should be discussed and planned for. Do compliance issues exist with EPA or OSHA? This could pose a critical risk for investors and the firm. Is there a contingency plan? Will compliance issues change over time? Government regulations were also discussed under market issues.

Supplier power, which is of great interest to investors and lenders, should also be discussed under operations. In 2001 starting or expanding a business requiring large amounts of electricity in Southern California would represent a critical risk. Many new enterprises and smaller businesses are very dependent on a few suppliers, which have considerable pricing power. The prostate cancer seed implant company has only two possible suppliers of radioactive isotopes, one of which they have a long-term contract with. Investors and lenders will want to know if higher costs resulting from supplier power can be passed on to your customers.

A family-owned California giftware importer buys from several Chinese manufacturers who also sell direct to U.S. mass merchants. The smaller giftware importer has reduced each supplier's power by contracting with alternative sources in Singapore and the Philippines. In her business plan the importer lists exchange rate fluctuations and political government changes as critical risks. Forward contracts are used to offset the exchange rate risks.

All business or strategic plans should list major past, present, and potential suppliers, their prices, features, benefits, and competitive advantages. Suppliers should then be ranked by desirability. This exercise requires the entrepreneur to consider alternatives, critical risks, and contingency plans.

A business or strategic plan should state industry metrics for measuring supplier and customer quality and methods for controlling and improving quality. For a service business, customer satisfaction, percentage rework and wait time might reflect quality. Controls to improve quality might include better training of personnel, less rigorous schedules for operators, and asking customers about expectations. For a manufacturing business, quality might be defined as consistent tolerances, meeting performance specifications, and exceeding failure rates. Quality improvement might result from inspection of incoming suppliers, regular maintenance of equipment, and continual training of personnel.

FINANCIAL STATEMENTS AND PROJECTIONS

Investors and lenders want to examine line-item financial statements for the past five years, monthly projections for the next year, and annual pro formas for the following two or three years. Include this material in your business plan. For a start-up or early-stage business, past and present financial statements have little ability to predict the future. Generally they contain start-up expenses with no or little revenue. They show how the founders have spent their initial investment.

For latter-stage firms, past and present financial statements reflect the ability of the business model to scale-up revenues, control expenses, and generate cash flow. Audited statements help to create credibility even though they stretch a small business's limited budget.

Future projections must state the assumptions on which they are built. For instance, revenue for a home health-care service is driven by the number of patients released from local hospitals. The installation of one-day bathroom remodeling units is driven by the number of home improvement fairs attended by the firm. Revenues of an e-commerce site for beauty parlors are driven by the number of salons that subscribe plus the number of services offered. Looking at cash flow and expenses, payments of accounts receivable and accounts payable might be based on industry averages. Line-item expenses including payroll and material might be based on past company experience, industry standards, the business model, or a multiplier of unit costs.

Sudden increases or decreases in revenues or line-item dollar costs or dollar costs as a percentage of revenue require separate explanation. The projected revenues for the compact disc scratch removal device firm doubles in year three, because they plan to sell them via two new major multistore chains. Per unit manufacturing costs decrease significantly each year, showing economies of scale, but also total cost reductions from less subcontracting and more internal manufacturing.

Financial statements are important not only to investors and lenders but to operating management. Investors use financial statements to establish valuations, risks, and potential returns on investment. Lenders use financial statements to evaluate the need for cash and the ability to repay it through cash flow or collateral. Both parties are interested in the sources and uses of funds. Management uses past and present financial statements and pro forma projections for the same purposes as investors and lenders but also to help them manage and measure the business. How and why do line-item expenses from sales force compensation to insurance costs to material costs change over time? How do sales and profit trends compare to the industry standards? What opportunities exist to reduce costs? Of course, management will use pro forma projections against which to measure actual costs.

Entrepreneurs and small-business people must understand and analyze the enterprise's key control points that measure and control results and productivity. Key control points will vary by business enterprise and are discussed in Chapter 3. The business plan should track and predict such key control points as average revenues, costs, and margins by account or by product or service line. Have they risen in the past or will they rise in the future? Other key control points might include days of sale in accounts receivable and inventory, capital expenditures, and working capital ratios. Also, labor and materials as a percentage of revenue might be a key control point in certain industries.

For pro forma projections prepare a best, worst, and most probable case scenario. Assign probabilities of success to each case and clearly state the different assumptions of each scenario. If in two years we can open a particular major account, and if no major overseas competitors enter the market, and if we continue our present strategic alliances, then the probability of achieving our best case remains at 75 percent. As these assumptions change, so do the probabilities of reaching our best, worst, or most probable case. Each year these sensitivity-related projections should be compared to actual results. The business plan represents a long-range sales forecast and expense budget. Each year or quarter compare actual results to the sales forecast and expense budget, explain variances and discuss corrective action. Every year or six months repeat the process by preparing a new business plan with new assumptions, probabilities, and financial statement projections. Business plans should represent a continuous process not an event.

The business plan should include not only past and present profit and loss statements, and cash flow statements along with future pro formas, but also balance sheets. Past, present, and projected balance sheets have a major impact on cash flow statements. A business plan should contain five years of actual historic balance sheets, if available, monthly projections for the first year, and year-end statements for the next three or four years. These balance sheet pro formas will be based on the best, worst, and most probable profit and loss statements with their attendant assumptions.

However, the pro forma balance sheets must also carry their own group of assumptions concerning capital expenditures, debt, and equity financing. The best-case balance sheet pro forma projection might assume a certain dollar amount invested at a certain price per

share; the worst-case projection might assume a lesser dollar investment, at a lower valuation. The best-case projection might assume no
need to buy a building but only equipment, while the worst case
might assume the need to buy facilities and equipment.

Similarly assumptions must be made concerning the terms and
conditions of future working capital and long-term loans. What percentage of accounts receivable and inventory can be borrowed? What
will the length and debt service be of any term loans used to purchase
fixed assets?

Also, the business or strategic plan should discuss and quantify
off-balance sheet liabilities, such as the rental amount and terms of contracts or leases. Guarantees and warranties for products and services
should be noted, quantified, and possibly listed as critical risks. Estimate
the cost of replacing returned products or providing warranted services.

EXECUTIVE SUMMARY AND
MISSION STATEMENT

The executive summary may get the entrepreneur a phone conversation
with an investor and the phone conversation may result in a meeting.
The executive summary is a sales tool directed at investors and lenders
to get their attention and interest. To save time, write the executive summary last, not first, even though it will appear at the beginning of your
business plan. Use the executive summary to restate the key merits and
risks of your enterprise. Include key points from each section: management, customers, markets, competitors, products or services, operations, channels of distribution, sales organization, marketing, human
resources, information technology, financial statements, critical risks,
and timetable of events. This five-page executive summary should then
be placed at the start of your business plan. Five pages represent the initial attention span you will receive from busy investors and bankers.

Professional equity investors receive hundreds of business plans
a year but only invest in a few enterprises. Executive summaries are
the most frequently read section of the plan. Be sure to include:

- The company's origins, activities, management, and perform-
  ance to date
- The product's or service's distinguishing features and benefits
- The attractiveness of the market
- A summary of key financial statements and projections
- The amount of money being sought; equity, debt, or both;
  and how this money will be used to enhance growth and
  profitability
- The possible exits

The executive summary should contain a short mission state-ment at the beginning or better yet at the end. In no more than five sentences the mission statement gives the company's longer-range vision and objectives. Obviously, you don't want to include a mission statement that does not reflect the quality of your enterprise. It is often easier to write the mission statement after writing the business plan. A start-up shouldn't be grandiose in the mission statement, because this often reflects naiveté. The mission statement of a start-up might be "To build a $25 million business selling radioactive seeds and value-added related services to urologists," or "To build a $20 million specialty con-sumer electronics firm, selling through mass merchants using our CD scratch remover as the initial platform."

The order of topics presented in your business plan may vary depending on the intended reader and the objective. For investors you may lead with product or services, markets, and financial statements. For lenders you might lead with management, customers, and com-petitors. For internal purposes I would suggest the order outlined in this chapter. For investors you would add a discussion of merits, risks, and exit strategies.

SHORT HISTORY

The executive summary (or a separate section) should contain a short history of the business, including when it was started and important events to date. This narrative sometimes describes how the products or services were chosen and developed, and what role management has played in bringing the business to its present state. This section also should mention past problems or setbacks, how they were dealt with, and how to avoid them in the future.

CRITICAL RISKS AND CONTINGENCY PLANS

Once you have written the business plan, make a list of critical risks and contingency plans covering what could go wrong, what you will do to prevent that, and what corrective action will you take after-wards. Most business plans do not contain realistic critical risks or meaningful means of dealing with them. This leaves the entrepreneurs unprepared and the investor skeptical.

Planning makes good things happen. We react better to problems if we have a plan for dealing with them. Critical risks alert the entre-preneur to potential problem areas and prepare him or her on how to prevent them or how to deal with them. Realistic critical risks and con-tingency plans communicate experience to the investor and instill confidence. For example, what action will you take if competitors lower prices or suppliers raise them? Can you wrap a service around the product and maintain price or must you meet competition? Do you have alternative suppliers? Can you raise price or must you live with lower profit margins?

Critical risks and merits change over time as businesses mature. Your business or strategic plans should reflect these changes. Some business or strategic plans contain both critical risks and merits, especially if they are used to raise different rounds of equity financing.

For an early-stage firm risks might include funding, management, and product acceptance; for a latter-stage firm risks might include scalability, competition, and labor shortages. For an early-stage firm merits might include comparables, a proven model, and industry growth, versus key customers, strategic partners, and excellent results for a latter-stage firm.

TIMETABLE OF EVENTS

A schedule showing the timing and interrelationship of the major events necessary to launch or grow the venture and realize its objectives represents an essential part of any business or strategic plan. In addition to being a planning tool and showing deadlines critical to a venture's success, a well-prepared schedule is an extremely effective aid for raising equity funds. It instills confidence in management's ability to plan and act, plus it demonstrates why and when each financing round takes place.

Prepare a month-by-month schedule showing the timing of key activities such as product development, trade show attendance, recruitment of major team members, and purchase of equipment. Show the timing of primary tasks necessary to accomplish major goals. Show the deadlines or milestones critical to your venture's success, such as completion of the prototype, hiring of management members, leasing a facility, purchasing computers and software, calling on customers, and starting operations.

Discuss the activities (for example, equipment installation) most likely to cause schedule slippage and necessary corrective action. Discuss the impact of slippage on the venture's operation and capital needs.

As you can see from this chapter, properly prepared business and strategic plans represent powerful tools for entrepreneurs and small-business managers. You need a road map to make the journey.

ENTREPRENEURS' MAJOR MISTAKES AND WEAKNESSES IN WRITING BUSINESS PLANS

- Underestimating competition and overestimating markets and revenues.
- Not stating the assumptions on which pro formas are based.
- Confusing profits and cash flow.
- Not presenting the best, worst, and most likely scenarios.
- Not stating realistic critical risks and contingency plans.
- Not quantifying how the features and benefits of your products or services can increase a customer's revenues, decrease their costs, and reduce working capital needs or capital expenditures.
- Analyzing markets rather than market segments.
- Not discussing strategic partners.
- Not understanding competitive barriers to entry and customer switching costs.
- Not clearly differentiating the product or service, channel choice, sales organization, and marketing approach.
- Neglecting to discuss operational excellence and to analyze capacity issues.

QUESTIONS AND EXERCISES

1. Does your enterprise have a business plan, marketing plan, or strategic plan?
2. How do you use it? Who reads it? When was it revised?
3. Compare the subjects in your business, marketing, or strategic plan with the topics in this chapter. What subjects are missing or out of date?
4. What action has your firm taken as a result of these plans?
5. Do the plans address past, present, and future issues?
6. Do the plans realistically deal with changing competitors, products, customers, and markets?

CHAPTER 2

Proper Financing

As previously mentioned, there are three strategic alternative means for you to become an entrepreneur. Each alternative has different risks, merits, rewards, advantages, and disadvantages. You may choose to start a new business by developing and introducing a new product or service; buying an existing business, managing it, and possibly some-day selling it; or cloning an existing business model, possibly by fran-chising someone else's idea.

Whatever strategic alternative you choose, you will need to finance your enterprise by either debt or equity financing. These forms of financing have different risks and rewards, advantages and disad-vantages, costs of capital, and expected returns.

You must engage a qualified attorney to assist you in raising the first dollar and then all subsequent amounts of debt and equity. There is a proper format and sequence for doing this. Unless early-stage financing is done properly, later stages become more restrictive and expensive. Ask successful entrepreneurs and small-business owners for referrals, and know exactly what skills, knowledge, and experience you seek in an attorney. Interview several attorneys at several law firms. Be sure to consider that the top hourly rates of an experienced attorney may be cheaper in the long run, because the total hours and total cost of an experienced attorney may actually be less than that charged by other, less experienced attorneys with lower hourly rates. Ask the attorney for a list of entrepreneurial clients with your needs from your industry and call a select group for reference.

In addition to hiring an attorney, you must also engage a quali-fied independent accountant to help in preparing pro forma state-ments: forecasts of future revenues, expenses, profits, assets, liabilities, cash flows, and resulting needs for outside financing from investors, banks, or other lenders. The process and format for preparing pro forma and cash flow forecasts is discussed in Chapter 3. Again, look for independent accountants with start-up or early-stage experience in your industry; talk to several candidates and check references.

The entrepreneur must look at financing as a long-range continual process. Entrepreneurs spend most of their time and energy financing their enterprise and then marketing and selling their product or service. Today you start with an idea, some human resources, and minimal funds. To break even in year three and reach your revenue forecasts in year five how much outside money will be needed each year for operating losses, inventory, accounts receivable, and capital expenditures? Does the cash shortfall lend itself to equity or debt? What are the best financing sources? If equity, how much ownership do you want to give up at each round, so that you maintain an appropriate number of shares for yourself and other key employees?

DEBT FINANCING

Although banks represent the major source of debt financing for early-stage firms and small businesses, you should also consider:

- Family and friends
- Asset-based lenders
- Suppliers
- Government agencies
- Customers
- Cash flow improvements

In either debt or equity financing, the lending source or investor will insist that the owner has made a major investment of his or her own assets in the business. As an entrepreneur or small business owner you must accept this risk.

Often, family and friends are also included in this first round or early-stage investment. This early-stage, high-risk investment often takes the form of low-interest debt convertible into stock at a very favorable price or debt with warrants to buy equity at a very favorable price. Debt gives the investor a somewhat senior position and the ability to write off the investment sooner should the company not succeed. The interest on the debt gives the start-up or small business a tax-deductible expense or tax shield.

The second round of financing may include a bank, asset-based lenders, and government agencies for debt, plus private value-added investors, suppliers, and customers for equity. The third round of financing may include a venture capital investor for equity; the fourth round, a corporate partner with a strategic interest in your business for equity; and the fifth round, an initial public offering. We will discuss these later rounds under equity financing.

You must have a plan for each round of debt and equity financing before you start round one. How much debt and equity will be required in each round? What sources will be approached? How much ownership must you give up? Most entrepreneurs and small-business managers only use a 12-month time frame in planning their financial needs. Eventually, this wastes the entrepreneur's and small business manager's time, increases the cost of capital or funding, and dilutes eventual ownership. To make intelligent decisions now you must plan what the desired capital structure should be in 36 months. Though needs and sources will change along the way, you will benefit from a flexible long-range, multiround plan.

For a start-up or early-stage firm, how long will it require to get to cash neutral or break-even and what cash deficits will result? How will your start-up or early-stage firm finance those deficits? Operating deficits will require equity financing, while capital expenditures might lend themselves to debt or leasing.

In running your financial projections for a growth-stage firm, determine how many marginal dollars of inventory, accounts receivable, and capital expenditures (capX) are required for each marginal dollar of revenue. To grow your enterprise from one million dollars to three million dollars of annual revenue over four years might require another $400,000 of accounts receivable, $300,000 of inventory, and $250,000 of capital expenditures. How much can you finance through internally generated cash flow, such as accounts payable, earnings before income taxes, depreciation, and amortization? How much will you have to borrow or raise in equity funds?

If your business will generate good quality accounts receivable, these can be sold to a financial factor at a discount. You receive less than face value immediately, probably 80 to 85 percent, and the factor collects the funds. This is common with small apparel firms and importers. The 15 to 20 percent cost/discount is high, but the factor replaces your accounts receivable collection function. On the other hand, you may lose some customers who prefer not to deal with factors who can be tough in collections. The factor will charge you back for uncollected accounts receivables. Some factors also loan a small percentage on your inventory value and may take possession of inventory. Again, the costs are high.

If your business requires a large investment in capital equipment, consider leasing that equipment from the manufacturer or a third party with an option to buy. As in leasing an automobile, total costs of ownership over the life of the equipment rises, but monthly cash flow requirements decrease. Many equipment manufacturers offer leasing programs, some bundled with maintenance, upgrades, and training. Some commercial leasing companies specialize in early-stage firms and offer more favorable terms in exchange for equity.

Government agencies represent an important source of debt and equity funds for start-ups. Many cities, counties, states, regions, universities, and not-for-profit organizations have microloan programs for start-ups that create new job opportunities, are owned by minorities, or support certain technologies such as biotech. The local Commerce Department or Small Business Administration (SBA) office should have a list of these organizations. Often city specific or state specific periodicals will publish the list. Add to these two sources an appropriate Web site search, and you should have uncovered most of these programs. Some of these organizations combine low-cost consulting services with loan packages.

A number of loan programs exist for minority-owned businesses. The SBA can make or guarantee loans to minority entrepreneurs for up to $100,000. Also, minority enterprise small business investment companies (MESBICs) make loans to and investments in minority-owned firms. MESBICs use private funds and government loans as sources of their capital.

As mentioned in the Introduction to this book and as discussed in Chapters 3 and 7, proper pricing and proper working capital controls will suffice to finance many small businesses and early-stage firms. The cheapest funds are those generated internally. Besides pricing at what the market will bear to maximize dollars of income over time, consider increasing your billing cycle from once a month to twice a month. Consider offering customers incentives for paying faster or prepaying a portion of the invoice. Equipment manufacturers and furniture retailers often finance themselves through customer deposits, which function as partial prepayments.

Alternatively, consider working with suppliers on longer payment terms. An extra 30 days can save you interest payments and equity dilution.

Service businesses face extra challenges in this area because they have no inventory and few fixed assets. Also, accounts receivable collection depends on customer satisfaction or successful completion of a project, and payroll cannot be deferred. Early-stage service businesses need owner-infused equity and good margins to overcome these challenges.

Going to the Bank

Most successful entrepreneurs and small-business owners will want to obtain or at least consider some bank financing. Generally speaking, a reasonable amount of debt with its tax shield is cheaper than relying totally on equity, which dilutes ownership, especially in early-stage firms.

The best way to approach a bank, as with equity investors, is through a referral. Often your accountant, lawyer, or business associates can provide an introduction to the proper person, which saves you time and energy. You may wish to start at the bank where you have a personal account. As with equity investors, targeting banks with the highest probability of lending you funds saves the entrepreneur's valuable time and energy.

Look for banks with small business, SBA, start-up and/or appropriate industry experience. Some banks have experience lending to early-stage service firms; some do not. Some banks specialize in small construction and retail loans. Look for banks that have enough capital and services to meet your longer-term needs. You may need a $150,000 asset-based loan now, a $250,000 working capital loan next year, or some letters of credit for importing in two years.

If you need an SBA-guaranteed loan and you qualify, look for a bank that does SBA lending. Locate a higher-level loan officer who will be in the job for several years and with whom you can develop a relationship. If that is not possible, meet the junior loan officer's superior to establish continuity. Lastly, check the bank's loan loss record. Many smaller community or neighborhood banks meet most of the previous selection goals, but every three years they purge weaker loans because of internal capital constraints.

Certain banks are SBA-approved lenders, which means that under certain conditions the SBA will guarantee 85 percent of your business loans from that bank over $150,000 and 75 percent of your business loans under $150,000. The bank performs the usual due diligence and must approve the loan as meeting its and the SBA requirements. Since these requirements and conditions change from time to time, check with your bank to find out about eligibility. Also visit the SBA Web site: www.sba.gov for a list of SBA-approved lenders and necessary requirements for loans. The SBA is no longer the lender of last resort, and time frames for approval have shortened. The SBA merely assumes part of the loan's risk once an approved bank has performed the same due diligence it would for any loan approval. The SBA has guaranteed more than 400,000 loans totaling over $50 billion since its creation by the U.S. Congress in 1953.

Be sure to ask your banker about the Low Doc loan program, which applies to SBA loans less than $100,000. Under this program the entrepreneur needs to fill out only a one-page loan application, and the SBA responds through your bank with an approval or nonapproval within a week.

Should a bank or an equity source turn you down, ask why and ask for referrals to other lenders or investors. Try not to be discouraged and remember that every problem represents an opportunity.

A bank, like an equity investor, will want to see your business plan, historical financial statements, and pro formas. A well-written, complete business plan (as described in Chapter 1) serves as a sales aid, reflects your competence, and allows the bank to process your loan more efficiently.

The astute banker wants to know: Do you really need the money? How much is needed? How will it benefit your business? Will the $100,000 loan allow you to hire more people to provide your service, or allow you to buy more efficient equipment to lower your costs, or will it only allow you to pay down accounts payable incurred from past operating losses? Do you need $100,000, $200,000, or $300,000? The entrepreneur and small-business person must quantify how the loan will increase revenues, lower costs, increase profits, support working capital requirements, or pay for capital expenditures.

The entrepreneur or small-business owner must show the banker two methods to repay the loan: cash flow and collateral. Will an increase in revenue and/or decrease in costs resulting from the loan create enough free cash flow to meet interest payments and pay down principal? How many times annual or monthly interest and principal payments is the cash flow or coverage ratio?

Should that method (cash flow) of repayment fail, the entrepreneur or small-business owner must show the banker available collateral that can be monetized. Collateral would include the business's assets such as equipment, accounts receivable, and inventory plus the entrepreneur's personal guarantees. As a small-business person or entrepreneur you will be asked to guarantee the loan with your personal assets. The more and the better the collateral, the better the terms of the loan.

Banks ask for personal guarantees to prevent owners, entrepreneurs, and managers from walking away from difficult situations. Banks don't want to run your business, and they also don't want to take your house. Personal guarantees make entrepreneurs and small-business owners uncomfortable. However, if you have confidence in your business model, the risks of a personal guarantee are not that great. You can negotiate the guarantee by guaranteeing the first or last $100,000 of a $200,000 loan or by guaranteeing a certain amount after liquidation of certain assets.

Entrepreneurs must remember several people make the loan decision and all those people receive a bonus based on their loan's results, success ratios, and actual dollars of margin. Banks and bankers are in the business of making loans, not turning them down. However, your loan officer or banker is paired with a credit analyst. The loan officer's job is to generate business; the credit analyst's job is to select the best opportunities. The loan officer may say yes and smile, only to have the loan turned down by the credit analyst.

The Six Cs

In evaluating loans, bankers refer to the *six Cs:* conditions within the industry, character and competence of management, cash flow, capitalization, and collateral. The entrepreneur and small-business manager must present their business plan and loan request in terms of the six Cs.

Conditions within the industry include market size and growth, market segments, customers, prospects, competition, and competitive advantage. As mentioned, most entrepreneurs overestimate the market and underestimate the competition. The banker will need a clear and simple definition of your business: hardware, software, contract services, programming. If the banker cannot understand your business and business model, your chances for a loan diminish. The banker will need a clear understanding of the changing landscape in terms of customers, technology, and competition. Do critical risks or opportunities lie in these changes? The banker will need a clear understanding of the firm's ability to maintain or raise prices, and the firm's ability to maintain or lower costs. On a macro basis, what happens if interest rates rise, the general economy recedes, or government regulations change?

Competence of management/ownership includes industry, functional, start-up, and small-business experience, plus past successes and failures. Is there a track record of success for each management member and are the important functions covered? Does the start-up need a salesperson? Does the small business need a controller? Equity investors spend a great deal of time investigating management and researching markets, but since banks also rely on collateral and personal guarantees, they spend less time in these areas. Banks and equity investors both insist on key-person life insurance as a condition for a loan or investment.

Character of management/ownership reflects past records for honesty. Does the balance sheet include family loans? Is there a conviction record? Was there a past bankruptcy? Are owner's excessive salaries creating losses that the bank is being asked to finance? Are the owners willing to put in more capital if necessary?

The pro forma and historical financial statements, if any, must include properly prepared cash flows, which reflect not only revenues and expenses but also changes in accounts receivable, accounts payable, inventory, and capital expenditures. If pro formas differ significantly from historical statements, the banker must know why. The entrepreneur must state the assumptions that drive growth or change. Audited historical statements, if they are available, can result in lower rates. Bankers rely more on historical financial data, while equity investors rely more on future pro forma projections. Bankers want stable, reliable, realistic, and predictable cash flows that will allow for repayment of debt and acceptable coverage ratios of interest payments and debt service.

Capital reflects the funds the entrepreneur or small-business owner has invested in the enterprise. Banks and equity investors want management and ownership to have some downside risks. For startups and early-stage businesses, banks generally want paid-in capital plus retained earnings to be equal to their loan. However, with working capital loans based on a percentage of accounts receivable or long-term loans made against a percentage of fixed assets, banks may liberalize their debt to equity ratios. Under such circumstances the bank might approve a loan in which the owner's investment was less than the bank's loan. In presenting your loan requirements to a bank consider the debt-to-equity ratio and your personal investments. Banks and equity investors will not accept situations where they have a great deal of risk and the entrepreneur does not.

The last item of the six Cs is collateral, which we discussed previously as one of two repayment methods.

Tailor your business plan presentation to the six Cs when dealing with a bank. Understand the role of each decision maker and target your selection of a bank.

For smaller loans, some larger banks use credit scoring, a computerized loan-review process which simplifies the six Cs to certain quantitative data, gives weight to each category, and then scores each category based on available historical information. On these smaller loans, rather than incurring the expense of reviewing a business plan, analyzing markets, management, and cash flow, the bank uses software to computerize the evaluation. The applicant fills out a simple application form and the computer totals up pluses and minuses to measure the risk, weighing such factors as years in business, management qualifications, financial ratios, projections, collateral, and promptness in paying bills, liens, lawsuits, judgments, and credit ratings. The loan is approved or denied based on the total credit-rating score.

Types of Loans and Loan Structure

Banks and other providers of debt financing offer short-term loans for repayment in less than a year, and long-term loans for repayment over several years. Short-term loans rely on collateral such as accounts receivable and inventory that convert to cash through sales and customer payments within a year. Long-term loans rely on collateral with longer-life fixed assets, such as machinery, buildings, land, leases at less than market value, and sometimes patents and trademarks.

The entrepreneur who applies for a loan must explain how much is needed and why; how it will be used to increase revenues and profits or decrease costs; how much will be structured as a short-term loan, with accounts receivables or inventory as collateral; and how much will be structured as a long-term loan, with fixed assets as collateral. A service business with no inventory or fixed assets must rely on short-term borrowing using accounts receivable as collateral.

The amount and length of a term loan will depend on your ability to repay, cash flow, and debt coverage ratios, plus the life of the assets used as collateral. A machinery loan might require repayment in five years, while a loan collateralized by real estate might carry a 10-year repayment schedule. An early-stage or small business with substantial cash flow can borrow a higher percentage of its fixed assets than a similar enterprise with less cash flow.

Short-term loans secured by accounts receivable and inventory are often called *working capital revolvers* because the amount of the loan varies from week to week depending on the dollars of accounts receivable and inventory. A bank or other lending facility might loan an early-stage enterprise or small business 60 percent of all accounts receivable under 60 days old and 30 percent of all finished goods inventory under 120 days old, with a limit on total dollars.

As mentioned, short- and long-term loans to most early-stage firms and small businesses will require personal guarantees from the owners and possibly key managers. Entrepreneurs often ask equity investors to help guarantee bank loans.

In making the final choice of a bank for debt financing, compare costs such as interest rates, fees, and compensating balances. Also compare the required collateral and personal guarantees. What percent of each type of collateral can you borrow? Must you personally guarantee all or part of the loan? What cap is put on total borrowing—$400,000 by one bank, $150,000 by another? Compare any restrictive covenants on spending, salaries, capital expenditures, or reporting. Then compare the lending sources based on these previously discussed items:

- Industry, small business. and SBA experience
- Loan officer level and turnover
- Ability to fund future growth and potential needs
- Loan loss record

For each item, weigh its importance as a 1, 2, or 3. Depending on your personal circumstances and business, the number-one concern might be personal guarantees and the total dollars that can be borrowed. For an entrepreneur or small-business owner competitive interest rates should not be the number one concern. The difference of a percentage point on a $100,000 loan is $1000 of annual interest, on a $400,000 loan it is $4000 of annual interest. Other issues are much more important.

Once you have that loan, maintaining a good relationship with your bank or other lending source is essential. The rate of return for a bank on a commercial loan is much smaller than the rate of return for an early-stage investor on an equity investment. Banks borrow money at about three or four percentage points less than their lending rate. This low point spread or margin does not tolerate much risk, and bankers don't like surprises. Equity investors also don't like surprises, but their expected rates of return are over 30 percent per annum.

Therefore, keep your banker informed about any storm clouds on the horizon. Bring the bad news early and don't report the good news until it happens. If a chance exists for you to lose a major customer, let your banker know this before it happens. If a chance exists for you to open a major new account, let your banker know after the first order.

Bankers, other lending sources, and equity investors are your partners, and they like frequent communication from the entrepreneur and small-business owner. Through meaningful communication, let them know you are managing the enterprise, and ask for their advice on appropriate matters such as credit and collections.

Through meaningful communication, discuss future lending needs. Anticipate that the terms of short-term loans will change each year depending on market conditions and your enterprise's needs. Banks operate in a dynamic world and need to make a profit. As their world and your world changes, the interest rates, dollar caps, percentages loaned, covenants, and personnel will change. Each year you will negotiate new terms and conditions. For this reason, successful entrepreneurs and small-business managers maintain contacts with several bankers and lending sources to continually compare terms and conditions. Generally, bankers do not talk with each other about clients, so approaching a number of banks makes sense.

In Chapter 1 we discussed a start-up firm that manufactured and sold handheld devices to remove scratches from CDs. At that firm manufacturing is contracted out and sales of the device are made through major music retailers. Forty percent of the business occurs in the last quarter of each year.

The firm bootstrapped its way to $1 million of annual sales in year one, relying on early collection of accounts receivable and late payment of accounts payable. In year two management decided to do some manufacturing functions internally and projected $2 million of annual revenues. At this early stage, without a proven track record, outside equity funding would be very expensive and so management decided to seek a bank loan.

The entrepreneur asked his accountant, lawyer, and business associates for recommendations. They suggest two large downtown banks which have small business departments that specialize in loans to companies involved in consumer products sold through retailers. The entrepreneur received a personal introduction to the vice-presidents of small business lending at both banks, who in turn introduced him to the appropriate loan officers.

At the first meeting the entrepreneur presented a cash flow showing the need for a $400,000 loan to support increased levels of accounts receivable and inventory plus the purchase of certain equipment. The cash flow also showed the ability to easily cover interest payments and a certain amount of debt repayment.

The entrepreneur supported his revenue and cash-flow forecast with detailed schedules on unit sales per month and per account, plus product costs and payroll data. The business plan efficiently covered the 6Cs.

Both bankers suggested a similar loan structure. They would loan up to 65 percent on qualified accounts receivable, most of which are to top-rated retailers, and 30 percent on all finished goods inventory. This working capital revolver matures in one year, at which point it must be renewed or paid off. One bank caps the working capital loan at $350,000 and will charge an 8 percent interest rate. The other bank caps the working capital loan at $250,000 and will charge a 7 percent interest rate. Both banks are willing to loan another $50,000 at 7.5 percent interest over five years using the new manufacturing equipment as collateral. This term loan is payable in equal installments over 60 months.

Both banks asked the entrepreneur and his partners for personal guarantees, which they accepted. Stock in this company represented their major personal asset. This early-stage firm chose the bank with the higher working capital loan limit and the higher interest rate. Their margins are high so the additional dollars of interest expense is not critical. However, liquidity to support the high growth expected over the next several years represents their number one concern. At the end of one year all parties will reevaluate the situation.

EQUITY FINANCING

As mentioned previously, there are many sources of equity financing. Generally four or five rounds are necessary for successfully financing a new enterprise. Entrepreneurs spend and often waste a great deal of time pursuing the wrong investors at the wrong stage of their business's development. Entrepreneurs need to target equity investors who are experienced, comfortable, knowledgeable about their industry, and appropriate for the present round of investment. Raising equity funds is a selling process and you must target investors(customers) with the greatest needs and highest probability of success.

Entrepreneurs must estimate their financing needs three years in advance, plan each round, and target the type investor. The plan and estimate may change monthly, but this allows you to organize what often becomes a chaotic, wasteful process. Again, a qualified attorney and an accountant must be part of the planning process, because unless early equity rounds are structured properly, latter rounds will become more difficult. Issues concerning pricing of each round, warrants, or options for future rounds, and dollars raised at each round must be planned by a qualified adviser. You require a qualified accountant to assist you in preparing best, worst, and most probably case pro forma financial statements along with appropriate assumptions.

At each round the entrepreneur wants to choose investors who can help with the next round. For example, you want early-stage private value-added investors who have credibility as successful business people and can lead you to the next round of professional investors or venture capitalists. Similarly, you want successful, credible venture capitalists who can lead you to proper underwriters for a public offering.

In each round of equity financing a significant risk exists for raising too little or too much money. If the entrepreneur raises too little capital, growth may be sacrificed and the next round might require a shorter time frame with some desperation, resulting in a lower valuation. Such a scenario would also require more of the entrepreneur's limited time. If the entrepreneur raises too much, this might cause unnecessary dilution, since valuations in earlier-stage rounds tend to be much lower than latter-stage rounds. However, you have the security of knowing the enterprise is well funded should the private equity market dry up as it did in 2001. All these risks can be mitigated by planning dollars needed and sources far in advance, doing appropriate networking, and possibly receiving commitments in advance.

Equity Rounds

When entrepreneurs first conceive of their business, they need seed money for market research, customer focus groups, lawyers, accountants, travel, telephone bills, and personal support. At some point, the entrepreneur must leave his or her day job to start the new enterprise. At this point you are selling integrity, knowledge, and a dream. Therefore, round-one financing comes from the founders, their families, their friends, employees, and "angels," who specialize in seed and early-stage money and understand the market, product, or service. Angels are private-equity investors; often they are successful entrepreneurs or wealthy professionals, who have the experience to add value to start-ups or early-stage enterprises and the risk tolerance to be comfortable investing in it.

There is little quantitative information to value the new enterprise except comparables and the probability of success. Qualitative information would include the maturity of management and the business model. Does management have both domain and small business experience? Has this business model for importing men's shoes already been proven in the women's shoe business? Seed and early-stage investors depend not only on facts and numbers but on intuition based on past experience. The founders must contribute their own funds plus sweat equity, work without pay. Some founders use personal credit card debt as seed money.

At this early point, the entrepreneur must decide what percentage of the company he or she eventually wants to own, how much must be reserved for each round of future financing and, if appropriate, for employee stock options. Then, working backward the entrepreneur can arrive at the percentage of total equity available for seed investors.

"Seed investors" often buy debt in the start-up which is convertible into stock or carries stock warrants. At this stage both debt and equity contain 100 percent down risk, but should the company fail, the investor can take a tax loss on debt sooner than equity. Also, debt or convertible preferred stock allows early-stage investors to receive some income while they wait.

Choose family, friends, employees, and angels who can afford to wait for or lose the money invested without impacting their lifestyle and who have the funds and risk tolerances to participate in future rounds. Seek "angels" with experience in your industry and possibly the business skills to assist you. Such an investor might become your business partner. Private equity investors who understand your business model and industry prove easier to sell, take less time to make a decision, are more helpful over the long term, and often put a higher initial valuation on the enterprise. A start-up selling radioactive implants to treat prostate cancer received seed and early-stage equity from urologists and medical physicists. A B2B e-commerce start-up for packaging received early-stage equity from executives of large container firms. A printing company start-up received early-stage financing from its employees in the form of convertible debt.

Seed money generally is used to test the business idea. Will uranium manufacturers supply the needed radioactive material to the start-up, and at what cost? Will nuclear physicists at hospitals buy the newly designed implants, and at what price? Will urologists recommend the procedure?

The next several rounds can be classified as early-stage investing. The entrepreneur has data showing the need, market size, potential customers, competition, competitive advantage, and possible financial outcomes. The latter is represented with pro formas containing various scenarios using various assumptions. Angels, private value-added investors, specialize in early-stage investing, but, as mentioned, also are worth approaching for seed money. These private investors often know each other and often syndicate their investments, that is, invest as a group with one person being the lead investor. They like to invest in industries they know and prefer local firms. Ask investment bankers, consultants, lawyers, industry executives, and business brokers for referrals. Once in the network, angels will refer you to their associates. Lawyers, consultants, and accountants who specialize in early-stage firms have a Palm Pilot filled with names. For credibility, you will need an introduction.

A few, but not many, venture capital organizations invest in early-stage firms. Again, ask local investment bankers, consultants, lawyers, accountants, and entrepreneurs for names and introductions. Contact other entrepreneurs who have raised equity funds in comparable industries for names of appropriate venture firms. If a private investor or venture capital firm turns you down, ask why and also ask for the names of other more appropriate people or firms. A number of reference books, along with local business publications, list venture capital firms by location, stage of investing (seed, early, growth, or mature) and industry interests. Addresses, phone numbers, Web sites, and officer names are also listed. Such publications include *Venture Capital Journal*, *Venture-One Venture Capital Source Book* (877-522-8663), and *Pratt's Guide to Venture Capital Resources*. More than 800 U.S. venture capital firms have active portfolios into which they have invested nearly $80 billion over the last 20 years.

Initially, target local venture capital firms with early-stage investments and with an expressed interest or possibly investments in your industry. This increases the probability of success and reduces the time involved. Equity investors, especially venture capitalists, share information about clients because this is a tight, often syndicated community. They do not like deals that have been "shopped around." Therefore, approach only two value-added private investors, or two venture capital funds, or two strategic partners at a time. You do want to compare multiple offers because this will allow you to negotiate better terms and reduce the time frame, but use the rifle rather than the shotgun approach. Once you target a venture fund, consider contacting one of their portfolio firms or someone on their advisory board for a referral.

Private equity investors and venture capitalists often participate in local entrepreneurial groups, forums, conferences, universities, small business fairs, and charities. Get your name on the list for e-mail notices of events and news. Attend these events to meet appropriate investors.

Other sources for early-stage investing include European and Japanese operating companies and overseas private investor groups, plus venture capital organizations owned by major American corporations and universities. The United States has become a leader in entrepreneurial ventures because of available capital, education, and market opportunities. For example, the B2B e-commerce packaging firm mentioned previously received early-stage funding from a Swedish investor and a Japanese conglomerate. Similarly, a growth-stage Wisconsin genomics firm received third-round funding from the German government in exchange for setting up a sequencing facility in eastern Germany.

Companies from Intel, Johnson & Johnson, Dell, and Staples to Du Pont, Motorola, JC Penney, and General Motors have strategic corporate venture funds for investing in promising firms related to their industries. Foreign investors and corporate equity funds often seek strategic reasons for the investment. The entrepreneur's firm might have a product or service that can prove helpful to the parent firm.

Strategic investors should be sought in early stages but generally don't participate until the business has proven itself. Strategic investors reap potential rewards beyond the financial one. The investment creates a value-added synergy for the investor. For this reason strategic investors place a higher valuation on the business which represents a major benefit for the entrepreneur. Often the strategic investor becomes a valued customer or supplier.

For example, the early-stage firm manufacturing radioactive implants to treat prostrate cancer received seed money from urologists and its early-stage round from a distributor who wanted exclusive sales rights to a certain market segment with a predetermined volume and price for the radioactive seeds. This multimillion-dollar investment was made for a small fraction of the business because the investor perceived significant value from the distribution and pricing agreement.

The next several rounds of investing are known as growth rounds. The entrepreneur's or small-business person's firm has customers, employees, sales, and some historical financial statements. The concept has proven itself, growth and scalability seem possible with more capital or debt, but critical mass for profits and positive cash flow remains at some future point.

These growth rounds prove most appropriate for venture capital organizations, strategic investors, banks, and other lenders. The large amounts of equity money required, risks, and returns prove most appropriate for venture firms and strategic partners and least appropriate for family, friends, and angels. Entrepreneurs must realize that each round overlaps the other and boundaries become blurred. Venture capitalists and strategic partners look for annual returns in excess of 30 percent on investments of several million dollars. Angels and private value-added investors look for returns in excess of 60 percent on investments of several hundred thousand dollars.

The final financing rounds involve raising money from public markets through initial public offerings (IPOs) and secondary offerings. Such offerings may involve private shareholders selling stock to the public, but more often involve the entrepreneurial venture raising new funds for growth. At this stage as in others, debt funding, if available, from various sources should also be used.

What the Equity Investor Looks For

Banks and other lending sources want to know how much money you need, how it will benefit your firm, whether your business will generate enough cash flow to repay the debt, and whether your firm or you have collateral to support the debt repayment if cash flow does not meet projections. Bankers look at the 6Cs and rely on your business plan and pro formas for information.

Equity investors have similar interests, but emphasize future returns, management, market opportunities, scalability, and exit. As with debt sources, a well-written, well-supported business plan sends a professional message to the investor. Chapter 1 deals with writing a business plan. In submitting your business plan to professional equity investors, remember they claim to receive at least 70 each week (many unsolicited), read 15, and meet with four prospects, which results in six to eight investments a year. For equity investors, the business plan must have a three-to-five page executive summary, which convinces the investor to read the entire plan, the initial purpose of which is to get the entrepreneur an appointment. The executive summary must allow the equity investor to understand the opportunity within a few minutes, so include key information on markets, management, products or services, competitive advantages, merits, risks, and the exit.

Typically, through referrals the entrepreneur has been granted 15 minutes on the phone with the investor. If the investor has some interest, he or she asks for a business plan. In the 15-minute phone call and the executive summary, the entrepreneur must clearly state the merits of this investment and his or her ability to make it happen.

Equity investors, especially venture funds, look for scalable business opportunities in rapidly growing large markets. Outside equity investors are not interested in a one-store retailer whose revenues will grow from $500,000 to $1 million in five years. This lends itself to an owner-manager situation with debt financing. Outside equity investors would be more interested in this same retailer if its growth could be replicated in a hundred company-owned or -franchised branches. Equity investors look for firms in rapidly growing large markets where the rising tide will raise all the ships, such as digital telecom services. Equity investors look for scalable products or services that will create new markets, like a small business Internet portal, or solve problems or meet needs in existing markets, like DSL services. Venture capitalists in particular look for large markets that can create large, new companies.

Equity investors pay particular attention to what drives the market, because should the market drivers change or not be sustainable, the market size, along with the competitors, will fall. Is market growth based on fashion, number of computers, Internet users, or the sale of compact discs? Similarly, is competitive advantage created by styling, size of line, just-in-time delivery, brands, or price or service issues? How sensitive is the market to business cycles? The entrepreneur must show a clear understanding of the business model, its key drivers, and competitive advantage.

To capitalize on these market opportunities equity investors pay particular attention to the quality of the management team. They want experienced management that can execute against the opportunity and solve unanticipated problems. Management should have proven ability to innovate, a clear plan, but the willingness to reevaluate this plan in light of market changes. Inexperienced management with a good plan may receive funding if a more experienced appropriate manager can be recruited to run the business. Equity investors often prefer stronger management with a weaker plan to the opposite.

Equity investors look for management with both industry (domain) and start-up experience. Investors try to assess the leadership potential of both the entrepreneur and the management team. Investors also assess management's skills and capabilities in marketing, sales, organization, administration, process, communication, operations, research, development, engineering, finance, accounting, control, human resources, conflict resolution, tax, and legal issues.

Entrepreneurs who become finalists for equity funding will undergo thorough background checks including credit, driving violations, and criminal records. Don't say you graduated from a university if you only attended. Don't exaggerate your résumé. Honesty and trust rank high with equity investors.

Be prepared to offer proof of management expertise such as years in the industry, working for successful firms in the industry, success stories related to the introduction and growth of new products or services. Be prepared to offer proof of start-up, new business, and entrepreneurial experience. The radioactive seed implant team all worked for competitors in the prostate cancer treatment industry. Be sure to let the equity investor know about weaknesses where your team needs help. Possibly you lack a financial or sales management person. Acknowledging weaknesses builds trust.

Investors look for a balanced management team with qualified, experienced people in each key function or the ability to recruit such people. They also look for succession planning. If the top programmer or researcher quits or becomes sick, who takes over?

In the Introduction we discussed the importance of competitive advantage and differentiation. For a business to grow, succeed, and become scalable it needs a defensible competitive advantage. An entrepreneur who does not have one should rethink his or her basic idea or business model. Sophisticated equity investors demand that your business have such a competitive advantage. Differentiation and scalability are table stakes for the type of smart investor you require. The greater and more defensible the competitive advantage, the more scalable the business model, the higher the valuation placed on the new enterprise. Intellectual property such as patents and trademarks help defend a firm's competitive advantage and add to valuation. Usually such trademarks and patents help in obtaining equity financing even though they prove expensive to defend and not terribly effective in actually limiting competition.

Equity investors look for both long- and short-term differentiation and competitive advantages. Long-term, sustainable competitive advantages rely less on product or service differentiation and more on barriers to entry created by marketing and operational issues. After three years of successful growth can your early-stage venture keep out larger organizations with greater human and financial resources, such as larger corporations with brand names, an extensive sales force, and existing customers buying a product or service similar to yours? Does your firm have sustainable barriers to entry?

As the new enterprise moves from start-up through growth to maturity, can it develop a strategy for customer intimacy, market segmentation, operational efficiency, or new product or service development to create barriers to entry and keep competition out? For example, a firm specializing in customized vitamins and herbs for women has differentiated the product offering and selected a growing market segment, working women ages 30 to 50. Sustaining the competitive advantage requires thousands of loyal customers and network marketers to create the ultimate barriers to entry. Also, a low-cost contract manufacturer will help create economies of scale. Continual management communication with customers and network marketers creates a pipeline for new product development. Management not only had experience starting successful firms in other industries, but also had experience working in the herb and vitamin business. However, management had no experience in network marketing.

Related to differentiation and competitive advantage, equity investors have concerns about pricing power. Can the early- or growth-stage firm maintain or raise prices as it matures? How much power will distributors, channel partners, customers, and suppliers have as the firm matures and how will this impact profits and cash flow?

To receive equity financing the entrepreneur must be able to prove scalability and sustainable differentiation. Therefore, understand and be prepared to present believable market drivers and competitive differentiators. If the number of current and future cases of prostate cancer drive the sale of radioactive seeds for treatment, give numbers from reliable sources such as the American Cancer Association.

Present potential equity investors with a list of your firm's competitors and the features and benefits that differentiate each one. Why and how will your advantage be sustainable? Does your start-up have a more reliable source of radioactive material, better relationships with urologists, or target underserved market segments, such as freestanding doctor-owned clinics? Prepare some proof, such as testimonials. Then, translate market growth and competitive advantage into market share percentages, plus unit and dollar sales figures. Be sure to realistically state and deal with weaknesses; this builds trust and demonstrates your knowledge of the business.

Equity investors will want to talk with your key management people, your most important customers and prospects, and competitors. Such conversations can prove awkward so plan how to handle this.

Generally, equity investors expect 30 to 60 percent returns on these high-risk early- and growth-stage investments. Equity investors want a proven formula for success, which just needs more funding to scale it and make it profitable. They also want to exit the investment within five years to harvest their returns.

The entrepreneur or small-business person must present the investor with several viable alternatives to exit the investment. One alternative might involve a strategic purchaser, such as a competitor or firm in a related field. Such a purchase might create cost savings or a more efficient sales organization or a more balanced product line for the new combined organizations. Another exit might involve an IPO, if market conditions were right and the firm was large enough.

Equity investors look for entrepreneurs and small business managers who share their common goals as to strategy, structure, process, and most importantly the exit. If you do not intend to sell your business, have an IPO, or provide some other reasonable liquidity vehicle for the investor, then don't seek equity investors.

Of course, equity investors want to review your best, worst, and most probable case pro forma profit and loss statements, balance sheets, and cash flows. Have an accountant help you with these and include plenty of assumptions on how you arrived at the numbers. That is, what are your revenue forecasts, line-item expenses, and asset/liability figures based on? State the assumptions behind the numbers, because assumptions tell the investor how much you know about the business. Be sure to explain why your pro forma numbers may vary from past actual results and from comparable public firms. Also, use different comparables for different stages of the business. Show various scenarios where upside is significant and downside can be mitigated. This subject was also dealt with in Chapter 1.

Where relevant, audited financial statements prepared by a CPA for past periods create credibility. Equity investors pay particular attention to sources and uses of funds and cash flow. What do you intend to use their money for—product development, research, equipment, working capital, or salaries? For each additional dollar of future sales, how many dollars of accounts receivable, inventory, and salaries are required and where will they come from?

Be prepared to substantiate your firm's investment merits and defend the critical risks. If an overseas competitor entering the market represents a critical risk, or if you source overseas and exchange rates create a critical risk, you must realistically address these issues.

Merits and risks change with each round of financing. For instance, in a seed-stage round, risks might include obtaining funding, does the technology work, will customers buy it, and recruiting qualified staff. In the next early-stage round, risks might include scalability, critical mass, expense ratios, and predictable revenues. In the next growth-stage round, risks might include execution, implementation, critical mass, competition, and exit. Similarly, each round of financing carries different merits from a good idea and an experienced management team in early-stages to strategic alliances, customers, revenue growth, and profitability in later rounds.

Equity investors often reduce their risks by sharing an investment with other participants. Therefore, they look for investments that can be syndicated and will be very interested in the quality of earlier-round investors, because that creates credibility.

In meeting with sophisticated equity investors, remember you may have an in-depth knowledge of products and markets, but they have seen many similar firms and have access to databases on markets, competition, and other similar investments made by other angels or venture capital firms. The equity investor will often concentrate on technology, management, and market issues, plus financial evaluations. On the other hand, entrepreneurs usually concentrate on the company, products, and vision to establish and build credibility, maximize valuation, and find the best equity partners. Raising equity funding is selling, which requires targeting investors and, as illustrated above, understanding their needs.

In raising equity funds keep in mind the following:

- The purpose of investors placing a value on your business through due diligence is to gain understanding, not to get a number.
- Investors are interested in the future, not the past.
- Cash flow and the exit opportunities support valuations.
- Investors will discount any future cash flows and returns to reflect present value.
- To take more risk, investors want higher returns.
- Financial engineering by investors does not create value, but rather the business, its management, and the markets create value.
- For investors being in the right, a growing market is more important than being in the best company in that market.
- Raising capital requires a great deal of time, effort, and creative energy. Most entrepreneurs underestimate this.
- The entrepreneur must be prepared to tell dozens of people he or she does not know a great deal of personal information on compensation and net worth and a great deal of confidential business information.
- Don't delegate fund-raising to others. Use advisers but keep the responsibility yourself, because this is too important for the entrepreneur to delegate.
- Don't celebrate until you receive the money, and always have a fallback plan. Most entrepreneurs overestimate investors' interest.
- You need a competent lawyer, but make sure you understand and are satisfied with all the terms and conditions of the financing. You must live with the ultimate decisions.

Those are some best practices, but some common mistakes to avoid in approaching equity investors include

- Requiring a nondisclosure agreement (NDA) before describing the business. Most equity investors consider this pretentious.

Many equity investors will not sign NDAs. Have your attorney prepare an appropriate NDA, and try to get it signed. If this proves difficult, don't release sensitive ideas until all parties are comfortable with each other.

- Not making sure the business case is clear, persuasive, and defensible. What problem does your new enterprise, its products, or services solve; what needs do they satisfy; and who will pay for this? If technology is involved, will it work, does the market care, and can you protect it?
- Not adequately identifying market size and failing to prove scalability.
- Underestimating competition and overestimating competitive advantage and market size. Not proving competitive advantage.
- Leading with the numbers, because anyone can create a good spreadsheet.
- Trying to convince your investors that everything is figured out. Rather, point out areas that need further research.
- Too much information, or overload. Clearly present the important issues and wait for questions to present the details. However, do make references to market research studies that support your market data.
- Unrealistic revenue, expense, cash flow, and break-even point forecasts. This immediately hurts credibility.
- Not linking financing to achieving key milestones. For example, when the product meets performance specifications as tested by a reputable third party, then the equity investor agrees to invest another million dollars.
- Unrealistic valuations based on industry comparables. Insisting on one valuation method.
- Giving inadequate attention to liquidity or the exit strategy.
- Focusing too heavily on early-round valuations, rather than choosing investors who can maximize your exit valuation. However, larger investment firms are not always better at maximizing exit valuations than smaller ones.

Placing a Value on the Equity Investment

How does an entrepreneur or small-business person place a value on the new or early-stage enterprise? There may be several years' history of sales and earnings, or there may be nothing but start-up expenses, sweat equity, and pro forma statements.

With no or little history of sales and earnings, investors look at the maturity and experience of management, the maturity of the business model, and comparables. Key questions concern management's industry and start-up experience. Two business school graduates starting an e-commerce site for memorabilia had a great business plan but no industry experience. Two other graduates from the same school started an e-commerce portal for small businesses. Each of the second two had started and sold several businesses and one had started a comparable Internet portal. The Internet portal market and business model had been proven in other markets than smaller enterprises. No one had yet built a successful e-commerce exchange relying solely on memorabilia. The small business portal received valuation on its early-stage and growth-stage equity financing many times that of the memorabilia marketplace.

Whether seed, early-stage, or growth-stage, private company valuations generally depend on public company multiples and comparables along with recent private company transactions. Early-stage Internet companies, cable television, or telephone companies are often valued by the number of customers, visitors, prospects, average order size, or subscribers. Each customer, subscriber, or prospect is given a dollar value, which may be those used to value similar public companies. A larger dollar amount might be assigned to companies with faster growth rates or greater market opportunities.

If the private company has a history of revenues, profits, and cash flows, multiples of these may be used to value the firm. The multiple will depend on growth rates and industry comparables for public firms. The higher the growth rate, the higher the multiple. However, equity investors often discount these valuations for a private firm to reflect lack of liquidity or exit.

Well-substantiated pro forma future projections of revenues, profits, and cash flows also create a basis for present and exit valuations. Again, we apply comparable multiples against these projections. Generally the multiple decreases as the forecasted years move to the future. A multiple of next year's earnings will be higher than a multiple of earnings in five years, reflecting the difficulty of accurately projecting future years' results.

Equity investors are most concerned about their returns, the probability of success, and reflect risks in the initial valuations and the exit valuations. In presenting your business plan and establishing a value, what will revenues, profits, and cash flow be in year five when you plan to find a strategic buyer for the entire enterprise or possibly just for the outside investors? What are the best and worst case and the most probable multipliers to arrive at a valuation in year five? What valuation does the equity investor need today based on the assumed exit value to achieve the desired rate of return, whether 30 percent or 60 percent? This type of method often reflects net present value and discounted cash flow models.

Expected rates of return depend on the stage of investing because the stage reflects risk. Early-stage investing has more risks and higher returns than latter-stage investing. Seed and start-up investors expect 60 to 80 percent returns, while early- and growth-stage investors require 40 to 50 percent returns, and latter-stage, bridge, and mezzanine financing only 25 to 30 percent returns. These returns explain why debt financing, if possible, is cheaper than equity.

Most entrepreneurs and small business managers will run a number of forecasts reflecting more and less optimistic assumptions as to revenue growth, expenses, and cash flow. Possible key market drivers will be altered, which may also affect methods of valuation. They will assign a success probability to each forecast. The most conservative numbers might carry a 75 percent probability of success, the most optimistic 20 percent, and the middle range 50 percent. In early- and growth-stage investing, a probability should also be assigned to total failure or zero exit value. These weighted valuations, whether based on multiples of revenues, profits, cash flow, visitors, transactions, or whatever, are then added up and divided to arrive at an average value.

Investors respond well to these types of weighted average valuations because they are reasonable. If an investor feels your assumptions are unrealistic, just plug the new assumptions into your spreadsheet and rerun it. This methodology creates credibility and flexibility.

Another variation on this theme involves arriving at a most likely forecast of future revenues, earnings, and cash flows by doing a best- and worst-case scenario, then arriving at three valuations based on 100 percent, 75 percent, and 50 percent of the most likely case. This convinces investors that the entrepreneur is reasonable and conservative. The entrepreneur would be satisfied with the 50 percent valuation.

The early-stage radioactive seed firm for treatment of prostate cancer had projected the total market based on the American Cancer Society's forecast for new cases of localized prostate cancers. Management made assumptions based on past history as to what percentage of those total cases would be treated with seeds versus surgery. For those cases treated with seeds, a dollar value was assigned to the cost and number of seeds for each patient. These total unit and dollar market numbers were then divided by each competitor's expected market share. The early-stage firm projected unit and revenue growth based on market and market share growth. Management presented three different revenue forecasts based on different assumptions. Each revenue forecast resulted in a different five-year expense and cash flow forecast. Management assigned a probability of success to each forecast ranging from 70 to 20 percent. The probability of total failure or no exit value received a 20 percent rating. In averaging all these weightings, the most probable pretax profit in year five was $3 million. Management showed investors a PowerPoint presentation on present pretax profit multiples of their competitors with publicly traded shares. The multiples averaged 15 times pretax profits, which would give the seed company a $45 million value in five years.

As discussed previously in this chapter, the entrepreneur and small-business owner must do cash flow forecasts to determine how much new equity and debt financing will be required over what period of time. Allow yourself some extra time and money for contingencies. The machinery may not arrive on time or may not work properly, or your customers may delay initial orders. For example, the radioactive seed company needed to raise $2 million for the purchase of equipment, land, buildings, and raw material and for employee salaries.

Since the seed company represents an early-stage investment, the investors will want a five-time return on their money in five years, or a 38 percent compounded annualized return. Their $2 million investment must have a strong probability of producing a $10 million value at the exit in year five. Working backward from the $45 million total exit value the investor must own 10/45th or 22 percent of the company to receive the required compounded annualized return of 38 percent. You could arrive at the same percentage ownership by discounting the $45 million valuation by the required return over five years.

Since this investor will be a minority shareholder (22 percent), the investor will want some control over key decisions, such as the exit strategy and management compensation. This control issue might be handled through a board seat or a separate agreement. A private angel investor might be comfortable with a 22 percent ownership position, while a venture capital organization might want 33 percent. In both cases, investors in each round should be given the preemptive right to participate in the next round of financing, which will increase or at least maintain their percentage ownership. Some investors will ask for options to purchase additional equity at a predetermined price if certain events occur.

Valuation also very much depends on negotiations. How many investors are interested in your business at this stage of its development and how badly do you need the funds and want this particular investor? Similarly, the equity investor may have many biotech or optical technology choices or be most interested in your enterprise.

Valuation may also depend on terms and conditions, such as management warranties and covenants of financial data and noncompete agreements. The entrepreneur must determine the equity investors "must haves," and "want to haves," and their motivators for investing. If a management three-year noncompete agreement represents a "must have," it becomes a potential deal breaker. If a "want to have," maybe you can offer a trade-off with another type of financial covenant. If the equity investor is motivated to make this investment for strategic reasons, not just financial ones, you have more bargaining power.

The radioactive seed company had many potential early-stage investors but was most interested in one group of urologists and medical physicists, who could be helpful in adding value to the enterprise. The urologists and medical physicists were represented by an investment banker who asked for many changes in the forecasts, assumptions, and multiples. Management had prepared spreadsheets, which could be altered based on different inputs. The urologists and medical physicists negotiated a $2 million investment, part debt, part preferred stock, and part common stock, but with a 22 percent stake and rights to buy another 10 percent of the firm at a higher price in two years.

As you can see, quantitative valuation factors for early- and growth-stage firms reflect markets, comparables, market position, competitive position, distribution strategy, growth rates, profit margins, and management. Qualitative valuation factors include negotiations; why and how much each party needs the other.

Structuring the Equity Investment

Sophisticated equity investors generally want control over key decisions, but generally do not want to own a majority of the stock. A majority of the stock in an early- or growth-stage firm should reside with the management and key employees to provide long-term incentives and strong motivation. As mentioned, equity investors may ask for covenants, terms, and conditions which give them control over the exit and a strong say in management compensation and capital expenditures. Again, because equity and debt funding at the outset very much influence and restrict future funding and future operations, an experienced lawyer must represent the entrepreneur or small-business manager.

An experienced lawyer and accountant also must assist you in structuring any equity financing to balance investor and entrepreneur needs. Equity investors are most concerned about the risk–reward ratios, their influence on the firm's development usually through board representation, the entrepreneurs' investment or down risk, minimizing taxes, future liquidity through an exit, and voting control if results don't meet expectations. Entrepreneurs are most concerned about incentives for present and future managers (stock options), flexibility to accommodate the next round of financing, maintaining stock ownership should they depart the firm, and future working capital availability and debt financing.

The structuring process involves evaluating each party's needs and concerns, evaluating alternatives, and choosing a structure which best meets each party's needs as well as the company's financial needs. The structure of equity financing uses a range of security instruments from straight debt to debt with equity features to common stock. This would include senior debt, subordinated debentures, preferred stock, and common stock.

Structure also involves terms concerning liquidity, dilution, covenants, management arrangements, events of default, remedies, representations and warranties, amendments, and waivers. These terms are used to reconcile both parties' concerns and needs.

Evaluating an Equity Investor or Venture Capital Organization

Equity investors, whether family, friends, value-added professional investors (angels), or venture capital firms, become the entrepreneur's and small-business owner's partner. Since this represents a long-term critical relationship, you must seek the right partners.

Look for investors who can help you with this and the next round of financing, whether growth or IPO. Look for investors with experience in your industry and in your stage of development (early, growth, or latter stage). If you are funding a growth-stage genomics-sequencing firm, look for investors with experience in biotechnology, not real estate. Look for angels with excellent venture capital or investment banker contacts. Look for investors who can help you recruit management or introduce you to key customers and prospects. Does the investor or venture capitalist have a "been there, done that" track record?

Assuming you will need several rounds of growth financing, look for investors with resources to back you in more than one round. Such investors can save you time.

Ask potential investors about their time frame and process for making decisions. Look for short time frames and a decisive and responsive decision-making process. Does the formal decision depend on groups of people in different locations?

Since equity investors become your partners, ask for references from managers of present portfolio concerns. You need investors with a reputation for excellent business judgment and a tolerance for crisis management. Success has many parents, but failure is an orphan. You need a partner who can deal with both.

If possible, it proves helpful to have local investors. Again, this saves travel time and allows you and the investors to spend more quality time together. As mentioned, target investors who are comfortable with and know your industry. They are easier to convince and more helpful as partners.

Choose equity investors who share your goals, especially on liquidity. What time frame do you perceive for the exit and by what means? Common goals may encompass more than liquidity. One venture capitalist may encourage rapid revenue growth at the expense of profit, customers at any costs, while another prefers slower growth through internally generated cash flow. Which strategy best meets your objectives?

Often you will seek a group or syndicate of investors. In early- and growth-stage investing a critical means to limit investor risk is to limit each investor's investment. In evaluating equity partners look for lead investors, individuals or firms who have the knowledge, contacts, and reputation to bring other people or groups in. Often the lead investor has a larger dollar commitment and a larger percentage ownership than the rest of the group. Again, the lead investor will save you time and ownership dilution.

Approaching Equity Investors

To reduce the cost and risk of failure, the amount of time, energy, and resources involved, as well as to increase the probability of success, use references to introduce you to equity investors with knowledge of your industry. Again, the greatest problems and opportunities for entrepreneurs and small-business managers lay in raising money, marketing, and sales. Your probability of overall success increases by shifting time, money, and resources to marketing and sales.

The referral will result in a 10- or 15-minute phone conversation with a decision maker or gatekeeper (analyst, accountant, etc). The purpose of the phone conversation is to sell an appointment to discuss your firm. The investor either will have read the executive summary of your business plan or will agree to your sending the plan.

Once in front of the equity investor or investors, use all the techniques discussed in this chapter to convincingly present the opportunity, as it relates to your company in particular, and to your industry and market, in general. At the first meeting determine if there is interest and a good fit. If so, discuss the metrics to determine valuation and a fair pricing range.

Then, convince the investor that management's unique skills and industry knowledge will allow you to effectively execute the opportunity. Sell both your strengths as an operator and the management as a team. Stress competitive advantage and differentiation.

Prepare a formal 20-minute presentation using overheads, PowerPoint, or some form of graphic display. Be prepared for questions during and after the formal presentation. Rehearse in front of some tough mock audiences.

A second meeting with potential investors should be attended by your management team, but not by previous investors. For example, angels often want to be present at meetings with the next round of investors. The next round of investors want to know who provided the seed money, but they seldom want to meet them. End any meeting or telephone call with an investor by agreeing on the next step, which might be another meeting, reading the business plan, or meeting a potential customer.

Give yourself at least six months to raise money, but always be networking with potential investors. As mentioned previously, after the equity investor expresses serious interest, expect substantial due diligence prior to a "term sheet."

Forty-five days before the possible closing date the entrepreneur or small-business owner will receive a *term sheet*, proposing terms and conditions for the investment. Term sheets at least include premoney valuation, amount of investment, the names of investors and the lead investor, the type of security (common, preferred stock, warrants), rights, preferences and privileges, and conditions to closing. The term sheet results from all the steps, skills, and techniques described in this chapter. The entrepreneur and investor are engaged, which in most cases leads to a marriage or a closing. Pieces of the term sheet emerge as you proceed through the process described in this chapter. The objective of the activities described in this chapter is to arrive at a term sheet and a closing. The term sheet must address key concerns of both parties, which if not resolved would later become deal killers. Again, your attorney must scrutinize the term sheet. Once both parties sign the term sheet, it generally takes 45 days to prepare legal documents (investment agreement, stockholder's agreement, employee option agreements, employee confidentiality agreements, and legal opinions), perform final due diligence, and close.

THE RESOURCE MAP FOR FINANCING

The following list should be a helpful resource map for evaluating all forms, stages, and sources of financing:

Financial Characteristics
- Cost of money (required rate of return)
- Fund-raising expenses

- Depth of pockets
- Collateral requirements
- Risk-bearing abilities
- Reputation or signaling

Nonfinancial Characteristics

- Management skills
- Speed of decision making
- Industry and product knowledge
- Flexibility
- Other resources provided
- Control tendencies

ENTREPRENUERS' MAJOR MISTAKES AND WEAKNESSES IN PROPERLY FINANCING A BUSINESS

- Not engaging an experienced lawyer and accountant to assist in seeking proper financing.
- Raising too much or too little capital and debt.
- Approaching financing as a short-term event rather than a continuous process.
- Not using referrals for introductions to lending sources and equity investors.
- Not considering alternative sources for financing of each round.
- Not seeking value-added investors and lenders.
- Not targeting investors who understand your business, can make fast decisions, and add value.
- Focusing on the cost of funds rather than potential returns.
- Unrealistic valuations based on industry comparables.
- Not linking financing to achievable key milestones.
- Not selling the equity investor on competitive advantage, scalability, differentiation, and the exit value. Not presenting a clear, persuasive, and defensible business case.
- Leading with numbers, because anyone can create a good spreadsheet.
- Not communicating bad and good news properly to leaders and investors.

QUESTIONS AND EXERCISES

1. How many rounds of debt and equity financing are you planning for, from what sources, and for how much money?
2. How did you arrive at an equity value for your business and for the equity dollars you wish to raise?
3. How did you determine the dollars of debt and equity needed to finance your enterprise?
4. What collateral will be used for debt financing and what cash flow will be available for debt service?
5. How will you convince equity investors and loan sources to participate in your business?
6. Why did you choose the particular loan or equity source? Do they offer value-added benefits?
7. Evaluate your business plan in terms of the six Cs and in terms of what equity investors look for.

CHAPTER 3

Financial Controls

One of the areas of expertise that separates success from failure in managing new ventures and small businesses is appropriate financial control. Many well-funded, early- and later-stage firms with products or services that meet a need in the marketplace, good targeting, efficient sales organizations, effective marketing, proper pricing, and well-written business plans fail for lack of appropriate financial controls. Entrepreneurs and small-business owners must plan and control expenses relative to revenues and disbursements relative to receipts.

Many examples exist of high-revenue growth firms in the telecommunications, franchising, retailing, fashion, and technology sectors which failed to produce positive cash flow or a profit, and thus like fireflies in June had exciting but short lives. Because entrepreneurs have limited human and financial resources, financial controls prove even more important.

A manufacturer of solar heat–reflecting window shades doubled its revenues each year for five years until it filed for bankruptcy. Selling these shades, which reduced ultraviolet light and solar heat in rooms where they were installed, proved easy, because the product reduced ultraviolet fading and air-conditioning costs. Creating positive cash flow and profits from increasing revenues proved much more difficult. Accounts receivable and inventory were not monitored and grew faster than revenues. Manufacturing and sales-related expenses were not budgeted and also grew faster than revenues.

Manage the parts and you manage the whole. We manage what we monitor. Therefore, the entrepreneur and small-business owner must decide on the key financial and key nonfinancial control points for his or her business.

THE KEY CONTROL POINTS

All new ventures and small businesses have key control points, which if monitored and managed properly will help to grow sales, but most importantly, they will squeeze profits and cash out of revenues. These key control points will vary depending on the industry, organization, and type of business: service versus product, new economy versus old economy, or distributor versus manufacturer. As an entrepreneur and small-business owner, you must determine the key control points most important to your business's success, establish metrics to measure them, and then the means to monitor them.

Start by considering where your business generates, spends, or uses most of its revenues, receipts, or funds. In other words, follow the money. Are more of your revenue dollars used to purchase raw materials or to pay salaries? Is more cash flow used for inventory or for accounts receivable or for capital expenditures? What key metrics and margins communicate the business's present and future success: gross margin per product, revenue minus labor costs, average selling price per unit, the cost of raw materials, customer satisfaction, accounts receivable aging, cash flow, working capital (current assets less current liabilities) or net worth (assets minus liabilities)?

ACCOUNTS RECEIVABLE AGING

All for-profit businesses have revenues and therefore accounts receivable, uncollected revenues for products shipped or services provided. Many larger concerns feel they can delay payments to smaller or newer firms because the latter have little bargaining power. Many start-ups and early-stage firms "buy" business by extending credit to poor risks that cannot get credit elsewhere. Many early-stage and smaller concerns meet their demise from late payments or no payments. Three issues exist here: what credit terms does each customer deserve, how to monitor accounts receivable, and how to collect overdue invoices.

You should age accounts receivable by customer in descending order of dollar importance. A newly established designer of women's sportswear sells to department and specialty stores. A teleconferencing start-up sells to large financial institutions and suburban municipalities. Both firms monitor accounts receivable dollars monthly by account showing the dollars owed 0 to 30 days, 31 to 60 days, 61 to 90 days, and over 90 days. The customer with the largest total outstanding dollars of accounts receivable is listed first even through all those dollars may be in the 0- to 30-day category. The customer with the least total outstanding dollars is listed last. Both firms also run a separate report listing all customers that have any accounts receivable in the over-60-day categories.

Any customer in the over-60-day category receives weekly calls from the person responsible for collections. However, credit approval and limits are set very differently by the two firms.

The designer sportswear firm operates on 60 percent gross margins and will ship any opening order under $500 to a retailer who has been in business at least three years. Credit reports, which cost $55, are only used for opening orders over $500. After the initial order, only customers which have current outstanding balances will be shipped, plus all customers have credit limits based on the firm's experience and outside rating services such as Dun and Bradstreet, www.dnb.com, and Equifax, www.equifax.com.

The teleconferencing firm leases its lines and equipment from major telephone companies and thus operates on a 20 percent gross margin. Direct costs associated with a bad debt represents 80 percent of that debt or revenue versus 40 percent for the sportswear firm. Therefore, the teleconferencing firm has much stricter credit policies for new and established accounts.

For some new enterprises and early-stage businesses, accounts receivable may not be considered a key control point, because the receivables are small, high-quality, or regulated. For example, a prestigious retail furniture store requires customers to make deposits on purchases and has the remainder collected by a delivery person. An early-stage e-commerce exchange for utilities trading power supplies has 20 triple-A clients, which all must pay within five days of a transaction or face regulatory violations.

INVENTORY

Manufacturing firms, distributors, retailers, or any new enterprise or smaller business selling a product as opposed to a service must be concerned with inventory control. For example, the furniture retailer mentioned previously had minimal accounts receivable, but large inventories for immediate customer delivery and showroom displays. The teleconferencing firm has no inventory because it sells a service, but the designer sportswear firm has large inventories because it imports seasonal fashion-oriented goods.

For each stock-keeping unit (SKU), style by color, in the designer sportswear line, the president has computer access to units on hand, less units on order for future delivery to customers, plus units on order from overseas suppliers, which nets out to an available-for-sale report. She then compares the available-for-sale numbers to each item's forecasted unit sales for this season and sales to date for this year or season versus last year. What major customers have ordered, which have not? She analyzes the numbers behind the numbers, considers manufacturing cycles, shipping times, and economic order quantity, and then decides how much of each SKU to reorder and when. If manufacturing were not contracted out, the process and analysis would still be the same, but she would place a reorder with her own factory, which would influence production control.

The furniture retailer looks at each SKU and divides dollars and units on hand by annual dollars and unit historical and forecasted sales of that item to arrive at days of sales on hand or inventory turnover. Inventory turns can be measured using revenues or cost of goods sold as a basis. For some high-volume basic items, such as traditional dining room furniture, he never wants to be out of stock and always carries 100 days inventory, including floor displays. For unique items like designer contemporary sofas, which are only available from his store and which are higher priced and slower moving, he only carries 50 days inventory.

As an entrepreneur with limited financial resources, consider the cost by category of too much inventory and too little. You never want to be out of certain high-volume, high-margin items for which there are quick substitutes. The cost is a lost sale and lost dollars of margin. Also, high-gross-margin items have lower inventory and carrying costs and higher profits from a sale. On the other hand, the cost of too much inventory is higher interest expenses from larger loan balances, space costs, and possible write-downs from obsolescence.

Some small service businesses, such as consultants, plumbers, programmers, or accountants have human capital or people as inventory. You can hire more staff to service clients or reduce the staff. There is a cost of too large a staff, of underutilization, and a cost of too small a staff, lost customers, and opportunities. One of the key control points for this business is labor utilization rates.

CAPITAL EXPENDITURES

For equipment- or capital-intensive businesses, such as telcos or Web hosting, capital expenditures represent a key control point. Management needs detailed information on the purchase and use of capital equipment. For example, a start-up broadband regional telephone firm needs weekly updates on the purchase and laying of cable and installation of switching equipment. As this firm matures it will need weekly updates on percentage utilization of broadband capacity. This early-stage firm raised $25 million in the capital market. Cash neutral will not occur for three years. In the meantime, capital expenditures, miles of cable laid, number of black boxes, plus percentage utilization rates remain the key management control points.

BALANCE SHEET RATIOS

Early or growth-stage firms and smaller businesses with large working capital needs for rapidly growing accounts receivable and inventory continually monitor the current ratio, current assets divided by current liabilities, and the quick ratio, cash minus accounts payable. Firms with large needs for capital expenditures and long-term debt monitor debt to equity ratios, plus cash flow coverage of interest and debt payments.

What balance sheet ratios reflect the financial health of your business? Ask your accountant for advice and create monthly reports to monitor these ratios.

CRITICAL OPERATING MARGINS AND UTILIZATION RATES

What are the critical operating margins for your business: margins per customer, per salesperson, per item, or per transaction? What do the critical utilization ratios relate to: machines, facilities, capital, or human resources? How do these operating margins and utilization rates reflect the health of your start-up, early- or growth-stage, or small business?

For a temporary help firm the key margin is weekly revenues less weekly payroll, and the key utilization rate is the percentage of the available labor pool on assignment. For many firms gross margin by service or product represents a key control point, and for manufacturing firms percentage of plant/equipment utilization provides a key ratio. For example, the spread between the cost of borrowed funds and the interest rate charged on loans represents a key control point for finance companies. The percentage of available funds on loan represents the utilization rate.

If the entrepreneur knows what utilization rate plus what margin in dollars and as a percentage of revenue are required to break even, and if the entrepreneur can exceed those margins on each product, service, or transaction and reach those utilization rates, then the probability of being profitable greatly increases. This type of analysis greatly influences pricing decisions because prices impact both margins and utilization rates. We manage what we monitor.

Personal computers, laptops, and accounting software make all these numbers readily available to the entrepreneur or small-business manager. However, someone in your organization must have responsibility for collecting and producing this information. Since software is continually updated and must be compatible with the rest of your system, consult an IT professional or your accountant for recommendations.

SALES FORECASTS

Sales forecasts by customer, product, territory, and/or month, bubbled up from the sales force and channel partners, represent yet another key control point. Once sales forecast numbers and resulting plans of action are agreed to, the entrepreneur and small-business manager must compare actual monthly results to forecast or plan and take any necessary corrective action.

The sales forecast, the number, the resulting sales plan, and the actions necessary to reach the number act as a standard for measuring actual company results. Often entrepreneurs and small-business managers claim sales forecasts and sales plans just waste time and are more appropriate for larger concerns with greater resources, but the opposite is closer to the truth. At the other extreme, some entrepreneurs evaluate salespeople on forecasting and planning, and include these two functions as requirements in channel partners' contracts.

Whether you have one salesperson or five, whether you personally handle sales or use a channel partner, have the people closest to the customer prepare monthly or quarterly sales forecasts. The forecast sets standards; creates a meaningful dialogue with management; gets a commitment from the sales organization; makes people feel important, useful, and worthwhile; allows you to do a better job of planning operations; and allows the entrepreneur to better control limited human and financial resources.

Don't give salespeople, channel partners, or yourself a blank piece of paper to fill in and call it a forecast. That only creates frustration and inaccuracy. Use the following process to create an accurate and meaningful forecast.

Ask each member of the organization who sells your products or services to list his or her top 20 customers and prospects for the next 30, 90, or 180 days. For each present top customer, ask for a forecast in units or dollars for whatever time period is appropriate (a month or a quarter). For each of these top 20 customers, ask for a short narrative on what is changing that will influence your sales to them, such as a new decision maker, a new competitor, or an expansion or contraction of their business. Are your firm's sales trending up or down with each of these customers and why?

In fact, the salesperson, channel partner, or you should ask major customers to estimate their use of your services or products over the next quarter or month. Ask these customers what is changing that might impact their business with you. This helps your company plan operations to better serve them and obtains an early commitment of their purchases.

For each of the top prospects ask salespeople or channel partners for the present competitor who sells them, what items your firm might sell them and why, and for the decision maker's name. Also, when might you receive an order and for how much? This represents a reality check to determine whether this account is a suspect or a prospect.

Should your firm sell a one-time or first-time system with a long, complex sales cycle, ask the salesperson to track and report on the steps between search and purchase. For each customer and prospect, determine the probability of and timetable for moving from one step to another.

Then discuss with the salesperson or channel partner changes at your firm, at the competition, and in the general business environment or market which will affect next quarter's or next month's sales. Your firm or your competitor may be adding or deleting products or services; raising or lowering prices, hiring or terminating staff, increasing capacity, or changing payment terms. Can the salesperson quantify the effect of these changes on sales in his or her territory?

Discuss changes in the general business environment with the salesperson or channel partner. What impact will lower interest rates and higher housing starts have on your firm's sales? Will the new medication reimbursement program or health-care reforms impact next quarter's revenues? How are the market drivers changing?

If historical numbers are available, what is the trend, or run rate, and where does that point sales? Are industry or market data available and helpful?

Then ask the salesperson or channel partner to put all these micros together into best- and worst-case sales forecasts with assumptions and probabilities. The salesperson might forecast 100 percent probability for $500,000 of revenue next quarter and a 75 percent probability for $700,000. If the firm's new product is shipped on time and her largest account does not go on credit hold, she can reach the $700,000 figure. The next question to ask involves necessary action if these negatives do occur.

Each salesperson, channel partner, or management member responsible for a portion of sales prepares not only a sales forecast (the number), but a sales plan (the actions required to meet that number). The sales plan includes such items as the number of in-person calls a week on A, B, and C accounts and prospects; number of projected demos or trials; attending trade shows or other special events; and necessary sales results per week to reach annual goals. The sales plan for products or services with long, complex sales cycles will be less focused on the number of calls and more focused on the strategic and tactical action necessary to move major prospects or customers from one step in the sales cycle to the next.

In addition to the salesperson's or channel partner's plans, the person ultimately responsible for sales, possibly a sales manager (but probably the entrepreneur or owner), must prepare his or her own sales plan. This plan should include action related to hiring, training, compensating, staffing, deploying, motivating, evaluating, and automating the sales force.

LINE-ITEM EXPENSE BUDGETS
BY DEPARTMENT

Once the new enterprise or small business has its monthly, quarterly, and/or annual bubble-up sales forecast, it requires line-item expense budgets from department managers for those periods. Bubble-up line-item expense budgets, like the sales forecasts, set standards; create a meaningful dialogue with management; get a commitment from department managers; and make managers feel useful, important, and worthwhile.

The line-item expense budgets also act as a standard for comparing actual results. Each month the entrepreneur or small-business manager meets with department heads who have prepared line-item expense budgets to compare actual monthly expenses to budget and take any necessary corrective action.

As with the sales forecast, many entrepreneurs and small business managers claim line-item expense budgets are unnecessary for early-stage and small businesses. On the contrary, because of limited human and financial resources, expense budgets prove more necessary. Also, good financial controls in general, but accurate sales forecasts and expense budgets in particular, will help you obtain bank loans and equity financing.

Preparation of the budget should be delegated to the person closest to managing the activity related to the budget. The expense budget should be prepared by the person responsible for making those expenditures or by the person whose job relates or depends on those expenditures. In a new enterprise the sales forecast and expense budget might be prepared by the entrepreneur with the help of his or her accountant. In an early-stage business with six employees, one each assigned to sales, operations, product development, information technology systems, and marketing, each person would prepare an expense budget for his or her area of responsibility.

Again, don't give a manager or other employee a blank piece of paper and ask for a number. This only causes frustration. Meet with the person to plan the action, which creates the number. What information technology equipment or milling machines must be bought, when and why? How many people do you plan to hire and why? Can raw materials be purchased in a more efficient manner? Should we have a long-term power contract? What has been the historical rate of these expenses and why might that change? Are there industry standards?

Some entrepreneurs and small business managers find it helpful to ask for line-item expense budgets grouped into fixed costs, which do not vary directly with sales volume and cannot easily be changed; variable costs, which do vary directly with sales volume; and discretionary costs, which management has the ability to change on a short-term basis. Rent would be an example of a fixed cost; raw materials or sales commissions are examples of variable expenses; and advertising and travel are examples of discretionary expenses. This organization of expenses allows the entrepreneur or manager to discuss the budget by categories of control and influences. Which expenses are controllable, which are a function of sales, and which are table stakes to be in business?

The book's introduction mentioned a number of factors that prevent new enterprises and entrepreneurs from succeeding. This group of growth busters includes silos, poor communication, and poor delegation of tasks. Bubble-up sales forecasts and line-item expense budgets force entrepreneurs and managers to have meaningful communication up, down, and across the organization. Bubble-up sales forecasts and line-item expense budgets force entrepreneurs and managers to delegate tasks and responsibilities to the appropriate person and break down silos. This represents a major benefit of these two processes for smaller firms.

COMBINING KEY CONTROL POINTS

When the entrepreneur or small business manager combines the sales forecast and expense budget with monitoring key margins and utilization rates, this results in a powerful control mechanism for the entire enterprise. For example, the women's sportswear designer knows that if her firm sells $4 million of merchandise to retailers, and if each style yields at least a 35 percent gross margin, and if selling, general and administrative expenses do not exceed $1.2 million, her firm will have a $200,000 pretax profit. Also, proper monitoring of accounts receivable and inventory will stabilize cash flow.

The salespeople and channel partners forecast $4 million of annual sales, broken down by major account and major prospect. Based on past and present sales trends, changes within the company, at customers, competitors, and in the general business conditions, this number looks realistic.

The department managers budget $1.2 million of selling, general, and administrative expenses based on $4 million of sales. Based on last year's expenses, new hires, advertising, and some information technology updates, this number looks realistic.

Each item in the sportswear line is priced to yield a gross margin of at least 35 percent, taking into account necessary discounts and terms. Since items are imported, utilization rates at factories are not a concern. The overseas suppliers have quoted fixed landed costs in dollars.

This year, critical risks involve having proper inventory to ship, being able to maintain prices, not losing a key customer or salesperson, and the overall economy. Each month the designer, who is also president of the firm, reviews the actual line-item expenses versus budget with the department managers. This quarter, information technology expenses exceed budget because of an unanticipated hire, but lower credit department expenses offset this. She discusses these issues with the appropriate manager.

Each month the designer or president reviews actual sales and shipments versus the forecast in total and by major customer. Several customers will fall below forecast for the year but be compensated for by other customers exceeding forecast. She discusses these issues with the appropriate salesperson or channel partner.

Each month the designer also reviews gross margins (revenues less landed product costs) for each product line, major customer, and the company versus forecast. Margins are below 35 percent on a discontinued line and at a large multistore customer, but above 35 percent at major specialty stores and on signature items.

She continues this monitoring process each month, taking corrective action where necessary. We manage what we monitor.

If this firm manufactured its own products, factory utilization rates would also be monitored, because that would impact gross margins. Higher factory utilization rates, operating at a higher percent of capacity, would drive down fixed costs per unit and drive up gross margins as a percentage of revenue and in absolute dollars.

For example, a small regional phone company would employ the same process to prepare and use a sales forecast and expense budget, but would rely on percentage utilization rates to help predict gross margins. The percentage of its system's capacity being utilized becomes a key control point to forecast and monitor on a monthly basis.

CASH FLOW

Entrepreneurs and small business managers must concentrate on cash flow in addition to profit and loss statements. For a start-up, an early- or growth-stage business, or a small business, cash is king. What sticks to the cash register is what counts. Therefore, predicting and measuring cash flow represents a key financial control point. Unfortunately, most entrepreneurs and small-business people do not know how to accurately predict or measure cash flow and often confuse pretax profits (EBIT) with cash flow.

Whether you are preparing a business plan to raise equity or debt financing or you are doing your annual or quarterly forecasts or budgets, do a cash flow analysis. Also, forecast and measure cash balances plus receipts minus disbursements on a monthly basis. This allows you to anticipate surpluses or deficits which impact payables and bank borrowings.

Rather than revenues and expenses, the cash flow analyzes receipts and disbursements. Receipts and disbursements are not only driven by revenues and expenses but by such balance sheet items as accounts receivable, inventory, accounts payable, accruals, capital expenditures, debt service, bank borrowings, and paid-in capital.

Whether you prepare an annual or monthly cash flow to raise equity or debt financing or a weekly cash flow to project internal needs, you should use a similar format. Start with beginning cash at a certain date. Then add receipts to beginning cash. Receipts would include collection of accounts receivable (based on net sales or revenues), bank loans, and paid-in capital. Based on industry tradition or company experience, what percentage of each month's sales are collected over each of the next three months?

Subtract disbursements from receipts and add or subtract the difference to the beginning cash balance to arrive at an ending cash balance for the period. Disbursements would include payroll, payroll taxes and benefits, payment of accounts payable, repayments of loans, interest, capital expenditures, dividends, and return of capital. Payroll-related disbursements can be categorized by department or hourly versus salary or some other significant description. Payment of accounts payable can be categorized by factory or raw material costs, advertising, rent, or any line-item or combination of line-items. If it proves difficult to predict when a particular payable will be paid, consider due dates, terms, past history, and industry tradition.

Have your accountant assist in formatting the cash flow. On a monthly basis, compare actual cash flow to forecast or budget, note variances, and take corrective action. Look at the numbers behind the numbers. For example, perhaps February collections were below forecast and March payments of payables above forecast. Why was this the case?

An understanding of the dynamics behind your firm's cash flow will help you obtain debt and equity financing, avoid unpleasant surprises, and better run your business. Because of limited financial resources, the high cost of financial distress, critical risks associated with major decisions, and high failure rates, cash-flow forecasting and reporting are essential key control points for small businesses and start-ups.

NONFINANCIAL KEY CONTROL POINTS

As an entrepreneur or small-business manager, consider other nonfinancial key control points important for the success of your business.

This will differ by business, but might include customer satisfaction as measured by annual surveys, employee satisfaction as measured by annual 360 degree evaluations or quality control as measured by statistical sampling. In a 360 degree employee evaluation, participants have an opportunity to evaluate all the people and functions they work with in the organization. A key control point for an importer or distributor might be percentage of each order shipped complete or on time. For a business relying on first-time or one-time customers, the number of new accounts would be critical. For a modified rebuy business, your firm's percentage of a customer's business or number of repeat customers might represent a key figure. For a business with high raw material costs, analyses of purchasing effectiveness and vendor performance would represent key control points. For a business with high labor costs, you would want metrics for measuring productivity. For a business with high sales force costs, results per call might prove important. For a business with high marketing costs, financial returns on advertising or trade show costs might prove important. Again, follow the money.

As an entrepreneur or small-business person, you cannot do everything. What are the key metrics you must understand and the key areas you must manage for success? The key control points will change as a firm moves from start-up to early and growth stages and then to maturity.

ENTREPRENEURS' MAJOR MISTAKES OR WEAKNESSES IN CREATING PROPER FINANCIAL CONTROLS

- Confusing revenues and expenses with receipts and disbursements.
- Not concentrating controls on customers, revenue sources, or expenditures with the largest dollar value.
- Concentration on profit-and-loss items at the expense of balance sheet items.
- Not analyzing the numbers behind the numbers.
- Not having salespeople and channel partners forecast sales.
- Not having department heads or department members budget expenses.
- Not comparing actual results to forecasts or budgets and taking corrective action.

QUESTIONS AND EXERCISES

1. What are the key financial and nonfinancial control points in your business?

2. What are the critical operating margins and utilization rates at your firm?

3. What processes do you use for forecasting revenues and budgeting expenses?

4. How does your enterprise predict and measure cash flow?

PART TWO

MARKETING AND SALES

CHAPTER 4

Differentiation, Target Marketing, and Target Customers

If an entrepreneur cannot differentiate his or her product or service from the competition, the new enterprise will not receive outside equity financing and will have great difficulty finding and maintaining customers. Differentiation can be created by innovation or invention, and is not limited to product or service design. Differentiation can be created by excellence in sales or marketing, customer relation ships, cost and pricing, niche markets, operational efficiencies, or wrapping services around products. When done well, differentiation creates a perceived competitive advantage in the minds of customers.

The entrepreneur looks for differentiation and a competitive advantage in operational excellence, new product or service innovation, or customer intimacy. Can our firm exceed customer expectations or create new ones? Can we redefine how customers perceive value? Possibly our differentiation involves after-sale service, quick delivery, eliminating the middle person, convenience of purchase or a hassle-free experience. Possibly we have found a less costly means to manufacture the product or deliver the service, which we choose to pass on to the customer in lower prices.

Successful entrepreneurs understand the difference between the profit and loss on a single transaction and profit over the lifetime of their relationship with a single customer. This understanding helps to target and customize the offering for different customers and market segments. In the 1990s, when on-line trading and discount brokerage fees first emerged, the early-stage entrepreneurs, with few legacies and reduced human capital investments, accepted minimal profits per transaction because of customers' lifetime profit value. These same early discount brokerage firms customized their offerings to various market segments. A client could trade on-line, use a touch-tone phone to trade, or place orders through a broker. A customer could choose between a low fee with no service, an account with potential service, or a full-service advisory relationship. A customer could pay a fixed annual fee for all transactions or a more conventional brokerage fee for each transaction. Since barriers to entry in the security brokerage industries were low and extent of rivalry high, the large established firms, the gorillas, eventually followed the structure offered by these early-stage ants, the entrepreneurial start-ups. By the year 2000, much of the brokerage business had been commoditized.

Ideas for product or service differentiation often come from sources outside the entrepreneur's company, such as present and potential competitors, customers, trade shows, trade publications, and the Internet. Since an advantage of smaller firms is their flexibility and speed, these new outside ideas can be accepted and commercialized quickly. To maintain their differentiation, entrepreneurs must relentlessly pursue new solutions to the problems that their own latest product or service has just solved. An Internet portal catering to smaller businesses offers on-line credit, marketing, and human resource services. When customers buy these services they have difficulty navigating the Web site, so the entrepreneurs' next challenge involves creating better customer service, using an 800 number, and a more user-friendly experience. Continually solving new customer problems creates new opportunities for differentiation, erects more barriers to entry, and perpetuates a competitive advantage. Striving for continual differentiation generates a company culture, and entrepreneurs must hire people who enjoy this type of culture.

Smaller companies must focus on a particular value discipline, which strongly influences their choice of target customers and determination of market segments. Leaders and early adopters are the target customers for new product or service innovators and firms offering customer intimacy, but the late majority customers are the target for operational excellence. Leaders and early adopters, whether businesses or consumers, want the newest and the best regardless of price. These groups also expect a high level of customer service. On the other hand, the late majority customers, whether businesses or consumers, assign a higher importance to price and utility.

STRATEGIC VALUE DISCIPLINES

After a successful start many small businesses fail because they don't continue to focus on their strategic value discipline. Reacting to competitive and customer pressures, they pursue initiatives that have merit on their own but are inconsistent with their firm's initially chosen strategic value discipline. Entrepreneurs must aggressively respond to change but also not lose focus on their strategic operating model. For example, a successful Midwest brand-name, better-furniture regional chain was challenged by a new lower-priced national competitor. To meet this new competitive threat, the regional chain lowered costs and prices by reducing the number of designers or salespeople at each store. The national chain's competitive advantage or value discipline was operational excellence and lower prices. The regional chain's competitive advantage or value discipline was customer intimacy and fashion/style. By reducing the number of salespeople or designers on the retail floor and their time to make in-home presentations, the firm lost their customer intimacy focus. Also, the regional firm could not reduce expenses enough to be cost competitive with the national chain. As a result the regional market share of the smaller fashion-oriented firm declined.

THE STRATEGIC SERVICE-PROFIT CHAIN

As a smaller firm or a start-up, consider the importance of customer intimacy and high-touch customer service to differentiate your offering. Relate this to choice of market segments and target customers. In the Introduction we said customer intimacy and high-touch service represent possible strengths for start-ups and smaller businesses, which should be used to offset the weaknesses of limited resources and lack of diversification. Therefore, smaller firms must understand how to put the service-profit chain to work.

The service-profit chain demands that frontline workers, who touch customers, and the customer, whether a business or a consumer, need to be the center of management concern (remember the silo Growth Busters, in the Introduction).

Therefore, investments in people who touch customers, technology that supports those people, hiring and training practices that reinforce the service orientation, and performance compensation linked to customer satisfaction all represent important tactical issues that drive success. For many smaller businesses and start-ups, differentiation and success depend on happy employees who create satisfied customers.

Start-ups and smaller businesses often suffer from customer and employee turnover, which proves very expensive. Obtaining that first order proves difficult enough, but losing a new customer represents an even higher cost in dollars, morale, and image. Even as businesses mature, longer-term customers often contribute more to dollars of margin and income as a percentage of revenues than the newer customers. A key strategic decision of more mature firms involves whether to focus on opening new customers or maintaining and expanding existing ones. Entrepreneurs must concentrate on the lifetime value of loyal, repeat customers (apostles), especially those that refer new customers. These issues all relate to strategy, focus, differentiation, and targeting.

The lifetime value of a loyal dentist buying equipment and hand tools from the same vendor can reach $400,000. The lifetime value of a small retailer buying photo frames from an importer can be $100,000. The lifetime value of a consumer using a home cleaning company service at $50 a week can approach $50,000. Repeat customers drive sales, lower expenses, and increase profits. Entrepreneurs must focus on this strategy.

Entrepreneurs must realize the strong relationship between profitability, customer loyalty and employee satisfaction, retention, and productivity. Customer satisfaction and loyalty drive revenue growth and income. Satisfaction results from a customer's perceived value, which happy, loyal, and productive employees influence. Employee satisfaction, in turn, results primarily from the employer's high-quality support services and from policies that enable employees to efficiently deliver results to customers. A start-up contains few legacy issues and bad habits, and should therefore be able to embrace the service-profit chain strategy.

An entrepreneurial trash removal service in North Dakota and a lawn care service in Virginia both ask customers to interview potential employees. The founders of both firms spend a day a week in the field with employees and customers. These managers talk about and audit employee attitudes toward customers.

Nationally, customer turnover in trash hauling and lawn care approaches 33 percent annually. These two very diverse firms from North Dakota and Virginia quarterly measure customer satisfaction and turnover and pay employees a bonus based on those results. Quarterly customer telephone surveys ask questions not only about areas of satisfaction and disappointment but about the number of services (for example, recycling, compaction, disease prevention, tree trimming) used by each customer. The surveys also ask customers to make referrals and rewards them for doing this.

These surveys prevent disappointed customers from bad-mouthing your firm, which can destroy a small early-stage enterprise. These surveys encourage satisfied customers to become apostles, who recommend your products or services, lowering the cost of new customer acquisition. A smaller firm should have an advantage in customer care and intimacy allowing it to prevent negative word of

mouth and raise customers from the zone of defection and indiffer-
ence to the zone of affection and apostles.

Customers demand value; they demand that the results received
from a purchase match the price and other associated costs.
Entrepreneurs must offer value that reflects customer needs, which
might be accurate billing, training, or installation. Small businesses
can differentiate themselves in these value areas also. Some of these
value factors are demanded and expected to compete in an industry;
others can differentiate your business. To be a serious competitor, your
storm windows must fit correctly, but one-week installation service
and after-sale maintenance are strong differentiators.

Entrepreneurs create employee satisfaction for those who face
the customer by allowing these people to effectively achieve results
for customers and to meet customers' needs. In order to handle customer problems, service providers must have the decision-making
authority to resolve any situation promptly. Also, information regard-
ing a customer's concerns must be transmitted to the service provider
quickly through the technological infrastructure. Customer-related
results require proper training, equipment, support, compensation,
and decision-making authority for those interfacing with customers.
Any employee who interfaces with a customer, for example, the
delivery person, needs the respect of management to create personal
dignity. At the lawn- and tree-care concern and the waste removal
firm, the people who perform the work on the customers' premises
understand the importance of their job.

To nip potential satisfaction and value problems in the bud, the
owner or president of a start-up or small business should personally
do exit interviews for all employees who leave and all customers who
defect. This reflects customer intimacy issues, the importance and
inter-relationship of employee and customer satisfaction, and entrepreneurial differentiation.

Customer and employee satisfaction must continually be measured and linked to performance pay. Establish accurate metrics to
measure employee and customer satisfaction and then efficient means
to get this valuable feedback. As mentioned, you should do quarterly,
semiannual, or annual customer satisfaction surveys and employee climate surveys. The survey might include all customers, a representative
sample of all customers, or the top 20 percent of customers. These surveys can be done by phone, mail, fax, or on-line. Services such as
zoomerang.com will administer your on-line surveys. Always benchmark by asking customers and employees what is better and worse
since the last survey. Always promptly follow up with corrective action
on areas requiring improvement. Also, a Web site and 800 number for
customer and employee input at anytime will collect useful data.

Employee metrics would include satisfaction with training, management, teammates, compensation, equipment, support systems, and customers. Customer metrics would include satisfaction with products or services; all company employees including sales, engineering, operations, delivery, and service; price or value; as well as instructions, documentation, and billing. Customer and employee satisfaction metrics should reflect and reinforce each other. Customer and employee satisfaction surveys should be done for the same time periods.

Customer satisfaction surveys should be done for external and internal customers. In some cases employees in other departments or functions are the customer. Have sales rate the credit and engineering staff. Have credit and engineering rate the accounting and production staff. Even in a business with five people there are external and internal customers. Realization of this and the use of surveys prevents silos.

What action and results on the part of employees create customer satisfaction? How can you accurately measure these and translate the results into performance pay? In a start-up enterprise, 40 percent of an employee's compensation should reflect performance pay and half of the performance pay should be deferred to reduce turnover. Metrics for the 40 percent performance pay will depend on the person's position. For those facing the customer, from direct salespeople to the call center staff to engineering support, a significant portion of performance pay should relate to sales results, customer contact activities, and customer satisfaction. Employee activities and results that foster customer satisfaction should be rewarded with not only performance pay but recognition, such as service awards.

Negative customer feedback on the product or service or on employee or operational issues requires a quick response from the internal design, engineering, and operations staff. Customer perceptions of quality and value reflect the difference between expectations and the actual experience. The actual experience reflects results and the process through which results were achieved. Entrepreneurs must realistically set customer expectations and also measure them. Entrepreneurial organizations often oversell expectations, which creates customer disappointment.

DIFFERENTIATION BY ALTERING THE CONSUMPTION CHAIN, CHANNELS OF DISTRIBUTION, AND CUSTOMER EXPERIENCE.

Entrepreneurs want to offer customers differentiation by giving them something of value not available from competitors. Differentiation is not limited to product design or service, however. Companies have

the opportunity to differentiate their offering at every point of customer contact from moment of need to the point of disposal.
Successful entrepreneurs consider their opportunities to differentiate at any point in the customer's total experience, or the consumption chain.

Many start-ups fail because the entrepreneur does a bad job in
demand generation for initial or repeat orders. Often this results from
a lack of funds for advertising and promotion. Successful start-ups
differentiate themselves by discovering unique inexpensive and subtle ways of generating demand. For example, an Indiana fine paper
distributor color codes the last box of his product in a printer's stock
room. On that box is the distributor's toll free telephone number
and Web site for reorders. Customers like this timesaving idea, and
it allows salespeople to spend more time with larger customers
and prospects.

Another means of differentiating your product or service involves
how, where, and when it can be purchased. For example, a New York
neighborhood travel agent specializing in travel to India offers tickets
and information on a Web site and on a 24-hour, 7-day-a-week, 800
number. On weekdays the retail location opens at 6 a.m., closes at
9 a.m., and then reopens from 5 p.m. until 11 p.m. In New York City
this reflects their customers' presence in the neighborhood. This neighborhood travel agent also uses permission e-mail to announce specials
reinforced by colorful direct-mail brochures. The business has doubled
its revenues each year since 1998.

Moving through the consumption chain, see if the customer's
selection process offers an opportunity for differentiation. Can you
make the selection process more comfortable, less irritating, or more
convenient? For example, a printed circuit board subcontractor in
Cleveland competes against many other smaller firms, but wins 55
percent of the available business by shortening the purchasing cycle.

The company's Web site is interactive, allowing prospects to
input requests for bids 7 days a week. Within 24 hours of receiving a
request, an engineer calls the prospect to qualify the project. Twenty
percent of the requests will be turned down because the subcontractor
does not have the proper capabilities. The remaining 80 percent will
receive a preliminary proposal. If acceptable, engineering and sales
visit the prospect two days later to review actual design specifications
and three days after that submit a prototype by overnight courier.
After many e-mails, a trial order is delivered and then a production
order written. This Cleveland firm has reduced the time and steps in
purchasing its products and the irritation in selecting a contractor.
Because of this speed, convenience and comfort, the firm grew from a
million dollars in annual sales to 15 million in five years.

For low-cost, high-volume products or services which customers frequently reorder, a company can differentiate itself by making the ordering process more convenient. A Wisconsin bakery products distributor gave all accounts above a certain dollar amount a free computer terminal loaded with its catalog and with programmed access to its on-line ordering Web site. This made ordering bakery products more convenient and created customer switching costs. Terminals were leased by the distributor and the expense recovered through increased revenues and decreased order processing costs.

Delivery affords many opportunities for differentiation. The local bakery products firm mentioned above and the regional fine paper distributor mentioned previously both deliver any order received before noon on the same day. An Omaha plumbing service thrives by guaranteeing a person at your house within three hours of the call, 24 hours a day, seven days a week.

You can differentiate your product by helping with installation or service. This represents an excellent example of wrapping a service around a product to enhance its customer value. The bakery products distributor trains the customer's bakery staff in proper use of certain mixes and icings. A software value-added retailer installs the software at clients' firms and trains people how to use it. A provider of refills for portable oxygen machines installs them for elderly customers and instructs them on proper use.

In the regional telephone business a major differentiator is backroom issues, such as the accuracy of monthly invoices, ease of understanding them, and ease of having billing questions answered. Start-up regional phone companies and DSLs that do this well gain market share from those that do not.

Smaller firms offering telephone equipment to consumers and businesses can differentiate themselves through leasing and finance terms. Often the small firm can provide competitive financing with the help of their larger equipment manufacturers and bank.

The bakery supply distributor also differentiates itself by leasing freezers to store frozen bakery products. Most bakeries have limited freezer space and many new bakery products must remain frozen until used. A competitor solves the disposal problem by buying back and removing the pails their frozen batter arrives in. Another firm offers frozen batter in 10-pound pails rather than 20 pound pails, which requires less freezer space but costs more per pound. Consider how you can differentiate your firm by helping customers with storage or disposal issues.

The same bakery products distributor packaged flour in 50-pound bags with handles rather than the 100-pound bags that competitors offered. Personnel in bakeries carry bags of flour from the storage area to the mixing equipment, which is often located on another floor. The 50-pound bags with handles proved much easier to move. Once delivered, do your customers have unfilled needs in moving your products? If so, does this represent an opportunity for differentiation?

Some industries contain customers who benefit from hot lines to obtain information on product use. This might be an 800 number or an on-line information center. A regional North American industrial cable firm opened the Mexican market by offering a bilingual 24/7, 800 telephone hot line and a bilingual Web site for after-purchase service. A subcontractor handled the 800 number.

A Canadian firm, which annually sells $10 million of emission control devices for trucks and city buses, contracts out after-sale repair services to trained mechanics in each major metropolitan area. The firm guarantees customers that they will repair or replace any malfunctioning part within 24 hours while no competitor does this. After-purchase repair and service represents a means for smaller firms to differentiate themselves.

Most of these ideas for differentiation are easy to copy even though they create switching costs for customers. Once successful, expect competition because barriers to entry are low. You will find some of these ideas for differentiation discussed further in Chapter 9.

Successful entrepreneurs who achieve significant differentiation from competitors often analyze their customer's experience at each point in the consumption chain. Therefore, ask yourself these questions:

- What are my customers doing at each stage of the consumption chain? What problems and opportunities does each stage present? What can my company do to enhance the customer's experience?
- Where are my customers located at each stage of the consumption chain and do they have concerns about their location?
- With who else or what other company does my customer share each stage of the consumption chain? With this knowledge can we enhance the purchasing experience?
- Do my customers move through various stages of the consumption chain at any particular time of day or day of month or month of year? Does this timing create opportunities or problems?

TARGETING AND MARKET SEGMENTATION

Successful entrepreneurs understand the importance of customer targeting and market segmentation. Early-stage entrepreneurial enterprises have limited human and financial resources, and cannot survive being all things to all people in this millennium's global markets. Entrepreneurs must target customers and markets where their firm has an easily definable, quantifiable competitive advantage. Once targeted, the ability to differentiate, create customer switching costs, and overcome competitor barriers to entry separates success from failure. This approach focuses scarce marketing and development resources on targeted customer groups, limits serious competitors, and allows the benefits of market leadership to develop more quickly, encouraging the entrepreneur to leverage past successes into other promising segments. Targeting creates a necessary dilemma because of dependence on a limited number of customers. Because issues of targeting and differentiation influence each other like chromosomes and genes, you must work on both issues at the same time.

Targeting decisions are made early in a firm's history without much experience and evidence. Often the first 10 customers or the first 5 repeat customers, who may arrive quite by chance, or who are based on previous relationships, are thought to be the target. Or the first 10 customers might bear no relationship to each other. Therefore, targeting represents a high-risk, low-data decision, which often runs counter to the entrepreneur's sales instincts. There are many segments and very little time to investigate small niche markets. When deciding on your target customer and/or market segment, use the decision-making methodology discussed in the Introduction. Consider alternatives, the merits and risks of each, along with the quantitative and qualitative data, which will help you make the correct decision, plus a plan and time frame for implementation. Then decide on the performance standards or metrics and the time frame necessary to measure the results along with the necessary corrective action, if you choose the wrong targets or the incorrect market segmentation.

Successful entrepreneurs continually test targeting and segmentation decisions, admit mistakes, and take corrective action. Perpetuating targeting or segmentation mistakes can prove fatal. Also, because business is a dynamic process, target customers, market segmentation, technology, competition, and strategy continually change. You must continually challenge and update yesterday's markets and targets. Entrepreneurs must understand that targeting can be challenging and mysterious. Most markets contain myriad segments and niches.

A Chicago-based sales automation software firm believed its target customers were Fortune 500 manufacturing firms, because its first 10 customers included divisions of Alcoa, U.S. Steel, several auto firms, an airline, a utility, and a railroad. All these firms were operations-driven, not sales-driven. The initial sales reflected relationships between the start-up's founders and the chief information officers in these Fortune 500 divisions. Because these firms were operations, not sales-driven, the new software was seldom used.

After years of struggling with marginal sales, the software firm changed its focus to mid-sized sales-driven firms with a large number of field salespeople. The target became pharmaceutical firms, consumer products firms, distributors, insurance companies, and service organizations with a lot of feet on the street. The mid-sized sales-driven, consumer- and service-oriented firms recognized the need for and benefits of sales force automation and had less decision-making bureaucracy, which shortened the sales cycle and increased the closing ratios.

Target customers, target markets, and market segmentation are determined by the dollars of present and potential revenue and income (scalability), the cost to sell and serve, and the probability of success. Let's say you want to know which market segments offer the best opportunity for your new emission control devices: autos, trucks, buses, material handling equipment, or underground mining equipment? These markets can be further divided by original equipment manufacturers, after-market distributors, and fleet owners plus by country of origin: North America, Central and South America, the European Union, South Africa, Australia, and Asia.

Dollars of potential revenue point you to the North American auto industry, but the cost to sell and serve this market segment is high and the possibility of success low, because of immense competition. Tier-three auto suppliers must have economies of scale to offer competitive prices. At this point in time, your small firm does not have economies of scale.

Further analysis of market and competitive data from government statistics, industry associations, and trade publications indicates various niches more appropriate for your strengths. Most entrepreneurs neglect market research and quantitative data that could help them make targeting and segmentation decisions. Sources for market research data include the Internet, which contains an ocean of information, as does government statistics, trade publications, and trade associations. The Commerce Department's Survey of U.S. Industrial and Commercial Buying Power is a good starting point. Also look at U.S. Department of Commerce Industry Search, www.doc.gov; Bureau of Labor Statistics, Economy at a Glance, Industries, www.stats.bls.gov; and *U.S. Industry and Trade Outlook 2000*, published by the Department of Commerce. Hire some interns to help with market research. Valid market data that support your value propositions and targets will help attain equity financing. The following sites and publications will help you identify other sources for the market research:

- Lexis-Nexis, www.lexis-nexis.com
- LENS Corporate Library, www.thecorporatelibrary.com
- One Source, www.onesource.com
- Boston Consulting Firm Publications, www.bcg.com/ publications

Imagine that you discover that the underground mining and material handling markets must use emission control devices because they operate in enclosed spaces. Plus, they are underserved. Large municipalities must retrofit existing buses to meet new federal emission control regulations. Your devices have a total cost and performance advantage in both these market segments. Although North America offers the greatest potential, Europe and Asia also have passed new emission control regulations for trucks and buses. South Africa and Australia have the largest number of underground mines. In the retrofit or after-markets the cost to sell and serve a customer is high if you use stocking distributors who receive a 33 percent discount for their services.

Because of your competitive advantage in performance and cost, government regulations, and the fact that certain markets are underserved by competition and others overserved, niches emerge where the dollars of present and potential income and revenue can be maximized over time. These same markets contain a higher probability of success and a lower cost to sell and serve.

Continuing this example, note that within a particular market this same analysis can be performed by customer. In the retrofitting of city buses, Detroit, Toronto, Chicago, and Cleveland become target customers. Because of their proximity to your facilities, you can easily sell and service them directly without using a distributor. The number of buses involved in retrofitting their fleets is large but within your capacity. The sales cycle can be reduced because of existing relationships with key decision makers. The lifetime value of retrofitting buses for each city exceeds $5 million.

Salespeople's efforts will be concentrated on these target customers and target markets. Salespeople will not call on auto or truck manufacturers but rather manufacturers of mining and material handling equipment and bus engines in North American and Europe. Salespeople also will call on municipal bus companies in certain U.S. cities plus major mining companies worldwide for retrofit work. South Africa and Australia will require an independent sales representative; possibly you will partner with another firm in Europe.

In addition, the company will customize emission control devices for each target market segment. Mining equipment needs a different configuration than material handling, and requirements for Canada and Europe (metrics) are different from the United States (decimals).

Customer Needs, Prospect Indentifiability, and Accessibility

Markets are segmented and customers targeted based on dollars of present and potential revenue and income over time, the cost to sell and serve them, and the probability of success. These criteria reflect segmentation based on customer needs, prospect identifiability, and prospect accessibility.

Segmenting and targeting based on customer needs, applications, or reasons to buy begins with understanding how customers benefit from the product or service. The idea involved in customer-driven or value-based segmentation is that the vendor must implement a separate marketing strategy for each needs-driven, value-based segment. Each segment represents a group of customers and prospects sharing a common set of needs or applications or reasons to buy different from the needs or applications and reasons of other segments. This approach centers on the customer and makes its way back to the vendor. This approach proves difficult in rapidly changing markets where buyers' needs and applications also change rapidly and customers are not always aware of their needs.

On the other hand, segmentation and targeting based on the prospects' or customers' identifiability and accessibility to the seller works outward from the selling firm toward the prospect. In this approach all members of each segment can be identified through the same criteria (e.g., location or size) and can be reached through common channels (e.g., trade shows). This assumes buyer characteristics can be associated with underlying needs.

Although more difficult to implement, the customer needs approach should prove more successful, since it is buyer-oriented. The identifiability approach provides easy-to-define customer groupings, but can claim no casual relationships to sought benefits. Entrepreneurs should look for segments and targets where these two approaches overlap, where, indeed, an easily identifiable customer or prospect group does have common needs and benefits related to your product or service. You might choose one approach to segmentation and targeting over another based on the product or service involved or the particular marketing task. For example, you might choose needs-benefit segmentation for pricing policy but choose the identifiable or accessible approach for advertising policy and channel choice. Organizing your sales force might require a hybrid approach. You organize salespeople initially based on major accounts, product lines, or geography, but then after numerous customer visits and a needs analysis, each salesperson prioritizes or targets prospects or customers based on benefits.

For an entrepreneurial, early-stage firm or small business, knowledge of and use of these two approaches should create a more efficient use of human and financial resources. Be sure to redefine targets and segments using these two approaches as markets, products, customers, and competitors change.

The entrepreneur and small-business manager also must acknowledge the cost of segmentation and the need to keep it simple. Obtaining the information for segmentation can be time-consuming and expensive. More important for a start-up, early-stage, or small business, too much segmentation can cause confusion and a diffuse focus and create excessive marketing, sales, engineering, product development, and operating costs.

For example, an electronics manufacturing subcontractor in Arizona segmented its market into eight pieces based on needs and accessibility: health care devices, auto, computers, telecom, industrial process controls, cell phones, personal handheld organizers, and slot machines. The firm used a different salesperson for each segment, advertised in appropriate industry publications for each segment, and attended trade shows for each segment. Selling expenses quickly rose to 22 percent of revenues and marketing expenses to 11 percent of revenues. Also, the factory and engineering could not operate efficiently manufacturing all these diverse products. Based on present and potential revenue and income over time, the cost to sell and serve, and the probability of success, management reduced the market segments from eight to four, resulting in increased revenues and decreased expenses.

In assessing the potential profitability of each market segment, management looked at the lifetime value of target customers, their possible product mix, their physical proximity to each other, and the marketing and sales costs necessary to convert them from prospects to customers (the cost to sell and serve). In evaluating the cost to sell and serve and the probability of success, consider not only the competitive grid for each target segment or customer but also the proximity or density of accounts, the number of highly qualified prospects within that segment, and probable closing ratios or conversion rates.

In looking at the marketing funnel for your product or service or for a target customer or market segment, consider the steps, closing ratios, conversion rates, probabilities, time frame, and costs of moving suspects to prospects to qualified prospects to customers to repeat customers. The marketing funnel will help you define the probability of success and the cost to sell and serve. The marketing funnel will vary depending on the type of product and buyer behavior.

The marketing funnel is the steps your company must perform to locate prospects and then convert them into customers. The steps to identify prospects might include trade shows, advertising, and telesales. The steps to convert prospects to customers might involve a salesperson visit, needs analysis, proposal, trial, and bid. The cost and elapsed time of each step must be measured along with the number of prospects who enter the funnel, drop off at each step, and exit as customers. The funnel must be modified for retailers and e-commerce and will vary for consumer versus industrial or commercial products or services.

For first-time or one-time purchases of high-ticket systems the funnel will have more steps (longer sales cycle) and require more time and cost than for a modified rebuy of less costly products or services. Commodity purchases may have the shortest sales cycle and be accomplished by telesales or the Internet. For first-time or one-time purchases of high-ticket items a market segment may consist of only a hundred potential customers. In such situations market segmentation based on dollars of present and potential income and revenue must be tempered with the number of potential accounts. If the universe of suspects is small, it may significantly reduce your probability of success. As you can see, the marketing funnel can help determine market segments and target accounts.

Once you have determined which market segments have the greatest needs for the features and benefits of your product or service, completed the competitive grid, and analyzed the marketing funnel, you need to look at the cost of maintaining these target customers or market segments. In order to create repeat customers ask yourself what after-sales services are required, such as training, documentation, and repair? Does the price charged for these services cover the cost? What marketing and sales costs are required to maintain these accounts, such as advertising, trade shows, direct mail, telesales, or in-person calls? How many in-person calls are required for a reorder? What is the cost in time and dollars? Does this market segment or target customer order at intervals, in quantities, and with a product mix that is profitable to sell and supply?

Quantify as much material as possible and prepare spreadsheets for various target customers and target markets using different assumptions for average order size, number of reorders, as well as required human and financial resources. What customers and segments produce the most dollars of contribution margin over time and the highest return on investment?

New Products and Services

For technology and new product or service start-ups, market segments are heavily influenced by the customer type. When an entrepreneur introduces a new product or service, whether it be a medication, medical device, Internet service, or video camera, he or she seeks customers who are innovators and early adapters. These are businesses and consumers who are leaders, enthusiasts, and visionaries. These are successful businesses and consumers who want the newest and the best and are willing to pay for it. These visionaries are adventurers, prefer early buy-in, are independent thinkers, and think and spend big. These consumers shop at certain better department and specialty stores and on-line sites. These businesses like to buy directly from the vendor's management. For new products or services the probability of success and dollars of potential income are highest with this rather small group.

Once the new product or service has proven itself, the more pragmatic and much larger early majority segment or type becomes targeted. The early majority are businesses and consumers who would like to be innovators, leaders, and early adapters, but don't have the necessary funds to accept the risks involved. Early majority customers have a wait and see prudent attitude and spend to budget. Early majority consumers shop primarily at moderate department or chain stores, and these businesses want to buy from vendor salespeople. As the product or service moves through its life cycle and prices decline along with demand, followers or late majority businesses and consumers become target customers. These consumers shop at lower-end chain stores and mass merchants, and these businesses are content buying from channel partners such as distributors or independent sales representatives. The late majority purchases based on utility and price. The last customer type are laggards or resisters who only buy for replacement based on price. Resale shops and used equipment dealers target this group.

A major challenge for entrepreneurs introducing new products or services is convincing early majority customers to try it. Innovators, leaders, and visionaries are an easier sell for new products, but the much larger group of pragmatic early majority are necessary for a successful introduction. Entrepreneurs often refer to this transition as "crossing the chasm."

The model, then, for new product or service targeting and segmentation involves selection and service within the context of the adaptation cycle. Segments are identified and prioritized on the basis of customer value-added and common application or use.

In the year 2000 a Bay Area start-up received venture capital funding to provide on-line services for small businesses. Services include public relations, on-line advertising, direct-mail and print ads, tech support, training, business software, recruiting, credit, sales, market research, travel, legal, and Web site design. Management defined the universe of prospects as the 15 million businesses with fewer than 100 employees. But how should management segment those 15 million accounts to increase the probability of success? Which are the target accounts? Which segments or customers have the highest present and potential revenues and income over time, the lowest cost to sell and serve, and the highest probability of success? How do various customer groups benefit and derive value from applying the service? How can the firm easily identify and then cost-efficiently reach these groups?

Based on benefits, needs, value-added applications, identity, accessibility, costs, the marketing funnel, and the new service adaptation cycle, targets and segments emerged. The target prospect or customer employs fewer than 25 people, may be a self-employed person, must be on-line, might reside in a more rural setting, and must be an early adapter. The marketing funnel involved reaching the target segments by linking the start-up's Web site to other on-line services' target prospects use, plus attending targeted trade shows, and advertising in select trade journals. Once at the small business site, prospects will be offered a free trial for one service after they have registered. Once registered, customers and prospects will receive permission e-mail. Special pricing will be offered for buying a package of services and a bonus for referrals. An 800 number will be available for service.

As this example illustrates, market segmentation for new products and services involves targeting specific early adapters and then customizing the means of reaching them. It also illustrates the marketing funnel for e-commerce and the similarities between old and new economy businesses.

CORE COMPETENCIES

Realistically understanding your firm's core competencies will also assist in targeting because it influences dollars of present and potential revenue and margin, scalability; plus your ability and cost to sell and serve and, of course, the probability of success. To help understand your core competencies, I suggest you prepare a competitive grid, for each market and market segment, which lists competitors across the top and competitive issues down the side. The grid should illustrate how the target customer decides between one competitor and another.

A St. Louis photo accessories distributor, who sells imported albums and frames to retailers (minilabs) using telesales people, competes against other photo accessory distributors, as well as against domestic and overseas album and frame manufacturers who sell direct to retailers. The entrepreneur lists her five major competitors across the top of a page, and down the side of the page she lists how a customer chooses. (She lists variety of items, minimum order size, retail/consumer sell-through, next-day delivery, back orders/fulfillment, relationship with salesperson, frequency of salesperson contact, accuracy of monthly billing, return policy/guaranteed sale, payment terms, retail mark-up percentage, promotions, and price.) Retail/ consumer sell-through would include items such as brand recognition, packaging, and taste level.

She considers both direct and indirect competitors, as well as replacements and substitutes, barriers to entry, and switching costs. Digital photography might replace photo albums and frames. Substitutes could include loose photos with no frames or albums. Indirect competitors for the photo frames and albums sold to minilabs and gift shops are mass merchants and chains that carry similar merchandise.

Customer switching costs could be created by this small firm by keeping database records of what items each minilab and gift shop bought and the date of order. This information would help the retailer analyze results and could be made available to the retailer in hard copy or on-line. Switching costs also could be created by aggregating and distributing data to customers on what product groups sold best in each region. Small firms have the ability to wrap value-added customer services around products.

The small photo album and frame distributor could create barriers to entry by having suppliers sign exclusive agreements on certain designs or by trade marking these designs with product names. Satisfied customers and happy vendors also create barriers to entry for the competition.

The entrepreneur looks at her firm's competitive grid and realistically identifies core competencies and competitive advantage. Core competencies include the working capital to support a broad product line and high stock levels, excellent relationships with Asian suppliers, a database of 5000 active customers and 3000 prospects, a highly trained telesales group, information technology and telephone systems that automate many processes, and management's ability to select appropriate merchandise. These working capital and systems core competencies allow the owner to offer a wide variety of tasteful items with small minimum orders and 99 percent complete next-day shipments. The training, information, and telephone systems allow the telesales force to build positive relationships with customers and call on the proper date for reorders. The large diversified customer base reduces the risk of returns and bad credit, allowing the firm to offer guaranteed sales and lenient payment terms. Because of good vendor relationships and management's high taste level, the photo albums and frames have excellent retail sell-through. To recoup the cost and reflect the customer benefits of these features, the product's prices are upper-moderate.

These core competencies and the competitive grid clearly point this firm toward certain types of retailers. Targeted retail segments include photo finishing minilabs, independent gift shops, vacation area retailers, cruise lines, corporate human resource departments for framing awards, and portrait photographers. Similarly, these core competencies and the competitive grid clearly point this firm away from mass merchants and large chains that insist on vendors counting stock in each store for reorders, prefer national brands, and want very low prices. Mass merchants and large chains buy directly from the same vendors that this small distributor does.

These core competencies and the competitive grid clearly point this firm toward an unexplored opportunity: selling direct to consumers with a business-to-consumer (B2C) Web site. Through focus groups and on-line market research, this small firm also discovers that working women between the ages of 25 and 45 prefer to purchase frames and albums on-line. They are the target market in this space.

Understanding her firm's core competencies and competitive grid has allowed this small business owner and entrepreneur to focus her firm's limited human and financial resources on market segments and target customers with the greatest present and potential revenue and income, lowest cost to sell and serve, and the highest probability of success. The global business universe contains space for many enterprises, each occupying its own niche. Success depends on finding that niche.

THINKING GLOBALLY

Entrepreneurs and small-business people must think globally in terms of customers, prospects, markets, and competition. The Internet, fax, telephone, regional trading agreements (NAFTA, EU), and efficient transportation systems have created a borderless world, a global economy, which presents both opportunities and problems for entrepreneurs. As a result, your competitive grid should contain both domestic and foreign competitors. The photo album and frame distributor has competition from Asian manufacturers and U.S. distributors. And the firm has export opportunities to Canada and Mexico.

Most small-business people and some entrepreneurs are myopic and don't seriously consider overseas markets. Ask yourself whether and where there is a demand for your product or service overseas. Do you have a competitive advantage there? How can you most efficiently reach the target customer? This section describes an accurate, fast method to answer these questions. Often, overseas demand exceeds the domestic market and can fund the new enterprise. Consider using an intern or part-time college student to help you collect the data you will need to start thinking globally.

Sources for information on overseas market potential by country or segment can be obtained on-line or in hard copy from:

- Country sites on the Internet
- USAID, Department of Commerce, American Chambers of Commerce, www.info.usaid.gov
- U.S. and overseas embassies, consulates, country desks, http://usembassy.state.gov
- Trade associations, professional associations, and trade missions
- Foreign branches of American banks, accounting and law firms
- International trade shows, trade publications, agents, and resellers

Internet sites include:
- International Bureau of Chambers of Commerce, www.eccw bo.org
- International Business Opportunities, www.hamamatsu.cci
- USA Trade Web site, www.usatrade.gov
- Lexis-Nexis, www.lexis-nexis.com
- National Trade Data Bank, www.stat-usa.gov
- SBA Website, www.sba.gov

U.S. Government tools include:

- Commercial Service International Contacts, www.usatrade.gov
- Agent/Distributor Service, www.usis.usemb.se/commercial/agent.htm
- Country Commercial Guide Index, www.state.gov/www/aboutstate/business/comguides
- Library of Congress Country Studies, http://lcweb2.loc.gov/frd/co
- Commercial News USA, www. cnewsusa.com
- Economic Bulletin Board, www.stat-usa.gov
- CIA World Fact Book, www.adu.gov/cia/publications/factbook
- Commerce Export Assistance Programs, www.trade.gov/td/tic
- Trade Opportunities Program, www. buyusa.com
- United States and Foreign Commercial Service (US & FCS), www.ita.doc.gov

Other resources include:

- *The Economist*, www.economist.com
- *World Trade, Export Today*, www.exporttoday.com
- *Journal of Commerce*, www.joc.com
- *Financial Times*, data sites, www.info.ft.com
- Regional international trade associations and clubs, www.fita.org
- Technology publication sites
- Foreign Trade Report FT 925, www.census.gov/mp/www/pub

Domestic and overseas trade fairs and industry events also represent excellent sources for obtaining information on foreign markets, strategic partners, and customers or prospects. Alert your salespeople at domestic trade shows to be on the lookout for foreign customers.

If you discover a country or region with scaleable present and potential revenues and income for your product or service, the next step involves gathering information on:

- Major cities, financial centers, demographics, income per capita, distribution of wealth, and contiguous markets
- Gross domestic product, interest rates, inflation, exchange rates, capital markets, profit repatriation, and tax laws
- Market growth rates, market segments, government regulations, competitors, payment practices, pricing sensitivity, product and quality standards
- Entry costs, import duties, available labor pool
- Export incentives, free trade blocks (NAFTA, EU), export duties
- Licensing, channel partners, intellectual property
- Local standards and customer preference (Does your product or service need to be modified?)
- Infrastructure available to support the business—information technology, transportation, telecommunications

Should you find a target market, market segment, customer, or prospect overseas that meets your requirements for dollars of present and potential revenue and income, you must then proceed with due diligence on cost to sell and serve and probability of success. Using the sources listed above, construct a competitive grid for your product or service in that overseas market. Your grid should answer these questions: Do you have a quantifiable competitive advantage in features, benefits, or image? How can you help these overseas customers or prospects to increase revenues, decrease costs, or reduce needs for working capital, and capital expenditures? What impact will tariffs, duties, import/export costs, and freight have on the product or service cost, price, and competitive advantage?

If, after applying these filters, the rewards still outweigh the risks, the next step involves exploring efficient, effective means of reaching overseas customers. You can sell direct from the United States or other country of origin; you can hire full-time salespeople in target markets; or you can use overseas sales representatives, agents, or distributors. Also, you may wish to consider indirect distribution through one of the following channel partners: commission agents, export management companies (EMCs), export trading companies (ETCs), export agents, merchants, remarketers, piggyback arrangements, or state-controlled trading companies. Your choice of an overseas distribution channel depends on the nature of your product or service, the type of customer, your company's size and stage of development, experience in exporting, and your available human and financial resources.

Indirect exporting involves using a second U.S. company as your sales organization. This company assumes the responsibility for finding overseas buyers and for shipping the product or providing the service. One way of penetrating foreign markets without becoming involved in all the complexities and risks of exporting is to use indirect marketing. Since smaller firms, especially early-stage businesses, have limited human and financial resources, indirect exporting works best. Choosing among the various types of indirect exporters depends on the services they offer and the needs of your company, customers, or prospects.

Many early-stage and smaller firms choose piggyback marketing, where an appropriate overseas company sells your product or service along with its own. Many smaller U.S. software, publishing, apparel, and pharmaceutical companies have overseas software, publishing, apparel, and drug companies carry their line. In this instance the entrepreneur must find a foreign company that reaches his or her target market with complimentary products or services. Correspondingly, your products or services must fill a void in their line and be needed by their customers.

As a direct exporter you select markets you wish to enter, choose the best channels of overseas distribution, bypass U.S. intermediaries, such as EMCs, and deal directly with foreign sales representatives, agents, distributors, retailers and end users. Direct exporting more closely parallels your domestic distribution.

The advantages of direct exporting for your company include more control over such areas as pricing, labeling, and distribution; greater profit margins; and closer ties to customers and markets.

Direct sales can accelerate export sales volume in the long run, even though a well-matched EMC/ETC may get faster initial results. The disadvantages include a greater commitment of human and financial resources and a possible loss of focus on the domestic business. Direct exporting costs more, but you can make more. Again, you must decide whether the reward is worth the risk.

In evaluating export opportunities, run some spreadsheets with various revenue and cost assumptions. Which alternative, if any, produces the highest dollars of contribution margin over time? How much capital is required and what is the return on investment? Who in your firm will be responsible for export sales? Also, it is worth considering that through exporting, your company might discover new product variations or a technology appropriate for the domestic market.

Other means of entering overseas markets with limited risks involve licensing, strategic partners, franchising, contract manufacturing, and joint ventures. Such arrangements allow you to eliminate the cost of duties and freight and possibly take advantage of a more efficient or less expensive labor pool.

A three-year-old Madison, Wisconsin, genomics firm with $5 million of annual sales formed a joint venture with a similar firm in Germany. A German venture capital group financed the newly combined enterprise and also invested in the U.S. firm. Synergies resulted from lower human capital costs in East Germany, highly qualified technicians and scientists on both sides of the Atlantic, and a relationship-based sales force calling on pharmaceutical firms in Europe and the United States. Many such opportunities exist for selling services overseas.

Be aware that to successfully sell your product or service overseas, you may have to make modifications to conform with government regulations, geographic and climatic conditions, buyer preferences, or shipping, branding, labeling, and packaging requirements. Be aware of cultural differences in sales, products, and relationships from one country to another. Acknowledge and respect these differences. Realize that one size does not fit all and don't impose American standards.

Hire a consultant to help you with pricing issues, costing, terms of sale, exchange rates, credit and payment risks, packaging, labeling, and documentation. A good freight forwarder and a knowledgeable banker also can be helpful in these areas.

Often, older products with small or shrinking U.S. markets have much greater potential in emerging markets. For example, a small Texas firm blending specialty chemicals for grinding, polishing, and electroplating relies on Central and South American customers for half its business. A Los Angeles-based financial service's advisory letter on commodity trading sells to more subscribers in

Asia than the United States.

A Seattle-based e-commerce exchange for the lumber industry failed in the U.S. market but succeeded in Northern Europe. A North Dakota miniature transformer firm has licensed its technology to a Swedish contract manufacturer. Royalties from this license equal the firm's U.S. pretax profit. An ornamental flower seed firm in Harrisburg, Pennsylvania, sells its packaged seeds to supermarket chains in Spain.

We live in a borderless, shrinking world with interlinked economies. As a small businessperson or entrepreneur you can benefit by understanding this new order, where performance standards for products or services reflect customer needs in a global rather than a domestic marketplace.

ENTREPRENEURS' MAJOR MISTAKES OR WEAKNESSES IN DIFFERENTIATION, MARKET SEGMENTATION, AND TARGETING CUSTOMERS

- Not differentiating your product or service or creating a competitive advantage through operational excellence, new product or service innovation, or customer intimacy.
- Not properly segmenting markets and targeting customers or annually evaluating changes in segments and targets.
- Not customizing products or services for each major market segment.
- Not quantifying the cost to sell and serve target markets and customers.
- Not taking into account your enterprise's core competencies and competitive advantages when evaluating target customers and market segments.
- Not considering export or global opportunities or potential domestic competition from non-U.S. firms.

QUESTIONS AND EXERCISES

1. What is the lifetime value of a customer in your business?
2. How does or will your enterprise differentiate itself? Create a competitive advantage through operational excellence, new product or service innovation, or customer intimacy?
3. What is your business's strategic discipline?

4. Who are your target customers, markets, and market segments? How and why did you choose them?

5. How does your enterprise utilize the strategic service-profit chain?

6. What strategy and tactics do you use to create happy employees and satisfied customers?

7. Can you differentiate your product or service by altering the consumption chain, channels of distribution, and customer experience?

CHAPTER 5

A Cost-Efficient, Effective Sales Organization and Marketing Approach

Once the entrepreneur has properly identified market segments, selected target markets and customers, and customized products or services to satisfy their needs, he or she must then create an efficient, effective sales organization and marketing approach to reach these customers and markets.

Strategically this involves reducing the sales cycle from customer search to purchase and developing a methodology for making the sales organization more productive. The major weaknesses of most early-stage firms involve funding, marketing, and sales, so entrepreneurs typically spend most of their time working on these three areas. As sales cycles become longer and product life becomes shorter, marketing and sales have become more complicated, and larger competitors with greater resources have therefore gained an advantage over smaller, early-stage firms.

For more complicated new systems sales, often one-time or first-time purchases, there are many steps in the marketing funnel and sales cycle. Often purchasing decisions are made by groups of people to spread the risks. Customer loyalty can no longer be expected in markets where global competitors, the ants and gorillas, constantly change. Therefore, start-ups must teach salespeople how to quantify in dollars and with spreadsheets how the features and benefits of their products or services can increase customer revenues, reduce their costs, or lower working capital needs and capital expenditures.

The entrepreneur's goal is to maximize sales force productivity and capacity. Proper sizing, deployment, channel choice, and architecture help to accomplish that goal. A start-up or early-stage firm has the advantage of a fresh start with few legacy issues. Use this as an advantage to create the right structure. Analyze the models presented in this chapter. Be careful about following industry tradition or a competitor. You may be following the loser or yesterday's model, not tomorrow's.

BUYER BEHAVIOR

Understanding buyer behavior for your product or service will help to properly hire, train, and organize your sales force. Ask yourself whether your target customers and target market are new systems buyers, established systems buyers, new product buyers, or commodities buyers. New-systems buyers are making one-time or first-time purchases. For example, the purchase of such heterogeneous products as a new medical device for monitoring anesthesia or sonic probes to help with prostate seed implants for cancer treatment or a new software program for measuring patient costs would be one-time or first-time purchases. Another example would be the purchase of a heterogeneous service such as that offered by an investment banker or lawyer who is assisting a firm with its initial public offering. Generally new systems buyers require long sales cycles with many steps between search and purchase, as well as group decisions and consultative selling and problem solving. The vendor and the vendor's salesperson need an expert image.

Established systems buyers involve a modified rebuy, which is when the decision maker repeatedly purchases the same product or service. However, selling is required for each repeat order because the product or service is not a commodity. Products or services in this group might include semiconductors, home health care services, auto insurance, industrial chemicals, and mutual funds. Generally, established systems buyers require shorter, less complicated sales cycles but often involve group decisions and more relationship selling. We buy from experts and friends. The established systems buyer, being an expert himself or herself, is looking for a vendor or salesperson who is a friend. This modified rebuy generally involves bargaining, politicking, and negotiating. Since you only have a portion of each customer's purchases of your category, the goal is to increase penetration of each customer.

New product buyers involve organizations that continually purchase new products as distinguished from new systems and so the purchasing people involved are experienced in the process. This is not a one-time or first-time purchase, but rather a continuous process of new product or service purchases. Purchasing agents and buyers for camera stores, computer or software retailers, or fashion apparel continually procure new products or services. In this environment, salespeople need good closing skills and no fear of rejection. This type of buyer requires salespeople who excel at presenting features and benefits, asking probing questions, and being good listeners.

Commodity buyers are experienced users purchasing a standard product or service using routine procurement functions. This requires route salespeople doing display and transactional sales. Commodity buyers do not require multilevel group sales, and actual decision making is often delegated to an administrative assistant. The buyer makes decisions based on relationships, price, delivery, convenience, availability, and customer service. As with established systems buyers, the vendor's goal involves increasing the share of each buyer's business, maintenance, and penetration. Since the salesperson takes orders rather than actively solicits, time management of many customer calls and use of information technology is very important. Commodity buyers would include the procurement of homogeneous products or services such as die castings, office supplies, injection molding, and airline tickets.

Your small business might sell to several or all of these types of buyers in which case you might create a hybrid sales organization. For example, a spice and flavoring firm located in Nashville, with annual sales of $7 million, services midsized food processors that buy the same ingredients from year to year, but it also sells to larger, branded firms that continually demand customized ingredients for their new products. The former represents a modified rebuy; the later, a new systems buy. This same ingredient firm continually updates its line with new standard products sold to all customers and calls on a large number of ethnic restaurants that buy commodities. After analyzing buyer behavior management decided to use stocking distributors to call on the modified rebuy midsized food processors, plus in-house telesales people to take reorders and offer new products to the ethnic restaurants. Management also decided to use their own national account sales people to perform consultative partnership selling to the major branded food companies. All three sales organizations sell the constant stream of newly developed products to their respective customers, but the distributors and telesales people have done a poor job of placing new products or opening new accounts. This remains a major challenge for the spice company as does using its Web site to assist in the sales process.

Should your firm decide to use field salespeople for all or some customers, look for candidates who have the experience or skills for dealing with the appropriate buyer behavior. Also, customize your training program to meet the needs of buyer behavior. For example, people dealing with new systems buyers require a lot of product knowledge and consultative sales skills training, while people dealing with established systems buyers require more training in negotiating and relationship-building skills. People calling on new product buyers need training emphasizing feature benefit selling and closing skills, while those calling on commodity buyers need more training in time management and information technology.

CHANNEL CHOICE

The next issue in creating a cost-efficient, effective sales and marketing approach involves choosing the correct channels of distribution to reach the target customer and appropriate market segments. Buyer behavior represents one of the criteria for this choice but there are many more. As illustrated by the spice company example, hybrid distribution channels often work best.

You can use your own direct salespeople and/or a combination of indirect channel partners, such as distributors, brokers, independent sales representatives, telesales, e-commerce, home shopping television channels, system integrators, value-added distributors, or retailers. Many smaller businesses, entrepreneurs, and start-ups use indirect channel partners because their cost is variable and fringe benefits are not necessary. Their compensation is entirely performance-based. Although these variable costs are appealing to an early-stage firm, this choice may not maximize dollars of gross margin over time. Also, once committed to a certain type of channel, change can prove difficult and expensive. Using the methodology outlined here will help you make the right choices to start with.

Choosing the proper distribution channels depends on the type of selling performed by the sales force, the type of customers called on, operating issues, type of product or service sold, areas requiring control, as well as capital and costs. Review these at least once a year to see what has changed and if these changes require an adjustment in your choice of distribution channels. Many of these issues are interrelated and repetitive.

Certain types of selling lend themselves to company-direct salespeople, others to an indirect sales organization or a channel partner. Long sales cycles with a great deal of consultative selling to first-time or one-time systems buyers lend themselves to a direct sales organization. The more influence a salesperson has on the sale, the more important a company-direct sales force is. Team selling and partnership selling lend themselves to the company-direct model. On the other hand, relationship selling to repeat customers, modified rebuyers, display, commodity, and order taking lends itself to using channel partners.

Most sales managers choose hybrid sales organizations by deaggregating the demand-generation tasks. For example, lead generation might be most efficiently performed by an outside direct-mail house or a Web site, and qualifying these leads might lend itself to an independent telesales organization. However, once you identify qualified leads, those with major potential require a visit from a direct company salesperson, while those with less potential can be seen by an indirect channel partner salesperson. In both cases, the salesperson will do a needs analysis, quantify benefits, demonstrate the product or service, offer a free trial, overcome objections, and attempt to close. After-sale service, installation, and ongoing account management might be best performed by a distributor. Look at the demand-generation tasks from search to purchase. What type of selling and sales channels will be most efficient?

Certain customer characteristics lend themselves more to company-direct salespeople, others to an independent sales organization. A large number of widely dispersed customers, frequently ordering small quantities, may be more efficiently reached by several outside indirect sales organizations than by your own direct sales force. If your firm's target customers are leaders (Wal-Mart, Cisco) or innovators, rather than followers, they may insist on a company-direct sales force. To enter new market segments, where you do not have customer contacts or knowledge, you may need a channel partner that does have these contacts.

Credit and hazardous material (for example, toxic chemicals) issues may sway you toward a channel partner who can more efficiently handle these risks. Consider how competition handles all these factors. Can you create a competitive advantage by doing it differently?

Customer needs and channel function requirements must be analyzed to determine the proper channel choice. This could vary by market segment, which means you may use a company-direct sales force for original equipment manufacturers and stocking distributors for the replacement market. For example, a situation in which customers require one-stop shopping for a basket of products or services and you provide only a few of them or only small lot sizes or large lot sizes calls for not using a direct sales force but choosing a channel partner who better meets the customers' requirements. Similarly, customers may insist on certain after-sale services, such as engineering, warranty, logistics, or transportation, which can be more efficiently provided by a channel partner.

Based on dollars of present and potential revenues and income, prospects and accounts may become designated A, B, or C. An A account requires more frequent calls than a C account and may require a different channel choice. You may use telesales people or e-commerce for C accounts and your own account representatives for B accounts.

Operating issues such as inventory, spare parts, service, maintenance, repair, customization, engineering, design, installation, programming, customer training, just-in-time delivery, safety, and credit services influence channel choice and may be related to previously mentioned items. Who can more efficiently provide each of these services, your firm or a channel partner? Which of these services does the customer value and which can be deleted? You must do value engineering on each service offered by your firm and your channel partners.

Certain types of products or services lend themselves to company-direct salespeople, others to indirect channel partners. Heterogeneous products, which can be more easily differentiated, such as biotech or consulting services or semiconductor fabricating equipment, lend themselves to a direct company sales force. Homogeneous products or services, which are more difficult to differentiate, like die-castings or injection molding, lend themselves to channel partners.

In reaching customers, higher gross-margin products or services generally use a direct company sales force, while lower gross-margin products or services generally use channel partners. New products or services, where the salesperson has a strong influence on the sale, do best with a company-direct sales force, while products or services toward the end of their life cycle are more efficiently handled by channel partners, telesales, e-commerce or customer service people. If you require tight control over pricing and limit customer selection, or you need feedback and good communication from the field, a company-direct sales force will better satisfy these needs.

Channel partners require performance pay that rewards positive action and superior results important for the success of your firm. To prevent channel partners from skimming the best accounts and low-hanging fruit, but not pursuing the middle market and smaller accounts, create performance pay that rewards the proper actions and results. You can pay a higher commission rate for one type of sale, customer, or product than another. You can give bonuses and rebates for product mix, number of new accounts, post-sale services, and inventory levels.

The last item in determining channel choice is to run the numbers for various alternatives. If you use a 100 percent direct company sales force, what will it cost, how much revenue and gross margin will it generate, and what operating income and cash flow, EBIT and EBITDA, will result? Do the same analysis using channel partners or a hybrid channel choice. Run spreadsheets using various assumptions at different revenue levels for different channel choices. What combination produces the most dollars of contribution margin over time? For each alternative, what percentage of sales do selling costs and salesperson compensation represent? What is your market share and number of customers? Is the channel or combination of channels supported by the other previously discussed criteria?

SALES FORCE ARCHITECTURE

Once you have decided on what channel or combination of channels you will use to most efficiently reach the targeted marketplace, you must decide how to organize these channels: major products or services, product or service lines, market segments, key accounts or customers, geography, functions (two-tier), no restrictions, or some combination of the preceding. The choice depends on your particular products or services, size and type of customers, target accounts, markets, market segments, type of selling, core competencies, channel choice, and objectives. Choose whatever type of organization or architecture best meets customer needs and best uses your firm's human resources, one that maximizes dollars of contribution margin over time by properly balancing expenses with revenues.

If your company offers, or plans to offer, a wide variety of dissimilar or unrelated products or services, especially if they are complex, or if your company's present or future products or services are or will be sold to totally different markets, you should consider a sales force organized by product line. A product line sales organization allows each of the various markets and each of the diverse or complex product lines to receive a high degree of specialized attention. It is difficult for one salesperson to effectively sell cost and activity tracking software to hospitals, human resource software to airlines, and supply chain consulting to tier-three auto firms.

If your company sells, or plans to sell, large quantities of products or services to a limited number of major customers, especially customers with many branches, you should consider a sales force organized by account. A sales force organized by account allows each major customer to receive a higher degree of specialization. It allows the salespeople to partner with major accounts, obtain specialized account specific information, and better understand the decision makers, decision-making process, and culture.

If your company sells, or plans to sell, similar or closely related products or services to a large number of widely dispersed customers in the same industry, then you should consider a sales force organized by geographic territory. This means that salespeople sell all your products or services to any appropriate customers within their assigned territories. Most early-stage and smaller businesses use this format because of its simplicity and low cost. Unfortunately, most early-stage companies and small businesses don't even think about the alternatives that might be more appropriate over time.

The geographic organization of territories allows salespeople to cultivate local markets more intensely by becoming more familiar with local problems, people, and conditions. Also, a person living in the territory often finds a more receptive ear than an outsider would.

If you offer a product that requires service after the sale and different skills for selling than for service, consider a two-tier sales organization with separate functions. In a functional sales organization, customers sometimes dislike the change of salespeople and salespeople sometimes dislike the change of customers. However, if your salesperson or salespeople show superior account development skills but a lack of interest in retaining or maintaining accounts, try the two-tier approach.

The most effective use of a sales force often involves combining elements of product, account, geographic territory, function, and no restrictions. Because of varying market structures, you may wish to use a different type of organization in different geographic areas or a different type of organization for different product lines. Remember, simple but flexible structures work best. Generally, smaller companies are more flexible than larger ones, allowing them more readily to use combinations or hybrids. However, combinations and hybrids can be more expensive and prove more difficult to manage.

In a smaller company, your most important resource is the human resource and your decisions concerning sales force organization and architecture must recognize this factor. If one of your salespeople has excellent contacts with certain major accounts, you may wish to assign him or her to these customers while organizing the rest of the sales force by geographic territory. If one of your salespeople has a very close relationship with a major customer, you may wish to have him or her sell all your products to that account while organizing the rest of the sales force by product line. If one of your better salespeople does well with smaller accounts but poorly with large, you may wish to place two salespeople in this territory rather than the usual one. Assuming appropriate market potential, the second person would call on large accounts, allowing the original salesperson to continue concentrating on the smaller ones. If one of your better salespeople has child care responsibilities and cannot travel overnight, but your sales force is organized by widely dispersed key accounts, you may wish to build a geographic territory of nonkey accounts within a day's drive of this person's home. The flexibility of a smaller business allows you to fully utilize the human resource element by combining various types of sales force organization or architectures.

Recently, several smaller health-care distributors and telecommunication start-ups created hybrid organizations by hiring part-time, flextime salespeople. Veteran salespeople who left larger companies to raise a family or care for a parent can return on a part-time, flextime basis working for these smaller firms. They must work at least 20 hours a week; they receive excellent comparable compensation but no fringe benefits, and they have smaller territories. These territories are often built around their contacts and are close to home. Smaller firms have the flexibility to do this.

STAFFING AND DEPLOYMENT

Once the entrepreneur has decided on channel choice and architecture, the next steps involve staffing and deployment. How many salespeople or channel partners do you need, how large should a salesperson's territory be, and how do you determine territory boundaries? Too many salespeople will increase direct-selling costs as a percentage of revenue; too few will not maximize absolute dollars of revenue.

Smaller territories maximize market share and minimize travel expenses, but they often cannot produce significant enough revenues to support a salesperson, whether on performance or fixed pay. Larger territories can produce significant enough revenues to support a salesperson but can be expensive to travel and may not maximize market share. A key issue is the amount of potential necessary to support one of your salespersons and the appropriate metrics needed to measure that potential.

As with channel choice and architecture, each year you must reanalyze the sizing and deployment of your sales force and make appropriate changes. Each year changes in salespeople, customers, products, technology, markets, and strategy impact deployment and sizing issues. Don't let legacy issues create chronic inertia for your small business.

To maximize the sales organization's productivity, each salesperson's territory must have equal potential based on present and potential revenues and income as well as present and potential number and type of accounts (call frequency) versus the salesperson's call rate or workload/capacity. The goal is for salespeople to economically make the optimum number of quality calls on the right customers and prospects. This will maximize dollars of contribution margin over time. Mapping software offered by Siebel, Saratoga Systems, Oracle, and Territory Mapper, among others, can assist you in these tasks.

Sizing and deployment involves both strategic and tactical issues. The entrepreneur must properly identify target accounts and market segments. He or she must determine whether new customers or a larger share of the existing customers' business represents the best opportunities. He or she must understand the cost of putting a salesperson on the road, a salesperson's break-even point, a territory's potential dollars of contribution margin, and how quickly a salesperson can be trained.

Next, let us explore how to create territories of equal potential based on present and potential revenues and number and type of accounts (call frequency) versus the salesperson's call rate or capacity/workload. The entrepreneur's first task in creating territory boundaries and deciding on sales staffing needs involves finding the proper metrics to measure each territory's potential revenues for the start-up's or small firm's various product lines. Many industry publications and associations, along with appropriate federal, state, and city governments have information on sales potential. Obtaining statistical data is simply a matter of identifying the associations, government agencies, and publications in a specific field and getting the information directly from the source. There are a number of publications that identify these sources: *Encyclopedia of Associations, National Trade and Professional Associations of the United States,* Associations on the Net (www.ipl.org/ref/aon), *Statistical Abstracts of the United States, The United States Government Manual, Guide to Special Issues and Indexes of Periodicals, National Directory of Magazines,* and *Standard Periodical Directory.* You can also use the Internet to search for and obtain these and additional data.

To create territories of equal potential, for example, the pharmaceutical industry has private market research firms that track prescriptions written for various medications by physician, pharmacy, and ZIP Code. The American Cancer Association has data on new cases of various types of cancer reported annually by state. Firms selling equipment, devices, and medication related to cancer use these data. Semiconductor equipment manufacturers use geographic data on the annual unit production of semiconductors by type to measure potential. The number of hospital beds, admissions, discharges, and Medicare cases by city provide metrics for hospital supplies and health care providers. The National Restaurant Association has data on number of restaurants by size and type by ZIP Code, which suppliers use to measure potential.

Using the proper metrics for your industry, decide on how much market potential is needed to support a salesperson. If a firm has, or wishes to have, a 1 percent share of its market segment and the break-even point for a salesperson, including all fixed overhead expenses, is $2 million of revenue, a territory must contain at least $200 million of market potential to justify this salesperson. A salesperson's break-even point depends on the dollars of fixed overhead allocated to that person. The less overhead, the lower the break-even point, and the lower required market potential. Market potential and territory performance can also be measured in units or in dollars. If a salesperson sells diverse products or services into many market segments, this calculation becomes more complex.

SALESPERSON'S BREAK-EVEN POINT

Most entrepreneurs and small-business managers don't understand a salesperson's break-even point or how to make a salesperson profitable. This requires having a method for comparing a salesperson's marginal costs to his or her marginal income.

First, determine the marginal annual cost of putting a new salesperson on the road, which should include:

- Total direct compensation (salary, commission, bonus, deferred compensation, and stock options)
- Fringe benefits (Social Security, Medicare, health insurance, pension plan, etc.)
- Reimbursed travel, entertainment, communication, and office expenses

For example, the total annual cost including compensation might be $150,000. Divide this by the number of days a salesperson works a year (for example, 240) and the number of calls a salesperson makes a year (for example, 480) to arrive at a cost per day and a cost per call. In this example the cost per day is $625 or assuming an eight-hour day, $78 per hour. In this example the cost per call is $312. Salespeople represent an expensive resource for an early-stage firm. Share these numbers with your salespeople in an effort to improve their time management.

Once you and the salesperson understand the cost of putting him or her on the road, you must then understand the salesperson's break-even point to determine what size territory and potential are required to support that salesperson. Add to the $150,000 cost of putting the salesperson on the road, the direct variable costs necessary to support that salesperson: training, samples, trade shows in the territory, local advertising, plus promotion and marketing expenses. When added to the previous amount of $150,000, you arrive at a new total of $200,000. Let's assume the gross margin after manufacturing costs, or after costs of providing a service, or after the cost of goods sold is 33 percent. The break-even point for this salesperson is $600,000 of annual sales, which will result in $200,000 of contribution margin after the 67 percent cost of goods sold. The break-even point for the salesperson can vary depending on how many dollars of selling, marketing, general, and administrative expenses are fixed (versus variable) and do not change because of a new salesperson. In other words, the break-even point for an existing salesperson might be higher then for a new salesperson because of existing overhead.

If the break-even point for your salesperson proves to be $600,000 of annual sales and you estimate the market share for your product or service at 10 percent, then the territory requires a $6 million market potential, based on industry data, to support a salesperson. Based on the $6 million, plus industry data, buying power indexes, number and size of present and potential customers; the physical boundaries of each territory emerge. These physical boundaries then must be compared to the customer call requirements and the salesperson's call capacity to arrive at a final determination of the territory boundaries.

Then, if the market for your product or service reached $24 million, you would consider hiring four direct salespeople. If the channel choice model pointed you toward a channel partner organization, then make sure the channel partners have adequate staff to cover a $24 million market.

If you presently have an existing sales force, use the appropriate market metrics to measure and equalize each territory's potential. Territories of equal potential maximize total revenues and help to properly motivate and compensate salespeople. Do you need to hire another salesperson, switch accounts from one territory to another, or change territory boundaries?

WORKLOAD

For each present territory and potential new territory, examine current and potential number and types of accounts, required call frequencies, and the salesperson's call capacity or workload. Classify prospects and accounts A, B, and C by present and potential revenue and income, cost to sell and serve, and probability of success. Based on this metric, A accounts need to be called on most frequently and C accounts least frequently.

A start-up selling real-time database software to petroleum traders has four salespeople calling on brokerage houses, commodity traders, banks, pension plans, and international energy companies. The more possible users each customer or prospect has, the greater the revenue potential. At commodity traders, the cost to sell and serve is less and the probability of success is higher. They also eventually need the most copies. Commodity traders represent the A accounts, the target customers, and prospects. Banks represent the other extreme and have a C classification.

The four salespeople at this firm call on A accounts and A prospects twice a month (24 times a year), B accounts and B prospects once a month (12 times a year), and C accounts and prospects once every other month (6 times a year). The Texas salesperson can make three calls a day and has an annual call capacity of 600. The Los Angeles salesperson can make two calls a day and has an annual call capacity of 400. The New York City salesperson can make four calls a day and has an annual call capacity of 800.

The Texas salesperson has 15 A accounts and prospects, 30 B accounts and prospects, and 30 C accounts and prospects. Multiplying the number of accounts and prospects by classification times, the required call frequency produces a workload for the Texas salesperson of 900 calls a year versus a call capacity of 600 calls. The salesperson cannot properly service and sell present and potential accounts. Possibly another salesperson is needed or C accounts should not be called on or frequency of calls on all accounts should be reexamined or a telesales person should be hired to assist the salesperson.

The New York City salesperson has 10 A accounts and prospects, 20 B accounts and prospects, and 15 C accounts and prospects. Multiplying the number of accounts and prospects by classification times the required call frequency produces a workload for the New York City salesperson of 570 calls a year versus a call capacity of 800. The New York City salesperson is underutilized and possibly needs an expanded territory.

The salesperson's call capacity is like a factory's production capacity; physical and time restraints prevent it from varying more than 10 percent from year to year. However, by changing the sales force organization or channels or by using automation, the call capacity can improve. A salesperson's call capacity could increase by having a customer service or telesales person qualify leads or occasionally handle smaller accounts. A salesperson's call capacity could increase with laptops, contact management software, and cell phones. E-commerce and Web sites increase sales force productivity and call capacity.

The number and type of present and potential accounts in a territory can be obtained from your customer lists, along with industry trade association, trade publications, telephone directories, federal, state, and city government (SIC) data, and the Chamber of Commerce. Use the Internet to search for data and possibly download it. Much of these data are available on-line or on CD-ROMs. The Commerce Department's *Survey of U.S. Industrial and Commercial Buying Power* lists by state and county the number of establishments by major SIC code, their shipments and receipts, and their percentage of the U.S. total for their SIC code. *Sales & Marketing Management* magazine aggregates some of these data in their "Annual Survey of Buying Power." Territories may have equal potential revenues, but one may have a large number of small accounts and another a small number of large accounts. In balancing territory workloads, the entrepreneur or small business manager must take this into account. Territories become defined then by classifying accounts as to importance, sales potential, and necessary call frequency, then by comparing current and potential accounts and current and potential territory revenues with desired market share and the physical call limits of a salesperson's workload.

Using these analytical, sometimes black box techniques to establish territory boundaries does not constitute an exact science, but it is a logical approach to improving salespeople's performance. As mentioned, computer software programs exist to assist you in this task.

For a smaller firm, as with channel choice and sales force organization, your salespeople, their needs, and their contacts also require
serious consideration in setting territory boundaries. Flexibility represents a competitive advantage for smaller firms, allowing the entrepreneur to temper the analytical approach to territories with important
human considerations. Smaller firms take into account where salespeople live, their personalities, personal needs, likes and dislikes, and
contacts. One salesperson may prefer a territory with smaller accounts;
another might do better with majors.

Sizing, deployment, and territory boundaries are also influenced
by mountains, bridges, highway systems, and market areas. Although
market information on buying power, potential sales, and number of
possible accounts is generally available by county, ZIP Code, city, state,
or region, sales territory boundaries may not lend themselves to city,
county, or state lines. Highway systems, rivers, bridges, subways, and
mountains must be considered. Major market and trading areas may
also cross state lines.

Since customers, products, competition, and salespeople continually change, entrepreneurs and small business managers must annually
reanalyze territory boundaries, workloads, call capacity, and potential
revenues. Remember, as an entrepreneur or small-business person, you
are an agent of change.

TERRITORIAL PROFIT AND LOSS

To help you manage and evaluate salespeople and channel partners
and create territories of equal potential, use a territorial profit and loss
statement. This represents an extension of the break-even analysis. For
each territory start with actual or forecasted dollars of net revenue
after discounts and returns. Subtract from net revenues the actual or
budgeted variable direct cost of putting a salesperson or channel partner on the road and analyze the resulting dollars and percentage margins. Then subtract the manufacturing costs or cost of goods sold for
that territory. Again, analyze the resulting dollars and percentage of
revenue margins. Compare these dollars and percentage margins from
one salesperson, channel partner, and territory to another. Based on
these variations, one entrepreneur realigned some territory boundaries, switched some direct salespeople to channel partners, changed
some salespeople's compensation and expense reimbursement plans,
and reduced spending on marketing. These margins reflect not only
the salesperson's and channel partner's costs, but the product mix
they sell and the pricing they obtain. Territorial profit and loss statements represent an easy and worthwhile analysis for the entrepreneur.
We manage what we monitor.

A men's sweater company with knitting facilities in North Carolina and annual revenues to retailers of $4 million did a quarterly profit-and-loss statement for their two salespeople and two distributors. Each salesperson and distributor received the following quarterly information compared to the previous year:

Net revenues after discounts and returns minus

- Salesperson's or distributor's total direct compensation (salary, commission, bonus, stock options)
- Fringe benefits (Social Security, Medicare, health insurance, 401k)
- Reimbursed travel, entertainment, communication, and office expense
- Cost of samples carried by salespeople and given to customers
- Prepaid freight into the territory
- Cost of in-service training for retail sales personnel at stores
- Local advertising, promotion, marketing expenses, and trade shows in the territory

Resulting in a salesperson's or channel partner's contribution margin in dollars and as a percentage of revenues minus

- Manufacturing costs for sweaters shipped into the territory

Resulting in a salesperson's or channel partner's net contribution margin in dollars

The entrepreneur used this information to analyze channel choice, deployment, and compensation.

HIRING SALESPEOPLE AND SELECTING CHANNEL PARTNERS

Since funding, marketing, and sales represent an entrepreneur's greatest use of personal time, we will spend some time in this chapter specifically on hiring, training, motivating, compensating, and evaluating salespeople and channel partners. Successful entrepreneurs know how to leverage human resources, especially the sales force. Also, entrepreneurs and small-business managers can use the same or similar techniques and processes as those described in this chapter for salespeople for hiring, training, motivating, and evaluating other members of their organization .

Effective hiring processes and techniques for salespeople and channel partners act as a filter to screen out less desirable candidates and increases the probability of hiring the best candidate. The more steps in the process, the more screens in the filter, the higher your probability of success. In its simplest form, the process involves preparing a job description, and candidate profile, sourcing, screening, and making the final choice. Sourcing is where and how we look for candidates, whether through competitors, customers, or Web sites. Screening involves conducting phone and personal interviews; checking references; making credit, drug, and drivers' license checks; knowledge and personality testing; and making a final choice.

The job description is a list of anticipated duties. Where do you want the salesperson to concentrate? Does the job description ask salespeople to target your most important customers, markets, and products? The candidate profile asks what salesperson experience, skills, knowledge, and personal characteristics these target customers, markets, and products require for success.

Another strategic issue to be reflected in the job description and candidate profile is whether you want salespeople to concentrate on new accounts or further penetration of existing customers. Where is the opportunity for growth better? Salespeople need to know this for proper time allocation. Also, opening new accounts versus penetration of existing accounts requires salespeople with different skills, knowledge, experience, and personal characteristics.

Similarly, if salespeople have a pricing window and negotiating price, and delivery and product or service customization is strategically important, it is imperative to list this as a duty in the job description and under desired experience in the candidate profile. If telesales is an important salesperson's tool, put it in the candidate profile and job description.

When creating a job description for a salesperson or channel partner in your organization, be sure to include sales and service duties, planning, reporting, company relations, administrative chores, and housekeeping. Review and revise the job description each year to reflect rapidly changing products or services, competition, customers, technology, and strategy. Each year ask your salespeople and channel partners to revise their job description, adding duties not listed and altering duties that have changed. Have them sign the job description, date it, and return it. An accurate job description acts as a checklist for training and evaluating salespeople.

Once you have developed the job description, it is time to translate it into a written candidate profile. Whereas the job description lists duties, the candidate profile describes the skills, experience, knowledge, and personal characteristics necessary for performing those duties. Which of these skills, experience, knowledge, and personal characteristics are musts and which are wants? Skills might include selling, communication, computer skills, and data analysis. Experience might include type of sales, industry, type of compensation, performance results, prospecting, national accounts, and type of customers. Knowledge might include understanding of customers, products, competition, and industry. Personal characteristics would include items such as confidence, enthusiasm, persistence, drive, passion, ability to be a team player, aggressiveness, desire, empathy, ability to accept rejection, honesty, initiative, and creativity.

Determining whether the candidate has these skills, this knowledge, and these personal characteristics is part of the screening process. For example, are you more interested in a salesperson who has been successful under a fixed or a performance pay plan?

Start-ups or early-stage enterprises can search for sales candidates through potential competitors, customers, recruiters, media advertising, and the Internet. Larger, more established firms might also source salespeople from within, from other employee referrals, suppliers, vendors, professional organizations, and outplacement firms.

Each of these sources has advantages and disadvantages. What source or combination of sources you use depends on your job description and candidate profile. The Internet works well when you are looking for salespeople with technical skills. Customers are a good source when you are looking for salespeople involved in relationship sales. Use the source that produces the best consistent results.

Begin the screening process by reviewing any résumés or applications received and comparing them to the candidate profile. Eliminate those candidates who do not have the experience, knowledge, and skills listed as "musts" on the candidate profile.

Call the remaining candidates for a telephone interview. Ask factual questions about their background, résumé, experience, knowledge and skills. See if the candidate sells and persuades you to arrange an in-person interview. How does the candidate present himself or herself over the phone? This, obviously, is an important part of most sales processes. Salespeople use the phone to sell appointments, take reorders, and resolve customer conflicts. If you are recruiting for a telesales position, give even more weight to the telephone interview. Set appointments for an in-person interview with those in which you are still interested.

Now you begin the art and black magic of in-person interviewing. The interview is an opportunity for the candidate to persuade you that he or she should be hired. The entrepreneur or small business manager's strategy is to create an interview situation that simulates an actual sales call in that particular industry.

For example, dental supply and device salespeople have four or five minutes of face time with dentists to present new products. Persistent follow-up with the dentist proves very important. If you are hiring salespeople to present your firm's new hand tools to dentists, structure a short introductory interview, which requires a lot of candi-date follow-up. If the salesperson who represents your transformers must give group presentations, have a group interview.

Inject some rejection into the interview to see how the salesper-son reacts. Salespeople must be able to handle rejection well. Ask the candidate or prospective channel partner to sell you his or her last product or service. Does he or she ask probing questions to find needs and opportunities, overcome objections, and close?

Although many entrepreneurs feel they are more interesting than the candidate, and want to sell the candidate on the position or company, good interviewers spend 80 percent of their time listening. Open-ended probing questions that cannot be answered with yes or no are the key to good interviewing. Some small-business managers and entrepreneurs like to ask why a candidate chose sales as a career or why the candidate wants to work for a start-up or small firm versus a larger one. Such ques-tions tell the entrepreneur a great deal about what is important to the salesperson. A candidate will return to the same subjects in answering these questions; for instance, the importance of family, customer satisfac-tion, an unfair boss, superior competition, and weak support services. The amount of time a candidate devotes to each subject reveals a great deal about his or her personal characteristics and areas of importance. Questions about the family or customers receive long, detailed answers, while questions about the boss or the competition are dealt with quickly.

You might ask a candidate or prospective channel partner to describe his or her greatest disappointment, problem, or setback and what he or she did about it. The candidate must choose between a pro-fessional or personal disappointment. What he or she did about it indicates the candidate's ability to deal with rejection and adversity, a very important trait for salespeople.

The entrepreneur or small-business manager must involve other members of the organization in making a final choice. Ask other mem-bers of the organization to interview and evaluate final candidates and channel partners. All outside customer-facing employees must under-stand that providing seamless service means that they have both outside and inside customers. Therefore have engineering, credit, marketing, shipping, service, and other appropriate department man-agers interview the final candidates. Should you already have another salesperson, get him or her involved in the selection process. Some start-ups will have a friendly customer or prospect interview final can-didates and channel partners.

Reference checking represents an important filter in the hiring process for salespeople and channel partners. During the interviews, ask for professional references and for permission to contact past supervisors, customers, and competitors.

Customers represent a reliable source of information about salespeople and channel partners. You must ask customers, competitors, and previous supervisors appropriate questions, which fill in the information gaps from the interview and résumé. An entrepreneur might ask a candidate's or channel partner's customer, "Did Susan follow up on and solve problems?" "Did she increase her share of your purchases or sell you new products?" "Was she enthusiastic and confident when faced with rejection?" "Would you recommend Susan as a salesperson to represent your firm?" "Do you feel Susan could successfully work in a start-up or small-business environment?" "Why or why not?"

If the candidate or channel partner sold a product or service noncompetitive to yours, and you know competitors in that industry, their input could be useful. They can provide information on the applicant's employer and possibly on the applicant as well.

Previous supervisors and principals represent critical sources of information about candidates and channel partners. Decide specifically what you want to know and formulate questions around this. Besides specific questions, you might also try a few of these more general ones: "What type of customer did the candidate or channel partner have trouble selling?" "Did you try to convince the candidate to stay?" "Why did you replace the channel partner?" "How does the candidate or channel partner compare to the replacement?" "Have you seen the candidate's résumé or the channel partner's promotional literature?" "What do you think of him or her?" "Would you rehire the candidate or channel partner?"

Some previous supervisors, principals, and clients or customers may not wish to discuss the candidate or channel partner. In these situations, be ready with another set of questions related to the company, not the candidate or channel partner, but obtaining similar information. "Do you require salespeople or channel partners to prospect for new accounts or provide technical services to existing accounts?" "Who are the firm's target accounts?"

Background investigations on finalist candidates and channel partners represent another useful filter. Contact the secretary of state for a driver's license check. Equifax Inc. of Atlanta, Trans Union Credit Information Co. of Chicago, Experion of Brighton, Michigan, and TRW of Orange, California, all offer a service that investigates appropriate court and financial records and, if necessary, verifies places of residence and past employers. The Internet lists many other providers of these services. These reports cost $50 each, and large credit agencies offer on-line computer access to their databases.

Intelligence, personality, and interest tests for salespeople can be administered and scored either by you or by outside services. Testing is avalable on-line or as hard copy. Such tests provide insight into the subject's learning and reasoning ability, emotional stability, confidence, and occupational interests. The problem lies in interpreting the results. Testing is a tool to help you hire outstanding candidates, not a crutch to make the decision for you. Don't substitute test results for your judgment. Narrow the field to the three best candidates, test each one, and compare results. Use tests to eliminate certain candidates, or better understand strengths and weaknesses, not to choose one over another. Also use tests to customize a training program for each person. If possible, test present salespeople and compare results of top and mediocre performers. Then use the best salespeople's test results as a benchmark for hiring and incorporate the results in your candidate profile.

TRAINING SALESPEOPLE AND CHANNEL PARTNERS

First pay salespeople more than they are worth, then make them worth more than what you pay them. How can a small business, an early-stage enterprise, or a start-up with limited resources and just a few salespeople meet this goal? Remember that it does not cost more to properly hire, train, and compensate a small sales force than not to. (Plus, size does not represent an advantage in hiring, training, compensating, or evaluating salespeople.) Success lies in understanding and using the proper process. For salespeople and channel partners to be successful, they need training in product, competition, and customer knowledge, as well as sales skills. They obtain this knowledge through initial training, field coaching, and sales meetings.

Salespeople and channel partners are no better than your ability to properly select and train them. A good training program forces channel partners to devote more time and resources to your company's products or services, making them more productive partners, not adversaries. Channel partners spend time where they are comfortable, have a commitment in human and financial resources, and obtain the best return on invested dollars.

For start-ups, early-stage, and small businesses, key strategic objectives for training salespeople and channel partners include reducing the time it takes to make a salesperson fully productive, teaching salespeople how to reduce the sales cycle from customer search to purchase, and reflecting buyer behavior in the training program. Strategic training topics include pricing, targeting, change management, group decisions, complex decision-making processes, negotiations, and differentiation.

Training a sales force well not only increases their productivity and capacity, but also improves sales force confidence and enthusiasm, reduces turnover, and makes salespeople feel useful, important, and worthwhile. A poorly trained sales force creates another excuse for nonperformance.

Training salespeople involves daily objectives and testing. At the start of each day of initial training, at the start of each "ride-with" and sales meeting, salespeople need to know the training goals. Goals will range from learning about pricing or closing skills to product knowledge and competitive information. At the end of each day of initial training and at the end of each ride-with and sales meeting, conduct a test related to these goals. Have the salesperson calculate prices for a particular project, perform a role-play on closing, answer narrative questions on product knowledge, or create a competitive grid. Knowing there will be a test to measure understanding creates more attention during training. Salespeople can then grade themselves using answer sheets. The answer sheets become lasting training tools and sometimes even sales aids.

The training checklist is a universe of topics that a salesperson or channel partner must understand to be successful at your company. The job description and candidate profile provide sources for these topics. The training checklist represents a key control point for sales management. Out of it flows a quarterly development plan for each salesperson, which represents yet another key control point.

The training checklist should contain the following headings:

- Product knowledge
- Competition
- Competitive issues and advantages
- Customer knowledge
- Market and industry knowledge
- Selling skills
- Company policy
- Time and territory management
- Administrative tasks
- Company organization and history
- Conflict resolution

Under each heading, the sales manager, owner, or entrepreneur fills in topics appropriate for his or her company. A heading for the subjects or topics appears across the top of each page, including the date completed, who completed it, and comments. Comments would indicate whether training was accomplished by field coaching, sales meetings, or initial training. Knowledge of products, competition, customers, and selling skills represent the most important topics and will be discussed in more detail.

Product Knowledge

Most entrepreneurial enterprises do an acceptable job of training salespeople and channel partners in product knowledge. After all, most entrepreneurs and early-stage firms are product-oriented rather than customer-focused. In fact, often salespeople and channel partners receive too much product knowledge at the expense of competitor or customer knowledge or sales skills. Product knowledge helps salespeople's confidence, but technology and operationally based firms often overemphasize this area. If your firm's customers are new systems buyers, making one-time or first-time purchases, product knowledge has more importance than if these salespeople call on managers making modified rebuys or commodity purchases. Essentially, you must teach salespeople and channel partners whatever product or service knowledge the customer requires to make the buying decision.

Entrepreneurial enterprises can more effectively teach product knowledge through hands-on experience. Salespeople and channel partners need to study the catalog, product manuals, videos, audiotapes, and Web sites, but product knowledge requires application, hands-on, and experiential training. Many firms accomplish this by having salespeople work at or tour a customer's location. What better way to understand how a product or service is used, the needs satisfied, and the problems solved? Other firms teach salespeople product knowledge by having them work in or tour their factory or other departments and functions, such as dispatch, installation, maintenance, design, the lab, or engineering. Riding on the delivery truck, filling orders in the warehouse, installing the product, repairing it, or answering customer service phones also can provide product training. Some firms rotate salespeople through key company functions to provide product knowledge and appreciation for other departments, a salesperson's internal customers. At the least, you should take a salesperson with you to see the product or service in use.

If possible, the salesperson or channel partner should use the product or service. Apparel salespeople should wear their product, software salespeople should use their product, and food service salespeople should taste their product. Where possible, have salespeople take the product apart and reassemble it, and work with models, prototypes, samples, charts, and graphs.

Competition

Salespeople and channel partners require knowledge of their competitors' products or services as well as their own. To sell effectively, a salesperson must know the competitive advantages or disadvantages of each appropriate style, model, or service in the marketplace.

As mentioned, most start-ups, early-stage enterprises, and smaller firms do an acceptable job of training their salespeople in product knowledge. However, they often do a weak job of training salespeople in competitor knowledge. Salespeople's understanding of the competition allows them to not only sell more effectively, but to understand strategic issues such as market segments, differentiation, and targeting. As the saying goes, the best defense is a good offense. Attack the competition where you are strong and they are weak.

Competitive grids for each product or product line or market help train salespeople. Marketing research firms can assist you in organizing and obtaining information for the competitive grid. Across the top, list your competitors. Down the left-hand side list the competitive issues, how the customer makes a choice. List price last, since you want to train salespeople in selling value. For each competitive issue, show how your product or service compares to the competition in features, benefits, and image. Is it better, worse, or the same, and why?

While compiling the grid, be specific. For instance, don't list quality as an issue. Instead, list how the customer defines quality, such as mean time to failure, natural yarn or fruit content, handmade, capacity, value-added services, design, materials, speed, freeze-to-thaw time, efficacy, and billing accuracy.

It is essential to be honest in appraising your competition. All companies' products and services have strengths and weaknesses. Accurate competitive knowledge allows the salesperson or channel partner to feel more confident; to present features, benefits, and proof more effectively and forcefully; and to make price less of an issue. Knowledge increases the probability of success; ignorance increases the probability of failure.

The competitive grid provides a great topic for sales meetings. For each competitive issue have salespeople and channel partners discuss whether your firm is better, worse, or the same as the competition and why. Salespeople and channel partners must understand that some competitive issues are expected, some demanded, and others represent value-added differentiators.

Entrepreneurs must keep a library or database of material, catalogs, and articles on each competitor, which remains available to company employees and channel partners. Sources for collecting competitive information include customers, interviewing competitive salespeople, trade shows, vendors, trade publications, catalogs, consultants, and the Internet. Knowledge is power. Know the competitor as you do your own firm. In collecting competitive information, emphasize ethics, the "spirit," and the letter of the law.

Customer Knowledge

Customers represent the most important asset of any organization. Salespeople and channel partners need training in how to collect, organize, and use customer information. Often the vendor with the best product or service does not get the order; instead, the salesperson who knows the most about the customer does. Do your salespeople know more about their customers and prospects than the competition does?

Your salespeople will have better customer knowledge if they maintain appropriate customer profiles. The entrepreneur or small-business manager should meet with the salespeople to design a customer profile. Determine what customer profile information provides your salespeople with a competitive advantage. A well-designed customer profile forces salespeople to ask the right probing questions which identify customer needs, budgets, time frames, opportunities, decision makers, and the decision-making process. Also, obtaining personal information on the decision maker allows the salesperson to establish a rapport and build the relationship.

The important profile issues are what information to include, how to collect it, and how to motivate salespeople to use it.

Most new enterprise and early-stage customer profile formats contain business information on the following:

- The decision maker
- The decision-making process
- Budgets
- Time frame
- Competitors
- History with your firm
- Credit
- Past use
- Potential dollars of purchases
- Locations
- Attitude toward your company
- The relationship of purchasing to other departments
- Needs
- Opportunities
- Problems
- Whether to sell at corporate or division levels
- Type of product or service used
- Key drivers of customer's business

- Sales history
- The customer's competitors and customers
- Key metrics (number of)

Most customer profile formats contain personal information on the decision makers, including education, past positions, hot buttons, issues not to talk about, hobbies, interests, families, important dates (e.g., birthday), decision-making styles, relationships with other employees, best time and way to reach them, and phone and fax number. When a new or different salesperson is assigned to the customer, this information proves critical. Customers appreciate the continuity. We buy from experts (business information) and friends (personal information).

The best salespeople obtain customer information on every call. After each visit, salespeople should write at least two new things they learned about the business and the decision maker. Salespeople and marketing can find important customer information from Web sites, catalogs, trade publications, trade shows, annual reports, and vendors.

Selling Skills

Now that salespeople and channel partners understand product, competitor, and customer knowledge, we must reinforce their selling skills. Many entrepreneurs and small-business managers assume experienced salespeople can sell. After riding with and coaching dozens of salespeople in entrepreneurial start-ups, my experience indicates most need improvement in sales skills. A sales force that understands strategic and tactical sales skills provides a strong competitive advantage in a commoditized world.

Outside trainers, seminars, videocassettes, audiocassettes, and books on sales skills are the place to start. Tom Hopkins, Brian Tracy, Miller Hyman, Sandler, and Wilson Learning are just a few resources. Ask your peers for references, read trade publications, visit trade shows, and search the Web. Several interactive selling skills programs are available on the Web. Prices vary according to your budget and need.

The entrepreneur's or small-business manager's job involves reinforcing and customizing these basic strategic and tactical sales skills. Knowledge is only power if we use it. Every industry, product, or service involves the individual use of certain broad selling techniques. Training salespeople in selling skills involves deaggregating these skills and then prioritizing the pieces most important for success in your industry. Long, complex sales cycles involving group decisions require different training than shorter, less complicated sales cycles with an individual decision maker. Selling to one-time or first-time new systems buyers requires different skills than selling to a modified rebuy, existing systems buyer, a new product buyer, or commodity buyers. Some salespeople call on multiple types of buyers and need to understand both strategic and tactical sales skills.

Strategic sales skills primarily used in longer, more complex sales cycles involve at least the following:

- Understanding the decision-making process, decision makers, budget, and time frame
- Organizational issues related to the buying center (Whom to call on first?)
- Champions and foxes (How can they help you?)
- The value-added proposition and alternative costs
- Quantifying benefits
- The decision maker's motives and key influencers

Tactical more basic sales skills include the following:

- Qualifying customers
- Precall planning
- Obtaining an appointment
- Using probing questions to find needs and problems
- Presenting features, benefits, and proof
- Overcoming objections
- Obtaining a commitment

In industries with long sales cycles, salespeople and channel partners must understand the decision-making process, including time frame, budget, decision makers, and steps from search to purchase. A salesperson selling enterprisewide software who obtains this knowledge has a competitive advantage over a salesperson who does not have this knowledge.

But, how does a salesperson obtain information about the customer's or prospect's time frame for purchase, budget, decision makers, and the decision-making process? The salesperson needs a fox and a champion. The fox is not a decision maker but a knowledgeable influencer. He or she can reliably and accurately answer a salesperson's probing questions on time frame, budget, decision makers, and process.

The salesperson also needs a champion. The champion is a decision maker who prefers your enterprisewide software and will support a decision to buy it. Your salesperson needs to supply the champion with information to help persuade colleagues and make the champion a hero.

In long, complex sales cycles, salespeople and channel partners must be trained to identify, track, and monitor the steps from search to purchase in the sales cycle. The salesperson or channel partner assigns a time frame, cost, and probability to each step. Success is defined by moving from one step to another within the time frame and cost budget. Each month the salesperson and manager discuss the status. Failure to move to the next step requires analysis and corrective action. Training salespeople in this process prevents unexpected disappointments.

For the entrepreneurial enterprise or small business to create a competitive advantage in customers' minds, salespeople and channel partners must receive training on how to quantify benefits. Using a spreadsheet to illustrate this, how do the features and benefits of your product or service increase customers' revenues, lower their costs, or reduce working capital and capital expenditure needs. Salespeople must be taught to prove this in dollars and cents.

All salespeople, whether their product has a short or long sales cycle, need training in basic or more tactical sales skills. Deaggregate the sales skills listed previously. Pick those pieces in the sales process most important to the success of your firm, and concentrate your training on those areas.

When moving from qualifying customers and obtaining an appointment to obtaining a commitment or closing, in general, the most common areas for reinforcement include probing questions to find needs and opportunities, presenting features, benefits, and proof, and overcoming objections.

To drive growth in many new enterprises, the salesperson must know how to efficiently find additional prospects with greater-than-average needs for the product or service. In such situations, teach the proven unique techniques that have produced qualified leads or develop and test new techniques. Test salespeople's skills and techniques with role-play.

Prospecting creates growth but the time required and risks involved are not worth the reward unless leads are qualified. You must teach salespeople and channel partners efficient ways to prospect for new customers. Track the closing ratio from prospecting. How can you train salespeople to improve it?

Salespeople and channel partners also need training on how to use e-mail and faxes to help set appointments or create interest in appointments. Salespeople also need training on how to deal with voice mail. Pressing zero to reach a gatekeeper who will find the person you are trying to reach represents one way to penetrate voice mail.

You must continually remind salespeople and channel partners that selling primarily involves listening, not talking. The answers to probing questions identify customers' needs. Salespeople should not present features, benefits, and proof until the customer and salesperson have agreed on the need, problem, or opportunity. To help train salespeople and channel partners, prepare a list of probing questions and what the answers tell you.

Also, presentation skills need continual refinement. Generally, salespeople and channel partners know the product or service features and sometimes mention benefits, but they seldom offer proof. In surveys of people who make buying decisions, results show salespeople who know how the product or service features benefit the customer and can offer proof of this obtain the orders. Test salespeople by asking them for a benefit and the proof whenever they mention a feature.

To help salespeople and channel partners close or move to the next step in the sales cycle, you must continually reinforce their training in overcoming objections. Salespeople must understand that objections show interest: no objections, no interest (and probably a credit problem). Make a list of the most common objections and how to overcome them. Discuss this list with your salespeople and channel partners.

Another key part of the selling process that requires constant reinforcement is closing, obtaining a commitment, or moving to the next step. Salespeople who do great presentations and probing questions often forget to close. Often the fear of failure, of a no, of a rejection prevents salespeople from attempting to obtain a commitment. Salespeople and channel partners must be trained that no is only no today and it takes a certain number of nos to get a yes.

Many sales managers believe that the key to closing is for both the salesperson and the customer to feel more comfortable. To create this comfort, they suggest the salesperson review what was agreed on, then make a partnership statement, and finally offer a choice. "Well, we agreed you need a better training program for your supervisors and that our content meets that need. I know this is an important decision, so I want you to have my home phone number. Would you like to start the program in October or November?"

Salespeople and channel partners require knowledge of products, competition, customers, and selling skills. The entrepreneurial enterprise or small business delivers this knowledge through initial training, field coaching (ride-withs, work-withs), and sales meetings. When possible, have suppliers help you with training or pay for training, because they are knowledgeable and have a vested interest.

Field Coaching

Even in organizations with no sales manager and one salesperson or one channel partner, management members must ride with salespeople. Field coaching allows management members to train, evaluate, and motivate salespeople or channel partners, share best practices, and establish rapport with customers.

Field coaching allows the entrepreneur to observe salespeople in planning and critiquing a customer visit, along with observing their knowledge of customers, competition, products, and sales skills. When the owner or manager of a small business rides with a salesperson to visit customers, the salesperson feels useful, important, and worthwhile, plus you establish rapport with customers. Field visits allow the entrepreneur a firsthand chance to learn more about problems and opportunities with customers, with products or services, with salespeople, and with competition.

Field coaching proves more effective if you and the salesperson have an objective. Focused ride-withs that alternatively concentrate on new products, new accounts, a particular product line, or market segment prove most effective. The focus also may involve training the salespeople on selling a major account. Ask the salesperson for his or her input on the work-with goal or objective and have a different focus for each ride-with.

Field coaching proves especially important for managing channel partners. If you use indirect sales representative organizations, distributors, or brokers, field coaching not only trains and motivates, it obtains a time commitment. An indirect sales force that you ride with will devote more time and resources to your products or services. The obstacle may be getting channel partners to accept field training. Training makes an indirect sales force more comfortable and competent with your products or services. Many firms have contracts which require their indirect sales force, their channel partners, to spend a certain amount of time at sales meetings and in field coaching.

Generally, we divide field coaching or work-withs into five parts:

- Your phone call to arrange time with the salesperson
- In the field precall planning
- The sales call itself
- The postcall critique
- The end-of-the-day summary

Many entrepreneurs spend the necessary time in the field but don't implement the correct process, and thus don't improve their salespeople's or channel partner's productivity. In planning each field coaching day agree with the salesperson or channel partner on the objectives, such as new product placement or opening new accounts. Before each customer call, review with the salesperson precall planning, such as the call's objectives and the strategy for reaching those objectives. Also, discuss competition at this account and what probing questions will be asked to determine needs. Review the customer profile and file, whether hard copy, digital, or hybrid. End your field training precall planning by discussing what happened on the last call, how long this visit should take (30 minutes or all day), what role you as the entrepreneur, manager, or owner will play, and how you will be introduced.

During the sales call observe and evaluate the salesperson's sales skills and knowledge of products, customers, and competition. Does the salesperson ask probing questions to identify key problems, needs, and opportunities? Does the salesperson present features, benefits, and proof, and quantify benefits in dollars? Does the salesperson overcome objections and establish the next action?

After each work-with sales call, do a postcall critique or analysis before driving to the next customer. Ask the salesperson or channel partner what went well and what went poorly, then give your opinion. After the call, what information, if any, did the salesperson add to the customer's profile? At the end of each field coaching day, summarize all these key issues with the salesperson, and ask, "What did you get out of our time together?" This question asks salespeople to evaluate the workwith, plus it allows you another opportunity to summarize key issues.

Sales Meetings

Periodic well-planned sales meetings provide a productive format for communication, motivation, and training. Similarly, you want to attend your channel partner's sales meetings or have them attend yours, and this should be included in their contract.

To justify the cost, time, and energy involved, the specific objectives of your sales meeting must be well thought-out. The objectives might include a combination of analyzing competition, pricing issues, opening new accounts, improving selling techniques, or product knowledge.

Whether you have a small sales force or a large one, whether you hold in-house meetings or conduct them at a channel partner, sales meetings can be made more interesting by having salespeople present certain topics and even run the meeting. Occasionally, invite a customer or prospect to speak about how he or she selects a vendor in that industry and the salesperson's role in influencing that selection. Allow time for questions and answers from the salespeople. Have each salesperson tell a success story. Include people from other company functions in the sales meeting, such as engineering, marketing, design, manufacturing, and customer service. A salesperson's customers are both inside and outside the company. Invite suppliers to participate in sales meetings and pay for part of the cost. Skits and role-playing that enact customer-salesperson interchanges represent powerful, realistic, nonthreatening, learning techniques at sales meetings.

For role-play, an Ohio-based electronic subcontract assembler of printed circuit boards has its purchasing agent play the customer.

Occasionally, this firm asks a customer design engineer to act as the customer. Videotapes of their role-play are given to salespeople for review.

At the end of each section or topic discussed at the meeting, hand the salespeople or channel partners a short test on the subject matter. After completing the test, hand them the answers and ask for their scores. This process ensures that participants pay attention and retain important information.

At the end of each sales meeting or each day of a multiday event, ask attendees to evaluate what went well and what went poorly, and to submit ideas for improvement. Ask salespeople to rate the subject, the presenter, and what they learned. These techniques foster involvement, ownership, and commitment plus provide valuable feedback for continuous improvement.

SALES FORCE COMPENSATION

As mentioned earlier, to attract, retain, and motivate the best salespeople, you should pay them more than they are worth. Then using proper techniques for hiring, training, organization, deployment, planning, nonmonetary motivation, evaluation, and automation, you should make these well-paid salespeople worth more than what you pay them. Remember that money is not a universal incentive. Salespeople reach complacency plateaus and comfort zones where nonmonetary motivation, for example, recognition, plays an important role.

Sales force compensation involves deciding how much your successful salespeople should earn in total dollars and then what portion of that total should be fixed versus performance pay. Total compensation depends on the complexity of the salesperson's selling tasks. The mix between performance and fixed pay depends on (1) balancing salesperson and company needs, (2) the type of salesperson you wish to attract, (3) the salesperson's influence on the sale, (4) the type product or service sold, and (5) rewarding the salesperson's specific actions or results most important to the company's success. Sales force compensation involves not only salary, commission, and bonuses, but fringe benefits, reimbursed expenses, and stock options.

The total compensation appropriate for a successful salesperson or channel partner is determined by the complexity of the sale and type of selling. A successful top salesperson involved in a long, complex, multistep, consultative, partnership sales process should receive over $100,000 annually in total direct compensation, regardless of the mix between fixed and performance pay. A successful salesperson involved in multilevel relationship sales that include modified rebuys of existing systems, which may require some after-sale service, generally receives

$60,000 to $100,000 annually in total direct compensation, regardless of the mix between fixed and performance pay. A successful salesperson involved in route sales of a homogeneous product or service requiring a multitude of daily customer visits, feature selling, and order taking from a person delegated by the buyer's decision maker generally receives under $60,000 a year in total direct compensation, regardless of the mix between fixed and performance pay.

The correct mix between performance and fixed direct compensation must reflect the company's and salespeople's needs. Basically, the company needs to attract, retain, and motivate salespeople or channel partners who produce a desired level of sales at a cost that generates profits and allows necessary percentage returns on sales and invested capital. Good salespeople and channel partners need a compensation plan that relieves them of basic financial worries, gives them pride in what they earn, reflects their qualifications and experience, and equals or betters that of the competition. A universal objective for all sales compensation plans ought to be simplicity. Also, a good compensation plan provides a certain level of stability so that salespeople have some downside protection for their incomes.

The mix of performance versus fixed pay acts as a natural filter in attracting certain types of salespeople. Review the candidate profile you prepared for hiring the sales force. Pay particular attention to the desired personal characteristics. Fixed-pay compensation plans generally attract salespeople who are team players, ambitious to climb the executive ladder, steady rather than top performers, more professional than commercial, and who prefer presold products. Once hired, salaried salespeople often develop rigid but comfortable routines and often expect considerable sales assistance from management.

Compensation plans weighted toward performance pay generally attract aggressive career salespeople with no ambition for promotion into management. These salespeople are lone wolves and top producers, but they are erratic and more interested in the sale than the selling technique. Sometimes these characteristics strain customer and company relations or result in a salesperson who prefers to highlight a large territory rather than saturate a smaller one. Does your firm's compensation plan attract the type of salesperson described in the candidate profile? As entrepreneurial firms and their products or services move from early to growth-stage enterprises to maturity, performance pay as a percentage of total compensation will most probably decline and the candidate profile will most probably change.

The more influence the salesperson has on the sale, the more performance pay should represent a higher percentage of total direct compensation. Closed biding; requests for quotes (RFQs); branded, presold, heavily advertised goods or services; team selling; rigid product or service specifications; the importance of price: all these things lessen the salesperson's influence on the sale. Also, people selling to government agencies or other businesses that require bids operate in conditions with no adequate measure of performance. Was the salesperson or the bid responsible for the sale? Here again, salary proves most appropriate. A salesperson may have more influence on the sale in a start-up because of good past customer relationships and no product or service history and less influence when the enterprise reaches its growth stage.

Certain types of products and selling lend themselves to a higher weighting of performance pay, while others lend themselves to more fixed pay. Presold, branded, heavily advertised products or services; cyclical, long, complex, sales cycles; higher ticket items; team selling; and after-sale service all lend themselves to more fixed pay. Nontechnical, unsophisticated products or services with lower unit prices and modified rebuys, which require constant customer revisits for reorders, lend themselves to a higher weighting of performance pay. A new enterprise will seldom have a presold, branded, or heavily advertised product or service. The type product also reflects the salesperson's influence on the sale. Does your firm's compensation plan reflect the type product or service sold and the salesperson's influence on the sale?

However, equally important, the sales force compensation plan must reward actions and results on the part of salespeople and channel partners that are most important to the company's success. Salespeople with better results in these key areas must receive superior pay. Most companies' sales force compensation plans do not meet these criteria. Often a disconnect exists between strategic corporate objectives and the activities or results for which salespeople are rewarded.

What positive action and results on the part of your salespeople and channel partners are important to your firm's success? If you plan to reward people for these activities and results, you require metrics to measure them. These actions and results will be different for a start-up versus an early- or growth-stage firm versus a more matured business.

Pharmaceutical firms reward salespeople for market share gains in particular medications. Several market research services track prescriptions written by doctors and filled by pharmacists. A bonus is paid for reaching specified levels of market share.

In another example, an early-stage textbook firm rewards salespeople for opening new school districts and for further penetrating existing customers. The company pays a bonus on the opening order and a progressive commission rate on revenues generated within a district. As revenues within each district increase, so does the commission rate.

A firm that sells emission control systems to diesel engine manufacturers rewards salespeople for account and territory profitability.

For each customer and territory, all direct expenses are subtracted from revenue to arrive at dollars of margin. A commission is paid on these margin dollars.

A food distributor pays its salespeople a progressive commission rate to reward growth. The rate on this year's sales until they meet last year's total is 6 percent. Once a salesperson exceeds this threshold, the commission rate jumps to 8 percent. The food distributor also pays a bonus for collecting overdue accounts receivable. For salespeople with established business, commission often loses its motivational impact. The established business functions like an annuity, and so you require a progressive rate to reward growth.

If salespeople have a pricing window or the discretion to give discounts, allowances, and promotions, a portion of their compensation should be based on dollars of gross margin for their territory. Similarly, if you wish to reward the sale of higher-margin items, you might want a compensation system that pays a commission on dollars of gross margin or pays a higher commission rate on revenues of one product line versus another.

If your firm has a long, complex sales cycle with many steps from search to purchase, consider paying a bonus for activities that lead to a sale or for moving major customers or prospects from one step to the next. Salespeople selling big-ticket items involving long, complex sales cycles often don't respond to rewards based on revenues, because it may take years to make a sale.

Many firms reward new product placement through their compensation plan. A salesperson or channel partner exerts the most influence on a customer's decision during a product or service introduction and the least influence during a product or service's decline. Some firms pay a higher level and rate of performance pay on new products and a lower level and rate of performance pay on mature or declining products or markets.

Brokers, distributors, and outside sales representative organizations generally receive 100 percent performance pay. Channel partners need specific rewards for positive action and results important to the success of your firm. For your indirect sales force to become partners rather than adversaries, they require training and correct monetary incentives. Apply the same criteria to your indirect sales force that you did for the direct people. A storm window manufacturer pays its stocking distributors a year-end bonus based on maintaining certain levels of inventory in key items and exceeding their revenue goals. An electronic component manufacturer pays its indirect independent sales representatives a commission based on gross margin rather than revenue, along with a higher commission rate for growth.

Before deciding on a final compensation plan for salespeople and channel partners, prepare spreadsheets of what each salesperson or channel partner might earn using various scenarios. If sales results meet forecasts, how much will the compensation plan cost in total dollars, and as a percentage of company revenues? What will each salesperson or channel partner earn? Run spreadsheets for different revenue levels, product mixes, prices, and different compensation plans. Which plan maximizes dollars of contribution margin over time? Which plan best meets the previously discussed criteria for the level and mix of compensation? How much does each salesperson's or channel partner's compensation vary under each plan? Which salespeople and channel partners are winners and losers under each plan?

Salary provides salespeople with a fixed amount of pay per period regardless of their recent activities or results. Nonetheless, when results exceed or fall short of expectations, you can adjust the salary accordingly. However, the reward for good performance or penalty for weak results is not immediate or direct.

A commission provides an immediate reward for successful performance. If sales increase, your people make more money; if sales decrease, they make less. Commission emphasizes the importance of writing orders and encourages the salesperson to engage in activities that culminate in order writing. Increased sales often require the salesperson to perform many tasks besides writing orders, including prospecting for new accounts, setting up display fixtures, counting stock, calibrating equipment, training, programming, or solving data entry problems.

With commission plans, sales compensation costs remain a fixed percentage of your revenues whether they rise or fall, thereby protecting profit margins and helping cash flow. When sales decline, the company is not saddled with a large fixed expenditure. For smaller companies and start-ups with limited capital, this feature is very important. New ventures especially benefit from commission plans, because initial sales costs are lower, reflecting the low sales volume. Sometimes new ventures use high performance pay compensation plans which do not properly reflect the salesperson's influence on the sale, type of service or product sold, type of salesperson required, or specific actions or results most important to reward. Sometimes these start-ups never mature because sales force compensation was poorly designed to start with. As the business matures, legacy issues can prevent changing to a more appropriate plan.

Because no career ladder exists in many smaller organizations, the opportunity to earn large sums from commission takes on added importance. In some small- and medium-size concerns, top salespeople regularly earn more than the sales manager, owner, or president. Commission also proves more appropriate for early-stage businesses, where the sales forces are often smaller but the territories are larger and have unlimited potential.

The major disadvantages of commission plans are that they lack emphasis on nonselling activities and encourage highlighting, or calling on a small number of large accounts at the expense of a large number of smaller ones. They can also result in high sales force turnover during weak sales periods, in excessive income from large nonrecurring sales, and in salespeople overselling unneeded features in addition to overloading customers with inventory. Commission compensation stresses the benefits (immediate orders) of shorter-term customer relations rather than the longer-term benefits of a growing relationship. However, proper sales training and supervision can overcome many of these disadvantages.

The rate of commission must allow a salesperson to earn a competitive and living wage from average results, but a superior wage from superior results. Also, the rate of commission must allow your company to maintain necessary profit margins and return on capital.

Some entrepreneurs and small-business managers abdicate their sales management responsibility by rationalizing that the compensation system will direct all salespeople's behavior. The ultimate example of this are companies that compensate salespeople on 100 percent performance pay, which may be a commission based on revenue or margins. In such a situation, the manager often does not spend enough time and thought hiring, training, planning, motivating, or evaluating salespeople, claiming that 100 percent commission will self-select the right people and self-direct them to work hard and smart, train, and evaluate themselves. These are dangerous assumptions.

Besides commission, bonuses represent an excellent means of using performance pay to reward positive action and superior results. Many firms defer bonus payments to year-end or future years because the bonus is paid on cumulative results. Some firms defer bonus payments to next year or future years to help with tax planning and lower turnover. Often a bonus provides an extra, deferred reward for some form of outstanding performance over and above forecast or goal. Often bonuses increase as salespeople or channel partners exceed goal. Entrepreneurs often pay salespeople and channel partners bonuses in the form of stock options.

However, if possible, pay part of a bonus quarterly to bring the reward closer to the actions or results. For example, a portion of the annual bonus can be paid quarterly if the previous quarter's performance exceeds a proration of the annual goal. If this is not possible, inform salespeople monthly about their performance progress toward the goal and remind them of the resulting bonus.

Entrepreneurs use bonuses to reward salespeople for new accounts, exceeding revenue goals, new product placements, product mix, gross margin, revenue growth, team results, company results, computer skills, product knowledge, call reports, or customer profiles. Decide which positive actions and superior results can be best rewarded by commission and which by bonuses. Bonuses provide the manager with additional goal-based flexibility for compensating salespeople.

Some combination of salary, commission, and bonus represents the most widely used form of sales compensation. Because the objectives of a compensation plan usually involve quickly and effectively rewarding a combination of actions, results, and behavior, rather than one isolated instance, combination plans prove most appropriate. Combination plans can be targeted to encourage the specific behavior, actions, and results most beneficial to your sales effort and to eliminate the disadvantages of straight commission or straight salary. The flexibility of a smaller or entrepreneurial venture allows it to take full advantage of combination plans. In entrepreneurial ventures, especially start-ups, early- and growth-stage firms, all employees including salespeople should receive half of their total compensation as fixed pay and the other half as performance pay. Half the performance pay should be paid in the year earned and half deferred to reduce turnover and reinforce long-term goals. Using the model previously described for sales force compensation attempts to meet these broader goals.

In addition to direct compensation, the sales force is also rewarded through reimbursed expenses. Regardless of product or service, any expense reimbursement plan should be fair, controllable, fast, simple, easy to understand and administer, and flexible. Salespeople and channel partners should have an economic incentive for controlling their expenses and for using expense money productively and efficiently. If no economic incentive exists because expenses are open-ended, salespeople and channel partners use them as an additional form of compensation. Similarly, management cannot ask its salespeople to pay for expenses when this would lower their total compensation to an unacceptable level.

Channel partners such as distributors, brokers, and independent sales representatives generally pay their own expenses out of their commission or margins. However, some start-up and early-stage companies do provide channel partners with travel, entertainment, sample, or trade show allowances.

In addition to direct compensation, fringe benefits (not discussed in this book), and reimbursed expenses, the sales force in an entrepreneurial venture should receive stock options. As mentioned, stock options can be given in lieu of cash as a bonus or rewarded under a separate program. You must consult a qualified attorney in these matters because the issuance of options today can influence your ability to raise funds tomorrow. Salespeople or any employee does not qualify for receiving options until meeting a certain term of employment and may not exercise the options until vested in several years. Options represent long-term compensation, which reduces turnover. A salesperson's option program may be totally dependent on company results or a hybrid involving both company and personal results. As an entrepreneur, you can also use options to hire the best performers from larger competitors.

NONMONETARY MOTIVATION

Money represents an important motivator of salespeople and channel partners. Hopefully, your compensation system rewards positive salesperson action and superior results important to the success of your firm, and reflects the salesperson's influence on the sale, the type of salesperson you desire, and the type of product your firm sells. But money is not a universal incentive. Salespeople reach comfort zones and complacency plateaus. A salesperson's motivation can depend on whether he or she is service-driven, achievement-driven, or, maybe, ego-driven. The compensation system requires proper structure but represents only one factor in driving salesperson behavior.

Salespeople, like entrepreneurs, have an insatiable appetite for recognition and a high need to feel useful, important, and worthwhile. Salespeople, including channel partners, want to be noticed, praised, and appreciated for their performance, and as the manager of a small business, or as the entrepreneur of an early-stage enterprise, you must reinforce and reward positive sales force actions and results with recognition. Recognition involves anything from a casual thank-you over the phone to an employee-of-the-month award.

Salespeople have a strong need to feel that their work serves a useful purpose and contributes significantly to the entrepreneurial company's success and well-being. A salesperson's motivation can be destroyed overnight by a feeling of worthlessness. Training programs, management's attitudes, good communications, appreciation of their work, and sensitivity to their problems all contribute to their sense of feeling useful, important, and worthwhile.

Although they hide it, many salespeople approach their jobs with feelings of insecurity and inferiority. They live with customer rejection every day. Their skills are intangible and difficult to describe, and nonselling coworkers, even family members, often don't respect or understand them.

As a small-business owner or the entrepreneur of an early-stage enterprise, keep in mind that salespeople must feel useful; they must feel a sense of worth in relation to the company. Temper your words and actions with knowledge of this need and treat salespeople as mature professionals who are performing significant work. What do you do to make your salespeople and channel partners feel useful, important, and worthwhile? Equally important, do some of your actions turn salespeople and channel partners off?

PERFORMANCE EVALUATIONS

Each quarter, the entrepreneur of an early-stage firm or the manager of a smaller business should evaluate the salespeople's and channel partners' results, activities, skills, knowledge, and personal characteristics. Hopefully, you and the salespeople informally review results on a continual basis, possibly monthly or weekly. Performance evaluations force the entrepreneur or small-business owner to manage the salespeople. As previously mentioned, some managers abdicate this responsibility to a performance-based compensation program.

The evaluation process starts by deciding what you wish to appraise. Prepare a list of activities, actions, personal characteristics, knowledge, skills, and results critical to the successful performance of a salesperson or channel partner for your particular company. Start by reviewing the job description and candidate profile used to hire each salesperson. The job description lists a salesperson's or channel partner's anticipated duties, the candidate profile his or her personal characteristics. Next, review the format of your training program, which lists the skills and knowledge necessary for success. Then add any other items not mentioned in the job description, candidate profile, or training checklist that contribute to effective performance.

The appraisal list will contain quantitative issues (sales results, quality of results, expense control, and activities) as well as qualitative issues (skills, knowledge, self-organization, time management, reporting, administrative, personal characteristics, and company and customer relations). Divide the appraisal list into 12 major categories:

- Sales results
- Sales quality
- Sales activity
- Selling skills
- Job knowledge (products, competition, customers, and markets)
- Self-organization and planning; time and territory management
- Participation
- Paperwork
- Expense control
- Customer relations
- Company relations
- Personal characteristics

Whether your sales force sells soft goods or durables, or products or services to consumer, industrial, or government users, these categories should prove helpful in deciding what to evaluate. These 12 interrelated categories apply to both long, complex sales cycles and modified rebuys, to both relationship and consultative sales, to direct salespeople and channel partners, to e-commerce, bakery products, motherboards, fiber optics, and telcos.

Creating a cost-efficient and effective sales organization separates success from failure for many entrepreneurs. Following the model outlined in this chapter will greatly increase your probability of success.

ENTREPRENEURS' MAJOR MISTAKES OR WEAKNESSES IN CREATING A COST-EFFICIENT, EFFECTIVE SALES ORGANIZATION

- Not annually reviewing buyer behavior, target markets, market segments, channels of distribution, sales force compensation, organization, sizing, and deployment to make adjustments reflecting changes in the market environment.

- Basing the above decisions on industry tradition and legacy issues rather than the enterprise's unique situation and last mover advantage.

- Not understanding a salesperson's break-even point or how to make a salesperson profitable.

- Not using job descriptions, candidate profiles, multiple sources, probing interview questions, and reference checking to hire the best personnel.

- Training salespeople in product knowledge but neglecting knowledge of competition, customers, and selling skills.

- Not using management for field coaching of salespeople and for selling major accounts.

- Not using present and deferred employee compensation to reward positive action and results important for the success of your enterprise.

- Motivating employees as a group rather than as individuals. Not realizing that different sparks light different people's fires.

- Not evaluating all employees quarterly based on results, activities, skills, knowledge, and personal characteristics. Not using this evaluation to agree on each employee's quarterly goals, objectives, and development plans.

QUESTIONS AND EXERCISES

1. Describe the steps in the sales cycle and marketing funnel from customer search to purchase for your product or services.

2. Are your firm's customers and prospects new-systems buyers, established systems buyers, new product buyers, commodity buyers, or some combination?

3. List the alternative channels of distribution for reaching your firm's target customers and markets and explain the rationale for choosing your current channel or channels.

4. What rationale did your enterprise use to decide on the number and size of each sales territory?

5. Write a job description and candidate profile for your salespeople.

6. Prepare a trining checklist and agenda for the sales force.

7. State the rationale for choosing the present or proposed mix of fixed and performance pay.

8. What nonmonetary means does your firm use to motivate employees?

9. What employee results, activities, skills, knowledge, and personal characteristics does your enterprise appraise for performance evaluations?

CHAPTER 6

Inexpensively Creating a Demand for Products and Services

Once the entrepreneur has targeted customers and segmented markets, creating an efficient and effective sales organization and marketing approach involves not only the selection of proper distribution channels, architectures, and the performance of approprtate sales management tasks, but also a search for ways to inexpensively create demand for the product or service.

A start-up, early-stage firm, or small business communicates product information to customers and prospects, and creates demand through salespeople, advertising, packaging, promotion, and publicity. The choice between channels and among alternative forms and media within each channel depends on the type of information you wish to communicate and the target market you wish to reach. Each alternative performs different functions and provides different kinds of information. The use of several channels, forms, or media reinforces the message and increases the likelihood of a purchase.

The previous chapter dealt with communicating and creating demand through salespeople. This chapter will deal with the other channels of communicating product information and creating demand. Those channels include press releases and publicity, the Internet and e-mail. trade shows, advertising, and more. Preselling, creating a demand for your product or service through advertising, promotion, and publicity, is helpful for most businesses, but essential for an entrepreneurial start-up, early-stage enterprise, or smaller business. Often, these firms or the products or services they offer are not known to their target customers, and the entrepreneur needs an inexpensive means of creating recognition. If a prospective customer or end-user has an awareness of your product or service and knows its features, benefits, selling points, or advantages, the salesperson's job or the retailer's job is that much easier.

The methods presented in this chapter are especially important for the introduction of newly developed products or services, as discussed in Chapter 9. Such products or services are unknown and unsought; therefore a low-cost means of creating demand becomes even more important.

Advertising and publicity reach customers and prospects less expensively than a salesperson's visit. However, with the exception of e-mail and the Internet, advertising and publicity are one-sided forms of communication. A salesperson can answer a user's questions and clarify benefits, whereas an advertisement does not allow feedback. Moreover, much advertising and publicity fall on deaf ears, readers or listeners who are not part of your target market. Only a small portion of advertising actually reaches your target audience.

Differentiation represents a key success factor for entrepreneurs, start-ups, early-stage firms, and small businesses; and advertising is an extremely effective means for developing that differentiation in a commoditized market. Advertising, promotion, and publicity create credibility and enhance the image of smaller businesses, entrepreneurial start-ups, or early-stage firms.

Many entrepreneurs and small-business owners feel their firms do not have the financial and human resources necessary to properly support advertising, promotion, and publicity. Costs seem out of reach, and the technical aspects of creating an ad or a Web site appear incomprehensible. This chapter shows how entrepreneurs and small-business managers can cost-effectively use advertising, publicity, promotion, the Internet, and packaging to create demand for their product or service, thus increasing dollars of revenue and dollars of income over time. We will discuss how to plan and maximize your advertising budget, how to choose among various types of advertising, how to communicate through e-mail, the Internet, packaging, sales promotion, and publicity, and how to create an effective message.

ADVERTISING STRATEGY AND BUDGET

Every entrepreneurial start-up, early-stage firm, and small business needs an advertising strategy and budget. Before you select the tools, decide what you want the house to look like, because strategy drives tactics. How does the advertising program support your marketing plan? Does it help your sales force to effectively and efficiently reach the target customers? Does it support your company image and create differentiation? Refer back to the decision-making model in the Introduction.

Consider how each alternative type of advertising supports your strategy, goals, and objectives. For each alternative, for example, e-mail versus trade shows, measure the risks versus the rewards using quantitative and qualitative data. Recognize that because data is incomplete and your time is limited, a leap of faith will be necessary. Once you have chosen the best alternatives, use the appropriate people and tools to execute or implement the decision. Set the performance standards or metrics necessary to measure the results of your advertising, publicity, or promotions. If results don't meet expectations, take corrective action. Don't be afraid to stop or change the advertising if goals are not met.

All advertising needs specific, measurable objectives. What do you want the advertising program to accomplish: new accounts, placement of new products or services, further penetration of present accounts, traffic at your store or your trade show booth, or registered visitors at your e-mail site? Incorporate in the ad, publicity, or promotion a means of measuring results, such as a coupon, special offer when mentioning the ad, click-through, bingo card, or special telephone number. Possibly have the ad feature one particular product or one store location. Use these metrics to compare one media or channel against another. Use metrics to compare one radio show or one trade publication, or one section of a newspaper against another. However, make sure the sample is adequate. Don't rely on a small sample of customers or responses to evaluate effectiveness, because they may not be representative.

Evaluate the number of responses against dollars purchased and the total cost of an ad. What was the cost per response, the cost per dollar sold, and your return on investment? Many experts suggest analyzing advertising, publicity, and promotion as an investment, not as an expense, because like a capital expenditure they produce income over time.

In choosing between alternative advertising channels, publicity, and promotional techniques, consider what your target customers or decision makers read, listen to, or watch. Consider where they live, work, and play. Consider how and where they travel. Does the decision maker read a particular trade publication or attend a particular trade show? What local newspapers, sections of newspapers, consumer magazines, radio and TV shows, and Web sites does the decision maker read, listen to, watch, or visit? Understanding the target customer and market segmentation (see Chapter 4) is essential in choosing proper advertising channels.

Advertising proves more effective when it is repeated and when it is reinforced in more than one media or channel. Running a large ad once in a trade publication or local newspaper will produce poorer results than running a smaller ad twice. It is not so much size but frequency that creates successful ads. Advertising on both local radio and cable television or in a trade publication and at a trade show will produce better results for each ad than just using one type media or channel. Therefore, you need a comprehensive rather than a piecemeal plan. The entrepreneur and small-business manager should create an advertisement, publicity, and promotional plan and budget for the next 12 months. This creates continuity and a unified theme or message.

The advertising budget consists of what your company can afford from internal resources along with what you can obtain from suppliers and customers. Most start-ups, early-stage firms, and small businesses buy from and sell through larger companies with substantial advertising allowances. Often, the smaller firm neglects to take advantage of the easily available advertising dollars from these sources. The astute entrepreneur and small-business manager should fully exploit these opportunities.

One of the most challenging decisions confronting an entrepreneur or small-business owner involves the amount of money to invest in advertising. The amount the firm can afford to spend on advertising usually differs significantly from what the entrepreneur or owner wants to spend. Most small businesses use the following criteria for determining an advertising budget: Is it affordable? Does it match the competitors'? Is it a reasonable percentage of sales? Does it meet sales objectives? Is it effective in performing certain tasks?

What percentage of sales should your business allocate to advertising? This depends on the stage of your business (early-stage or matured), its growth rate or CARG (cumulative average revenue growth), scalability, margins as a percentage of revenue, type of product, and type of competition. Start-ups and early-stage firms sometimes spend 30 percent of projected annual revenues on advertising, publicity, and promotion. This is especially true in technology, telco, and Internet industries with scalability and high growth rates. Advertising dollars drive growth and enhance scalability. Unbranded merchandise requires less advertising than branded merchandise. Markets where products or services, technology, and fashion change quickly, like branded software and designer apparel, will require more advertising than markets where change is less frequent. If your competitive advantage, type of product or service, and type of customer allow pricing power and higher margins, your firm can allocate a greater percentage of sales and a greater percentage of internally generated cash flow to advertising.

The budget for an early-stage firm or the introduction of a new product or service should view advertising as an investment creating a stream of income over time, not as an annual expense. Many entrepreneurs view advertising as a necessary evil, with little benefit, and allocate a small percentage of revenues after all other expenses are covered. Generally, this myopic view does not maximize dollars of revenue or dollars of income over time. As stated earlier, for every marginal dollar of advertising expense, how much can you expect in marginal revenue and income over time? What is the return on investment? Stated another way, to accomplish our revenue and income goals this year and over the next three years, how much must we invest in advertising this year and in the future?

A business-to-business (B2B) Internet start-up might want to create enough critical mass for breaking even in year four. This requires a certain level of fixed and variable expenses and revenue. To generate that revenue in year four, but stay within the break-even expense requirements, how much advertising is required at trade shows, on-line, in trade publications, and for direct mail?

Another approach is to follow industry tradition, practices, and competition. I call this follow the loser because it does not reflect each firm's strategy, needs, growth stage, or objectives. Industry tradition or competition might spend 2 percent of each sales dollar on advertising, but your needs, which include opening new accounts, introducing new products, and increasing market share might require spending 4 percent.

Entrepreneurs find advertising calendars helpful in reducing the budget and plan to bite-size pieces and putting them in a time frame. In which months will you attend and exhibit at which trade shows, run ads in which media, send out press releases, or run banner ads? How much will each activity cost and when does it need to be paid for? Total the cost for each month, for each activity, and the year. Are these totals above or below your budget? Then, reexamine the objective and anticipated result or payback for each advertising expenditure.

MAXIMIZING ADVERTISING DOLLARS

Regardless of your advertising budget's size or amount generated from internal sources, solicit your suppliers and channel partners for an advertising allowance, especially for the introduction of new products or services. Advertising should increase your firm's sales and, therefore, your purchases from the supplier and sales through the channel partner. Most entrepreneurial or smaller firms buy from and sell through larger firms, which have substantial cooperative advertising budgets. A small internally generated advertising budget can be greatly augmented from supplier, channel partner, and retailer cooperative advertising allowances. Most supplier's and channel partner's advertising allowances and retail cooperative advertising programs are not used by smaller or early-stage firms, because they don't understand advertising, are unwilling to do the necessary paperwork, feel amounts are too small, or don't want to invest their share. Therefore, contact your firm's suppliers, distributors, independent sales representatives, or retailers and explore this source of advertising funds. Some smaller entrepreneurial firms have asked landlords and trademark and patent licensors for cooperative advertising allowances.

If your firm makes perfume, approach your fragrance and packaging suppliers for an advertising allowance. If you rent tropical plants, approach the seed and fertilizer concerns you patronize. If you make power supplies for lasers, approach the battery companies.

If you sell a consumer product or service through major retailers, you should contact key retail customers and prospects concerning cooperative advertising. In such an arrangement, you and the store share the ad's cost, since both of you benefit from the sale of the product or service. The ad, whether in a newspaper or magazine, or on radio or television, announces that your product or service can be purchased at that particular store. Generally, the store will design and place the ad, eliminating your preparatory costs and allowing you the additional benefit of its lower advertising rate. Since major retailers continually buy large volumes of media space and time, their rates are lower than those available to you. Sometimes, the store pays half the ad's media cost, sometimes less. Normally, you receive a good-size order for the item being advertised, which automatically pays for some of your share.

If the perfume firm sells to Macy's, the store should be asked to pay for half the cost of a *New York Times* holiday advertisement; possibly the fragrance supplier would pay the other half. Similarly, if you sell an industrial or commercial product or service through distributors, approach them to share in the advertising cost of reaching the user. Again, you both benefit from the sale. If you manufacture office furniture and sell through distributors with showrooms and a sales force, you might ask a distributor to pay for half the cost of advertising in a regional trade publication.

Maximizing advertising dollars involves soliciting suppliers, channel partners, and retailers for funding and at the same time reducing costs. Rather than using an advertising agency to create and place advertising and press releases, hire independent specialists such as copywriters, graphic artists, and photographers. Leverage costs and human resources by contracting these services to other small enterprises. You can locate these independent specialists through networking, yellow pages, and the Internet. Look for creative people with industry experience who can reduce costs through using appropriate digital technology and software. Ask for references, samples, and costs of past work, along with examples of how they use technology.

Solicit suppliers, retailers, and channel partners for access to their creative people, ad slicks, printers, catalogs, and other sales-support material. Many larger firms differentiate themselves by providing these value-added services to customers, channel partners, or suppliers.

You can also reduce the cost of preparing advertising material by repeating successful ads in the same media or transferring them to other similar media.

Most important, in maximizing advertising effectiveness, choose media that can influence the target customers' decision makers. Run ads and submit press releases to media they read or watch. Run ads during periods when purchasing decisions are made. After measuring results, don't be afraid to admit mistakes and select different copy or media or period.

Investigate the possibility of shared advertising and take advantage of it. Does your industry have a trade association or syndicate that produces generic ads, allowing individual businesses to dub in local information. Smaller firms in the syndicate or association may pool their funds to produce greater media buying power, higher ad quality, or lower printing and production costs.

Choose an appropriate person in your organization to be responsible for advertising, publicity, packaging, and all other promotional demand-creating activities. You might have a committee but one person must be in charge. With appropriate input from other personnel, this person decides on the budget, raises outside advertising funds, hires contractors, chooses media, and decides on content. Many entrepreneurs do not understand advertising, publicity, and promotion, or do not have the human or financial resources to pursue it. The entrepreneur's probability of success increases by using the techniques described in this chapter to create demand for his or her product or service and leverage the human and financial resources necessary to accomplish this.

THE WORLD WIDE WEB

In the twenty-first century, entrepreneurial start-ups, early-stage firms, and small businesses must have a Web site, a Web presence, and a Web strategy. The Internet represents a cost-effective means of reaching targeted customers and prospects with an effective message. Technology, and the Internet in particular, has leveled the playing field between large and small firms and between the old and new economy. The Internet allows firms, their customers, and prospects to interact, in a manner similar to a salesperson's visit. With its capacity for sound, color, full-motion video, and visual appeal, the Web offers advertisers many of the same advantages as television ads but at a lower total cost and at a lower cost per visitor.

An electrical and electronic parts distributor in Minneapolis, with annual sales of $3.5 million, mailed catalogs to its 1000 retail and contractor customers, and then followed up with a five-person tele-sales force. The company now supplements the catalog with an inter-active Web site, which has doubled its customer base, reduced the telesales force, and increased annual revenues to $5.5 million.

The Internet allows small firms to inexpensively reach growing numbers of customers outside the United States. One quarter of Web surfers are located outside of the United States.

At the beginning of the twenty-first century, only 141,000 U.S. small businesses had Web sites out of a possible universe of 15 million. Digital marketing represents an opportunity to differentiate your firm, econom-ically reach a vast number of potential domestic and international cus-tomers and prospects, and enhance your image. The process, model, and methodology for successfully doing this is simple and cost-effective.

A Nashville gospel music producer and distributor sells compact discs and tapes to bookstores specializing in religious publications. The gospel music producer uses a small field sales force to sell multi-store chains, telesales people to sell and service average accounts, and trade shows and trade publications to advertise its new releases. Since inception in 1987, annual revenues have grown 12 percent a year to $2 million in 2001.

The owner's son received his MBA in 2000 from a state univer-sity and convinced his mother, who was the owner, to develop two Web sites: a business-to-business (B2B) Web site for retail customers and a business-to-consumer (B2C) Web site, using a different name, to reach the many consumers who did not presently buy the company's tapes and CDs. His mother reluctantly agreed and created a develop-ment budget of $75,000 and a goal of $400,000 in annual sales within two years for each of the two Web sites. The goals also included 300 visitors a day to the B2C site; 100 visitors a day to the B2B site; obtain-ing e-mail marketing lists of over 5000 businesses and individuals in target markets within one year; and limiting the marketing budget to 10 percent of sales, with a Web site development payback of less than one year.

First, the son, the newly minted MBA and entrepreneur, regis-tered domain names for these two sites by using Network Solutions, which charges $35 a year. To mitigate channel conflicts, pricing on each site would be the same as either wholesale or suggested retail prices stated in the print catalog used by the telesales people. To mitigate con-flicts of interest and channel conflicts, the consumer site would be given a new name, e-gospel, different from the company's trade name, Gospelwind. Next, the son divides the project into three parts: site design and functionality, technology, and marketing strategy.

He designs the two Web sites based on the firm's target market and market segments in both the business-to-business and business-to-consumer areas. The major reason businesses and consumers shop on-line is convenience and time savings. On-line shoppers, whether they are businesses or consumers, want to find, select, and purchase items in as little time as possible. Therefore, an appealing site must be well-organized and easy to navigate with items easy to find and an attractive product selection and assortment. To make the consumer and retail Web site easier to navigate, the owner's son incorporates left-hand and top navigational bars, brand-identifying logos, and attractive background colors and font types.

Registration clearly outlines the benefits and does not ask too many questions. Assuring convenience and creating time savings for visitors necessitates an easy checkout process with adequate customer service. Shoppers must trust that the retailer will protect privacy and efficiently execute the delivery of quality goods. This requires a clear and concise privacy policy.

On-line shoppers, whether businesses or consumers, abort transactions when Web sites are difficult, confusing, or just take too long to navigate. The "look-to-buy" ratio must be tracked to quantify the number of orders resulting from the number of visits. Also, the consumer will not want to purchase merchandise that is not presented in a flattering way. All Web sites require accurate quality product descriptions and appealing product photos.

Businesses and consumers often abort on-line purchases when they discover the shipping or freight costs. Therefore, the gospel music site will give customers access to shipping costs on the home page, or may bundle them into product prices or allow free shipping on purchases over a certain amount.

Businesses and consumers do not want to provide too much information in order to make a purchase. The gospel music firm decides only to ask for customer information needed to complete the order: name, address, telephone number, e-mail, fax number, credit information, or credit card information. More information will be asked for later with e-mail or telesales follow-up.

For customers to use and return to an on-line site, it must have appropriate product groupings for the target market, with easy-to-find prices, accurate product descriptions, and an easy route to buy the product (the fewer clicks the better), and it must not be overly graphic intense for slower connections. Not all likely and potential customers have broadband connections.

To allow for a personal touch, Web sites should store customer preferences and behavior and make recommendations based on last purchases. The gospel music firm decides to use cookies to track locations that users visit while in the site and use this electronic foot-print to send pop-up ads that would interest the user. Cookies are small programs that attach to users' computers when they visit a Web site.

To ensure more repeat usage of this site, the owner's son decides to create a community of interest. Gospel music fans will be able to interact and share their opinions on various entertainers. Gospel music retailers will be able to interact and share best practices for sell-ing these CDs, and share sales results for each entertainer.

Since businesses and consumers express concerns that customer information provided on Web sites will be sold to other firms and pos-sibly involved in fraudulent acts, the gospel music firm created trust through recognized certifications. They worked with Truste to create a privacy statement and complete an eighteen-page form detailing internal privacy and security practices. The annual Truste license fee was $299. They worked with Verisign to purchase a server ID, which creates secure connections for orders, customer data, and payments. Commerce site pricing was $895. They also looked at several more expensive security providers, PriceWaterhouseCoopers, and the Better Business Bureau.

On-line customers, whether businesses or consumers, need high-touch human interaction. The gospel music firm decided to differenti-ate itself from competition by excelling in this function. They provided 24-hour, seven-days-a-week access to an 800 number to answer ques-tions or complete a transaction. Between 8:00 p.m. and 6:00 a.m. and on weekends, this function was outsourced to a service provider. The remainder of the time several existing telesales people handled this function. To augment the 24-hour, seven-days-a-week 800 number, the gospel music firm provided e-mail support through a separate cus-tomer service e-mail address. Pictures and profiles of the customer service staff appeared on the Web site.

The owner's son accessed Forrester Research's list of highly rated sites and compared his site design to their top recommendations, which included:

- Consistent top bar that remains on every page of the Web site
- Broad product categories that are easily accessible on a left-hand navigation bar
- Product recommendations on the home page
- Lively, pastel colors.

Next, he compared his site based on user-friendliness recom-mendations, which included:

- The ability to register or sign in as a regular customer

- The ability to view the shopping cart as well as past orders and to check order status
- The deployment of privacy and security certification by respected sources

Last, the owner's son went to the gospel music competitor's business-to-business and business-to-consumer sites to benchmark his design. He also benchmarked his design against highly successful consumer sites such as Amazon and 1-800 Flowers, and against highly successful B-to-B sites.

The owner's son now developed strategy and tactics for technology and marketing. The technology solution has to be consistent with the marketing strategy, site design, and functionality. The technology must facilitate customer acquisition and retention, be reliable and dependable, and be able to handle the incremental traffic and revenue. It must also be viable from a cost-benefit and return-on-investment perspective. It should be scalable and functional, but the cost cannot exceed the derived benefits.

Based on the above, the owner's son decided the technology solution should incorporate the following features: secure credit card processing, the ability to track and monitor the site's traffic, customer fulfillment, and tracking information, the ability to store and process customer and company data and to present this information in an organized fashion. After reading a Gartner Group report, the owner's son also decided to include inventory and stock positions indicating availability of merchandise, plus, once an order is shipped, automatically e-mailing the customer a tracking number to trace it on the UPS site. The Web infrastructure must identify customers from prior activities, retrieve information on product preferences, and customize the shopping experience.

The owner's son then put the technology solution out for bid from an independent contractor with small business, B2B, and B2C experience, preferably in related goods. This was done through networking, Yellow Pages, trade associations, and e-Lance, a marketplace for free-lance Web designers and developers. He scrutinized the contractor's references, experience, skills, personal chemistry, reliability, time frame, and costs. He selected a qualified developer and designer at a bid of $50,000.

The next assignment involved creating a marketing strategy for attracting target retailer customers and consumers to visit the gospel music firm's Web site. The owner's son segmented the retailer target market into single-unit religious bookstores, multi-unit religious bookstores, plus gift shops, card shops, and music stores in the southeastern United States. He segmented the on-line target consumer market into working women ages 25-45 living in the southeastern United States, recently or about to be married women, and members of certain church groups worldwide. Based on historic account data from the present telesales organization and some on-line market research done through zoomerang.com, he decided on an appropriate on-line product offering, selection, categorization, and message for each target market. Messages varied from annoncements of excellent brand selection, to appropriate selection for various events or holidays, to highlighting certain entertainers and types of gospel music, to fast delivery.

Next, the owner's son again analyzed major on-line competitors for gospel music in each consumer and retailer market segment. This included some present competitors such as other production companies and gospel music distributors, plus, more important, some new competitors such as full-line bricks-and-clicks retailers, Amazon, AOL, and stand-alone gospel music consumer sites. He checked prices, Web site design, selection, and delivery information. Based on the competitive landscape, he confirmed egospel's value proposition to offer a wide selection of high-quality gospel music available at competitive prices in an easy-to-navigate environment. This value proposition would be communicated through a 100% satisfaction guarantee, open return policy, plus the previously mentioned easy to navigate Web site, high quality accessible customer service, and excellent fulfillment rates. The 100% satisfaction guaranteed and open return policy was prominently displayed on the home page.

The Web site personality would convey professionalism but with a warm, Southern, friendly, family-oriented theme. The tone would welcome and educate viewers and use a tag line, "Treasure the heritage." Key marketing messages to support the value proposition and personality would include: high quality at a good price, broad selection (with gift ideas); short, efficient purchasing process; secure, accurate order fulfillment; and information on individual performers.

The son proposed the following list of customer acquisition and retention tools for the two Web sites:

- On-line and off-line advertising
- Public relations
- E-mail campaigns
- Sales promotion
- Marketing collateral
- Search engine optimization
- Seasonal offers
- Web site content
- Comarketing and affiliates

- Customer service
- Customer registration

Previous market research done through telemarketers with present retail accounts and through zoomerang.com with prospective consumers, identified other noncompetitive Web sites visited by the target customers, publications read by them, along with events and trade shows they attend. The son decided to buy some banner ads on related gospel music and retail sites, offering useful information as the incentive for a click through. The consumer e-gospel site will also advertise in some special interest publications read by the target customers, and the B2B site will have a booth at retailer trade shows attended by targeted businesses.

The company will put its retail Web address on all store invoices, promotional material, and advertisements, along with announcing the Web site on a direct-mail piece. The company will put its e-gospel Web address on all consumer invoices, promotional material, and advertisements.

Next the owner's son listed both Web sites with appropriate search engines such as Yahoo, Google, Bigstep.com, Excite, AOL, Netscape, and Real Name. For $99, Big Step will register both sites in over 100 search engines. Appropriate search phrases are agreed upon, such as music plus gospel plus compact discs, religious music, and wedding music. Press releases announcing the establishment of both sites are sent to appropriate publications along with continual announcements of new releases.

As customers begin registering, their e-mail addresses are collected. As customers begin ordering, their mailing addresses are collected. Site visitors receive a monthly e-mail gospel music newsletter and notices of special promotions in exchange for registering. Registration must be kept simple and limited to one screen. Research shows each addition screen causes 25% of customers to abandon the registration or ordering process.

As both sites build critical mass, special seasonal promotions are offered to create repeat customers. Buy three holiday CDs and get the fourth one for half price. To increase the average order size, free delivery is offered on all orders over a certain size. Excess inventory and less popular performers are occasionally offered at a reduced price.

As both sites build critical mass, e-mail campaigns are used to create repeat customers and attract new ones. Targeted e-mail lists are purchased from Yesmail and Netcreations. Registered customers receive e-mail newsletters on gospel music, which may include seasonal promotions, tips on cleaning CDs, and lists of new releases. All e-mails and direct mail come from the owner's son and include a "forward to a friend" feature to leverage viral marketing. Eventually, the e-mail marketing function is contracted out to Click Action and Engage.

A mini-catalog of e-gospel's CDs and tapes is included with each consumer order, along with a thank-you note and a customer satisfaction survey card. A full catalog of Gospelwind's CDs and tapes is included with each on-line retail store order, along with a thank-you note and a retail store satisfaction survey card.

As mentioned, the owner's son wishes to attract new customers with on-line advertising at sites visited by the targeted retail and consumer customers. Although dealing with a small budget, he considers advertising in e-mail newsletters of large music distributors and certain well-known performers. However, affiliate site banner advertising on these same sites seems prohibitively expensive.

To create loyalty and repeat business, the owner's son contacts netcentives.com, cybergold.com, and webmiles.com to investigate travel awards for repeat customers on both sites. Loyalty and repeat business will also be promoted by both sites' user-friendly Web design.

Last, the owner and her son estimate the design and development costs of creating and maintaining the two sites. To this they add annual operating costs: payroll, contract services, advertising, and promotion. Then the total of these estimated annual costs is subtracted from estimated annual revenues to arrive at a margin from which the cost of the actual product must be subtracted. Several alternative spreadsheets are run using different price, traffic, and cost assumptions. Finally, a most likely scenario emerges, which indicates a very profitable opportunity.

As an entrepreneur or as a business manager of a small or emerging enterprise, the question is not whether to have a Web site and use permission e-mail marketing but how to use it. The Internet and e-mail today is what the telephone and U.S. Postal Service was in the mid-1900s. Effective e-mail campaigns and Web sites can generate significant marginal revenues and make your small company look bigger. Without them you are at a competitive disadvantage.

E-MAIL MARKETING

Most small and some larger firms overlook the power and efficiency of e-mail marketing for communicating with prospects and customers. E-mail marketing obtains higher response rates than traditional direct mail, off-line advertising, and Web banner ads at a fraction of their cost. It is best for your company to obtain the customer's or prospect's permission to send e-mail, because spam (unsolicited e-mail) creates customer hostility and results in low response rates. By giving permission, customers agree to allow your company or salesperson to e-mail programs, promotions, special events, new product or service introductions, newsletters, and updates. Limit the message to one a week, possibly two, and mix the topics. Keep the length to 150 words and limit each e-mail to one topic.

E-mail newsletters can be sent not only to customers but salespeople, channel partners, and other employees. Newsletters might include industry issues, best practices for improving profits, and product announcements. The more often you contact and serve a customer, the stronger your relationship. E-mails can be used to update the appropriate decision maker on order status and shipping information. The same e-mail might present and suggest other related products or services. Similarly, use e-mails to follow up after a trade show, customer seminar, or meeting with additional product information. It can also be a reminder about a business activity such as a reorder, trial, or benefit analysis. Some entrepreneurs send birthday greetings to customers and business proposals via e-mail.

If your firm has a customer service function, e-mail can be used to quickly answer inbound customer inquiries and do cross-selling of related products or services. Customer service people reluctantly do cross-selling in a person-to-person phone call, but have no problem using the less personal e-mail for suggestive selling.

E-mail marketing allows the entrepreneur and the company to customize messages depending on customer needs, which improves response rates. Customer replies to e-mail should be tracked and response rates measured and compared.

E-mails to customers or prospects should always contain a button for "send this to a friend." This represents an inexpensive form of referral and viral marketing. Consider having a related firm with a similar customer base attach your e-mail to one of their e-mails. Strategic partners, channel partners, and suppliers often do this.

PRESS RELEASES AND PUBLICITY

Publicity created by press releases represents the least expensive means of communicating the features, benefits, and image of products or services to customers and prospects, thus making publicity extremely appropriate for new product or service introductions and for early-stage enterprises and small businesses with limited financial resources. A product or service, especially a new offering, that receives publicity in a periodical acquires exposure, status, authenticity, and credibility, building confidence in its purchase. News is more readily accepted as being credible than an advertisement. However, with publicity that appears in the media, you do not have final control over what is published.

To create an effective publicity program, each month the entrepreneur or small-business manager should write a newsworthy story about one of his or her products, services, or customers, have photographs made, and fax, mail, or e-mail the package to select publications. If the product or service has an industrial end use (business to business), submit the material to appropriate trade publications. For consumer products, you must presell both the retailer (the gatekeeper) and the retailer's customer. Therefore for business-to-consumer products or services, submit material to both retail trade and consumer publications. In both cases, B2B and B2C, select publications read by your target customers, decision makers, prospects, and ultimate users.

Eye-catching photographs with captions and copy involving human interest stories produces good results. Many magazines and newspapers have on-line versions that create even more space to fill. Some magazines and newspapers are only on-line.

Be sure the press release contains information on how and where to purchase the product or service, along with your firm's telephone and fax numbers, mailing address, e-mail address, and Web site URL. You might use e-mail to submit press releases to publications. You might use e-mail to copy the press release or published articles to your customers and prospects.

Resources permitting, you might begin by consulting a public relations firm or independent public relations professional with small-business and industry-specific experience. You can find these firms and individuals through networking, yellow pages, trade associations, and Web searches. Be sure to ask for references demonstrating successful experience in your industry. You will quickly learn the techniques and be able to perform these functions admirably yourself.

To obtain free exposure for consumer products or services in certain consumer magazines and newspapers, first decide which section of the publication should receive your press release. If the product is an oven cleaner or squirrel trap, you would submit material to the home and garden editor. If the product is apparel, you would submit material to the fashion editor. If the service guarantees tire repairs for two years, you would submit material to the auto editor.

Next, buy reference books that list publications and their specific editors. For newspapers the reference book is *Editor and Publisher International Year Book*, www.mediainfo.com. For newspapers, magazines, and broadcast media, the major reference book is the *Gale Directory of Publications and Broadcast Media*, www.galegroup.com. Then select cities of interest, publications of interest, and submit the press release package to each appropriate editor by name. The results of such a program will amaze you.

You would follow a similar procedure for publicizing a business to business industrial/commercial product or service in trade journals, and a consumer item in retail trade publications. Listings of trade publications also can be found through *Standard Rate and Data Service* and the *Standard Periodical Directory.*

Make reprints of worthwhile published articles that appear as a result of your press release. Combine these reprints with sales bulletins, e-mail, and direct-mail pieces, and send them to salespeople, customers, and prospects. Recipients consider reprints important, and they will take the time to read them.

Publicity through press releases proves especially well suited for early-stage enterprises or small firms and for new product or service releases, because of nominal costs and excellent results. A start-up or small business with limited human and financial resources appears much larger and very successful when its name and products or services appear often in print.

Also consider creating positive publicity by the following activities:

- Write expert articles for trade publications or newspapers that are read by your target customers. A start-up offering on-line investment advice did this successfully.
- Publish a monthly or quarterly newsletter with articles of interest to your target market. Mail or e mail the newsletter to salespeople, channel partners, prospects, and customers. The newsletter might contain industry data or best practices along with product or service information.
- Offer to speak at trade shows, seminars, workshops, trade associations, or local civic and religious organizations. Choose shows, associations, workshops, and civic organizations attended by your target customers. Collect the names of those attending and with their permission put them on your mailing or e-mail list. Hand out sales literature after you speak.
- Sponsor your own seminars and workshops at trade shows or possibly as stand-alone events in appropriate cities. Many start-ups and small businesses use this technique to sell their software.
- Become involved in a not-for-profit arts, community, or trade organization that reaches your targeted decision makers. Serve on the board or on committees and make a small donation. Women entrepreneurs often network through women's business organizations. A small distance-learning firm sponsored a chamber music concert and invited customers.

- Obtain endorsements from friends and associates who have celebrity status. The mayor's picture is taken eating at your restaurant. The familiar president of a well-known bank publicly endorses your software.

TRADE SHOWS

In most industries, trade shows represent an effective means for start-ups, early-stage enterprises, and small businesses to create a demand for their product or service, especially when introducing new products or entering new markets. To accomplish this, you must choose the trade show attended by the appropriate decision makers in your target market; notify important customers and prospects by e-mail, fax, or direct mail that you have an exhibit; design an attractive, inexpensive display; and teach your salespeople how to make a two-minute presentation.

Many smaller firms efficiently sell to international customers at trade shows, which often are popular with foreign businesses. This is especially true with trade shows located in New York City, Miami, and Los Angeles.

Trade shows provide excellent opportunities for entrepreneurs to network with customers, suppliers, and competitors, even if you are not an exhibitor. Trade shows represent an excellent source of market research, competitive information, and new product trends. Trade shows also represent an excellent means to sell customers that are too small to justify an individual in-person visit.

Since exhibitor costs can be considerable—space alone can average over $200 per square foot in 2000—be sure to pick the trade show attended by the appropriate audience and the appropriate decision makers in your target market. Does the person responsible for purchasing your product or service attend a specific trade show? The year 2000 *Directory of Trade and Industrial Shows,* published by Successful Meetings, lists over 5000 trade shows. The Center for Exhibition Industry Research in Bethesda, Maryland, estimates year 2000 trade show attendance at 140 million. On-line listings of trade shows include expoguide.com and Trade Show Central (tscentral.com).

For commercial B2B products, you can attend industrial trade shows ranging from genomics to office equipment. For consumer goods, you can attend appropriate retailer trade shows, such as those for shoes, sportswear, consumer electronics, books, furniture, housewares, or gourmet food. In addition, there are a number of trade shows that present specialized consumer products directly to the consumer, such as ski equipment and apparel, sailboats and powerboats, as well as automobiles and camping equipment.

A Denver camping equipment start-up specializing in small, waterproof, long-lasting task lights successfully reached sporting goods retailers and campers by exhibiting at their trade shows. A Chicago-based firm offering a hand-held device for repairing scratches on compact discs created a twenty-million-dollar business in three years by displaying at the Consumer Electronics Show (CES) in Las Vegas. The product also appeared on many television shows and was highly praised in numerous magazine and newspaper articles. These trade shows and publicity created awareness at the store level and demand at the consumer level. Major music retailers had to offer the product, which had excellent sell-through and mark-up. New products, such as solar-heated swimming pools, one-day bathroom remodeling, fuel cells, sonic dental drills, laptop computer accessory packs, and many software programs were first introduced at trade shows by entrepreneurial firms.

In addition to the larger, well-known, and rather expensive shows, there are thousands of less expensive regional trade shows and some very specialized subindustry trade shows. For example, the Men's and Boy's Apparel Club of Nebraska holds two trade shows a year in Omaha. The New England Machinery Equipment Dealers hold a trade show in Boxborough, Massachusetts, each December. Separate trade shows are held solely for robotics, yarn, knitting equipment, video games, fertilizer, bicycles, fiberglass, ceramics, carpet cleaners, off-shore oil drilling, food-packaging equipment, community antennas, energy-saving devices, model railroads, hospital equipment and services, bread and pastry machines, welding equipment, hospital business machines, and poultry feed. Often, these less costly, smaller shows produce excellent results because of limited competition. For a smaller business, sharing your booth with another compatible firm can further reduce the cost of a trade show.

The average cost of making a customer contact at a trade show was $89 in the year 2000, compared to $168 for an average sales call in the field. The key to a successful trade show lies in effectively contacting a maximum number of qualified prospects and customers. To accomplish this, before a show opens, notify important appropriate decision makers that you will be exhibiting. Trade show attendees have a limited amount of time to accomplish their goals and must be selective. Through an e-mail, a fax, a direct-mail piece, a phone call, a trade publication ad, or an ad in the trade show program, sell targeted decision makers on the benefits of visiting your booth versus another. Will there be a demo of your product, a drawing for a Palm Pilot, a discount on their next purchase, a new product or service or application? Also, mention in any press releases and articles that your products or services can be seen at certain trade shows.

The exhibit itself should be eye-catching and quickly tell your story. The exhibit's purpose is to attract visitors who will talk to a sales representative or leave their card for a follow-up phone call from a sales representative. Customer contact represents the desired action. It requires an unusual display showing applications, benefits, and competitive advantages. If appropriate, you may wish to demonstrate your new or existing products or services, or use a video to illustrate their application. At your booth, distribute reprints of published articles and, of course, appropriate sales literature. Offer incentives for attendees to visit the booth and leave their contact information. Such incentives include gifts, drawings, and food.

Selling at a trade show involves some special skills. For example, customers become turned off by salespeople who smoke, drink coffee, or eat food at the booth. Customers also become turned off by salespeople who pace nervously, talk endlessly with fellow workers, or stand with arms folded across their chests. Salespeople at trade shows need to engage in a series of two- to five-minute pitches to a stream of strangers. You must teach these salespeople how to properly greet prospects, ask key probing questions, and give an effective two- to five-minute presentation. Questions such as "May I help you?" only receive a "No thanks" answer. On the other hand, questions that demand a response such as "Does your store sell candles?" or "What type cutting fluid do you presently use?" not only start the visitors talking, but help to qualify them as prospects. Ten qualified prospects might walk by while the salesperson is talking to a browser or even an unidentified competitor. Also, salespeople should not prejudge trade show visitors based on looks.

Train your salespeople and channel partners on proper trade show selling. Besides appropriate probing questions, they must be able to quickly quantify the benefits of your product or service in terms of increased customer sales, reduced expenses, or reduced working capital and capital expenditures. They have two to five minutes to accomplish this. Then, assuming the customer or prospect proves qualified and interested, the salesperson must collect and record information on needs, opportunities, and problems, establish a next action, and record information on name, title, company, phone, and e-mail.

Because trade shows are attended by your target market's decision makers, they offer an opportunity to perform market research and do networking even without an exhibit. Because trade shows are attended by your competitors, they offer an opportunity to collect competitive data, even if you choose not to exhibit. Many early-stage firms cannot afford to exhibit at trade shows, but their managers attend to network with customers and prospects, visit competitor booths, recruit key personnel, and attend industry seminars. Often start-ups hire college students to perform market research with decision makers at trade shows. The students approach attendees at workshops, seminars, and snack bars with a short questionnaire on buying habits.

After the trade show ends, start measuring the costs, results, and benefits. How many qualified prospects and customers were seen, how many left information about needs, how many were followed up on later, and what was the closing ratio or dollar amount in sales? Do the results justify the cost of the booth, display, people, travel, and entertainment? If so, repeat the show. If not, how can your results be improved or costs reduced, or should you try a different trade show?

TRADE PUBLICATION ADVERTISING

If you sell a B2B industrial or commercial product or service nationally or if you sell a B2C product or service to retail stores, then trade publications offer your early-stage enterprise, start-up, or small business an inexpensive opportunity to reach a specific market. Trade publications include both daily trade papers and weekly, monthly, and quarterly trade magazines. These publications are specialized in content and national or regional in distribution, and they are, most importantly, read by a targeted, well-defined, special-interest audience. *Standard Rate and Data Service*, which is available in hard copy, on-line or CD ROM, lists 9700 trade publications (magazines and papers), including *American Laundry, Automotive Engineering, Chemical Equipment, Design News, Forest Products Journal, Golf Digest, Hardware Merchandising, Frozen Food Age, Light Metal Age, Men's Wear Daily, Paper Trade Journal, Pulp and Paper, Rubber World, Sporting Good Business, Women's Wear Daily,* and *Yard and Garden Product News*.

If you sell a B2B industrial or commercial product or service nationally, determine what trade publications reach the decision makers you sell. Ask your major customers and prospects what publications they read, and study the results of market research surveys. You probably read the same publications as the decision makers. Because these publications have special-interest readership, your chances for getting good results are excellent. Moreover, because these publications generally have limited circulation, their rates are reasonable. As an example, a start-up semiconductor firm used a technical publication for reaching communication equipment design engineers and a general industry publication for reaching purchasing agents. For products and services sold regionally, many national trade publications offer regional advertising at reduced rates. Trade publications, like trade shows, offer an excellent opportunity to reach overseas markets. You might even advertise in a foreign trade publication, and attend or exhibit in an overseas trade show. Also some trade publications offer opportunities to advertise at reduced rates in their foreign editions.

If you offer a B2C product or service regionally or nationally through retail stores, you must first convince the appropriate retailer to buy your item before both of you can convince the consumer to buy it. Later in the chapter we will discuss how you reach the consumer, but it is equally important and much less expensive to reach the retailer, the gatekeeper to the consumer. As with the industrial market, determine what trade publications reach the retail decision maker. For example, a ladies sportswear company based in New York City advertised in one women's wear publication for reaching department store buyers and another for reaching chain store merchandise managers.

Trade papers and magazines contain certain specialized sections, editions, and days for different types of goods and services. In the apparel trade papers, Monday is knit goods day and Thursday financial services. Readership for sweater ads would be better on Mondays, and readership for banking and factoring ads would be better on Thursdays.

Personal computer trade publications contain specialized sections for components, test equipment, software, and quality control. A semiconductor manufacturer might receive better readership by advertising in the component section, while a test instrument firm might receive better readership by advertising in the equipment or quality control sections. In addition, most trade publications have special issues and increased circulation and rates for major trade shows.

Buyers, purchasing agents, and decision makers use trade publications as a source of general comparative product information, which influences buying decisions in the long run. Because of this, ads that feature user benefits produce the best results. In trade magazines you can use photographs to get the reader's attention and tell the story, but in trade newspapers with poor print quality simple art work produces the best results.

A small engineering firm specializing in water pollution control advertised monthly in various trade publications reaching the steel, utility, paper, and chemical industries. The ad contained pictures of pollution problems, such as dirty water or belching smoke stacks, and briefly listed the firm's technical capabilities. An e-mail address, Web site listing, return coupon, and toll-free fax and phone numbers generated many responses.

An entrepreneurial early-stage designer tie firm advertised twice monthly in the men's apparel trade paper, listing its products, price ranges, and markups next to a simple drawing of an attractive design. The ads invited interested retailers to visit its Web site to view an online catalog, call or e-mail for a catalog to be mailed, or visit the New York showroom.

CONSUMER PUBLICATION ADVERTISING

If you sell a B2C product or service nationally to a special interest group, such as skiers, or runners, or auto enthusiasts, and if it lends itself to visual presentation, then magazines can produce affordable results for your small business. Analyze which magazines reach your specific customer group.

A small optics company in Colorado made quality nonprescription plastic sunglasses for skiers. They ran a small ad each month in several ski magazines with pictures of an attractive couple wearing their sunglasses on the slopes. The ad listed major retail outlets by city that carried the glasses; it contained a return coupon, toll-free phone and fax numbers, an e-mail address, and the Web site location. The ads produced many consumer responses, which allowed the company to further expand the number of retail outlets and increase sales at existing outlets.

A dog trainer, in conjunction with an agricultural feed firm, devel oped a line of high-protein dog food. When offered through grocery stores and advertised in local newspapers, the product failed, because it was too upscale for that market. However, when it was advertised in *Dog World* magazine and sold through kennels, pet shops, and clubs as a premium product for show animals, sales increased dramatically. The advertisement contained a picture of a proud owner displaying her award-winning dog at a show. The advertisement also contained a toll-free phone and fax number, return coupon, e-mail address, and Web site information. Eventually, this entrepreneur offered a line of specialty high-performance dog foods and accessories directly to consumers through direct mail and the Web site. The Web site and the direct mail included a newsletter, which created a community of interest.

NEWSPAPER ADVERTISING

Newspapers are most cost efficient for advertising consumer products or services with wide appeal and local distribution. They allow you to concentrate advertising in a local market and at the same time reach a wide variety of readers. Newspapers are least cost-efficient for advertising most industrial or commercial products or services because the readership contains too small a percentage of potential users. Consumers use newspapers as a source of immediate comparative product and price information on which they base buying decisions.

Because newspapers deal with daily activities and have limited geographic distribution, readers use them to identify with their community. Readers have faith and confidence in the integrity and believability of their newspaper's contents.

In some cities, you can advertise in neighborhood, foreign language, and ethnic newspapers, which allows you to narrow the audience and reduce the expense. You can also narrow the audience by advertising in a particular newspaper section, such as Sports, Business, Food, Help Wanted, Fashion, Theaters, or Autos.

In addition, some newspapers have expanded sections with expanded readership on certain days, such as Business on Monday, Food on Thursday, Sports on Saturday, and Help Wanted on Sunday. You can take advantage of the expanded general readership of most dailies by advertising on Sundays. Depending on the readership and circulation, newspapers charge different rates for advertising on different days and in various sections. You should select the day and section which best reaches your target audience. Newspaper ads are least effective in targeting people under 30, and most effective in reaching older, educated high-income adults.

As mentioned, consumers use newspapers as a source of immediate comparative product and price information on which they base buying decisions. Because of this, a more descriptive advertising approach, which emphasizes price and benefits, produces the best results. Because readers have faith and confidence in the integrity and believability of the newspaper, it also provides a good medium for advertising new products. The major disadvantage of newspaper advertising is short life; generally, the reader discards a paper after one reading. Also, because of the relatively poor print and reproductive quality on ads, visual content must be kept simple, limiting the format of the message.

If you wish to advertise a price-competitive consumer product or service which can be purchased immediately in a specific local store or stores and which can be described in words better than in pictures, especially a new product or service, then newspapers can produce the best affordable results for your small business. The wider the item's appeal, and the more stores offering it within the local market, the more cost-efficient the ad. You will increase the ad's cost-efficiency, or results per dollar, by choosing the newspaper and section and day which best reaches your target market.

Although the number of U.S. newspapers has declined 20 percent in the last 40 years, this medium still accounts for 20 percent of all advertising dollars spent in the United States, about the same as television and direct mail. Newspapers also offer the advantage of late closings, or publication deadlines. Some papers permit advertisers to submit their copy 24 hours before an ad runs. Because newspaper ads produce quick customer responses, they represent an excellent means for promoting sales, grand openings, or new products.

Often, a smaller business's ad can become lost in a typical newspaper with 65 percent of the space devoted to advertising. Entrepreneurs and small-business managers can overcome this disadvantage by repeating ads, increasing their size, or using full four-color ads. Bold headlines, illustrations, and photographs also increase an ad's prominence.

The best location for a newspaper ad is on a right-hand page, near the right margin above the half-page mark, or next to editorial articles. The main news section and comics represent the greatest readership.

MAGAZINE ADVERTISING

Generally, magazines are much more specialized in content and more national in distribution than newspapers. Magazines allow you to reach a business audience having specific shared interests. Readers identify with their special interest or trade group through magazines. Magazines have better print quality, are more personal, and less likely to be as quickly thrown away as newspapers. Decision makers use magazines as a source of general comparative product information that ultimately influences buying decisions. The comments in this section apply to both consumer and trade magazines.

Magazines have more feature articles than news, and they are usually read at leisure in the privacy of a home or office, where the reader can more rationally select products or services that seem to meet his or her personal needs or the needs of his or her firm. Because magazines are read at leisure, they may be kept for months. Readers generally do not use magazines as a source of comparative price or specific product information upon which to base immediate buying decisions. Magazine advertising influences future purchases rather than immediate ones. Because of the excellent print and reproductive quality in magazine ads, visual content can be fully utilized. This allows more versatility than newspaper advertising does in the presentation of the message.

Magazines are most cost-efficient for consumer and industrial or commercial products and services with specialized appeal and national distribution. Magazines allow you to inexpensively reach a specific market. Again, some national magazines allow firms to further narrow the audience or market and reduce costs by advertising in regional editions.

Similarly, in most major cities, magazines exist which specialize in articles and listings about local events, politics, the arts, and restaurants. These magazines have local audiences with common interests in the arts, restaurants, and politics.

RADIO ADVERTISING

Within the broadcast media, radio represents the most effective consumer product or service advertising for a small business because specific types of consumer audiences can be reached inexpensively. Broadcast media do not lend themselves to advertising commercial or industrial business-to-business products or services in a cost-effective manner because the listenership contains too small a percentage of potential users. All broadcast advertising must overcome the recall problem. The listener has no practical way of saving the message for later reference. By 2003 wireless services will offer listeners an opportunity to dial special numbers which will replay radio commercials based on imputing the station numbers and time. This service will help to overcome the recall problem.

In addition, radio advertisements must get their message across in 15 to 30 seconds to a listener who is most likely engaged in some other primary activity. Because of these limitations, consumers seldom use radio as a source of immediate comparative product information on which they base buying decisions.

Radio programming and, therefore, radio audiences vary a great deal, making it easy for an advertiser to reach certain types of listeners and markets. Popular music stations reach young people, while classical music stations reach affluent adults, and talk shows reach homemakers and expressway commuters. You can further narrow the radio audience by advertising on foreign language programs, on sporting events, on Sunday night opera, or on Monday night jazz. Also, audience size and rates vary depending on the day of the week and the time of day.

The radio audience is more clearly defined than that of a newspaper, but audience members have less in common and fewer shared interests than that of a magazine. Radio listeners develop strong loyalties to personalities and stations. Because broadcasters use the spoken word to influence customers, emotions, urgency, and a more personal tone are possible. Like that of a newspaper, radio's audience is primarily limited geographically, and listeners must be able to purchase or use the advertised product or service locally. A few FM stations are now broadcasting in distant cities via satellite, allowing interested advertisers to reach more distant markets. Several satellite firms will soon offer national programming to vehicles.

If you sell a consumer product or service to a well-defined market, and the product or service lends itself to a 30-second verbal presentation, then radio advertising can produce good sales results at affordable costs. For example, classical music FM radio stations are an effective means of advertising theater, symphony, opera, fine restaurants, foreign cars, banks, art galleries, jewelry, and fur coats. As another example, popular music, AM radio stations are an effective means of advertising soft drinks, domestic cars, fast-food shops, records, blue jeans, rock concerts, and cosmetics.

Radio reaches 77 percent of the U.S. market daily and 95 percent of adult consumers each week. Radio commercials have late closings, allowing the advertiser to change the ad quickly to match changing market conditions related to price, products, or special events.

Because vendors are limited to one minute or less, you must keep the message simple but repeat the ads. Make sure the listener knows how to reach you; repeat your location, phone or fax number, e-mail address, or Web site. Repeat the benefits of your product or service. Use music, sound effects, and unusual voices to obtain the listeners' attention. Make radio ads conversational.

Convey a sense of urgency with words such as "now" and "today" and by suggesting buying action, which must be accomplished within a certain time frame. Make it clear what you want the listener to do and by when.

TELEVISION ADVERTISING

Television allows you to advertise locally or nationally and reach a wide variety of viewers. However, television like radio does not lend itself to advertising commercial or industrial B2B products in a cost-effective manner, because the listenership contains too small a percentage of potential users. Consumer products or services can be vividly presented in actual use because television appeals to both visual and auditory senses and conveys the impression that it is "live." Although television is an extremely forceful advertising medium, it shares radio's recall problem. Although most televisions will soon have instant replay and some will have storage facilities and even though most viewers have VCRs, presently the viewer has no practical efficient or cost-effective way of saving an advertising message for future reference.

Even though network television reaches a large and diverse consumer audience with tremendous realism, the present cost of network advertising places it outside the reach of most entrepreneurial start-ups or smaller businesses. In 2001, a 30-second commercial on network television cost well over $500,000, but a 30-second spot on a local cable station went for $200, making it competitive with FM radio and banner Web ads.

The growth of cable stations, satellite transmission, and the merging of personal computers and television will open new advertising opportunities for smaller firms. This will allow more targeting plus the ability to store and recall messages. Because some television shows are presented live, and because programming is becoming more specialized, viewers develop strong loyalties to specific TV personalities and to stations that appeal to their interests.

Local and national cable television channels allow you to reach special interest consumer groups such as animal lovers, travelers, gardeners, cooks, moviegoers, investors, and science and sports enthusiasts. In some cities, cable stations offer specialized financial or commodity market reporting from 8:00 a.m. to 3:00 p.m. Such stations lend themselves to inexpensive advertising by small financial service firms, such as investment counselors. Cable television represents an excellent means of reaching a particular foreign-language market.

The emotional impact and effectiveness of television advertising surpasses all other media. Television allows the advertiser to use color, action, symbols, image, reason, price, value, realism, fantasy, wish fulfillment, and status to their fullest extent. With television ads, entrepreneurs can demonstrate consumer product or service uses and benefits. However, few entrepreneurs have the skills, knowledge, or budget to prepare an effective television commercial. Generally, the television station involved will provide inexpensive design and production assistance.

DIRECT MAIL

Many early-stage entrepreneurial enterprises and small businesses use direct mail to create demand for their products or services. Successful direct mail requires an accurate database of decision makers at B2B target customers or an accurate database of targeted consumers. Successful direct mail involves many alternative forms: an interesting newsletter, copies of press releases, reprints of published articles, product literature, catalogs, brochures, statement stuffers, letters, postcards, discount coupons, CD-ROMs, compact discs, and videotapes. Whatever the form, it must reach the targeted business or household and be read or viewed by the targeted decision maker. As you can see, to a certain extent direct mail has been replaced by e-mail.

The database mailing list will contain names of customers, decision makers, and targeted prospects. Ask your salespeople and channel partners to submit names of decision makers and prospects. Add to this mailing list the names of people who visited your trade show booth, belong to appropriate trade associations, read certain B2B or B2C publications, or visited your Web site. For consumer products, consider buying lists from credit card firms or list brokers of consumers in certain ZIP Codes, with appropriate income levels, net worth, past purchases, hobbies, interests, occupations, or other demographics. Continually update and purge this mailing list to keep it fresh. For B2B products or services consider buying lists of decision makers, such as oncologists or chief information officers, or target companies in certain ZIP Codes and by SIC classification.

In some cases you may wish to draw special attention to a mailing by using Western Union Mailgrams or various forms of priority mail. Services such as Western Union will print your message on their letterhead and also do the mailing, which arrives in an attention-getting envelope within a few days.

Direct mail using accurate databases of target customers represents an inexpensive means for smaller and newer businesses to introduce new products and keep their names in front of customers and prospects between a salesperson's visit or a consumer's store visit. Direct mail can also pay for itself by generating an immediate direct response purchase by phone, fax, mail, e-mail, or Web site visit. Therefore, all direct-mail advertising, whether B2B or B2C, should contain clear instructions for making an immediate purchase including mailing, Web site and e-mail addresses, salesperson's and firm's phone and fax numbers, and any 800 numbers.

Half of all direct mail is discarded unread. To improve on this percentage the envelope must create enough mystery to be opened by the recipient. Once opened you have less than a minute to get the reader's attention. This can be accomplished with a headline, graphics, sample enclosure, or a diskette. The right message sent to the right customer or prospect produces powerful results at minimum cost.

In the minute you have to capture the reader's attention, put the most important benefits of your product or service into a headline. Whenever possible, back up claims and statements with proof, endorsements, numbers, and testimonials. Make it easy for readers to respond to your offer. Use high-quality paper, envelopes, graphics, and printing to reflect your image. Use envelopes with windows that resemble invoice envelopes. Always address the envelope to an individual, not to a title, such as purchasing agent, design engineer, chef, or occupant. Make the copy easy to read, leave plenty of white space. If the direct-mail piece includes an order form, make it easy to find, navigate, and use.

You can measure the results of direct mail in several ways: (1) direct response purchases or (2) deferred purchases, usually made through a gatekeeper, salesperson, or channel partner. Code your direct-mail pieces with special words, prices, products, or numbers so direct responses can be aggregated. Have salespeople, channel partners, and retailers ask customers how they heard of your product or service. What form of direct mail, radio, television, or print advertising are they responding to? Advertising responses of any sort prove difficult to accurately measure. However, as an entrepreneur or small-business manager with limited resources, you must continually attempt to measure advertising effectiveness and take corrective action.

Relative to the audience size reached, the cost of designing, producing, and mailing (postage), direct mail can have a higher cost per thousand (CPM) than any other advertising medium. A typical direct mailing costs over $400 per thousand customers reached; postage, printing, and paper represent 75 percent of that cost. Where possible, use follow-up phone calls, faxes, and e-mails to improve the response rate and return on investment. Use of direct mail in conjunction with other advertising media and sales channels and use of repeat ads will increase your success rate and lower your cost per response.

For all consumer products and some business products include a direct-mail piece with every shipment and invoice. The cost is minimal and you have the customer's attention. Consider piggyback mailings where your direct-mail piece is included with one from a strategic partner. Consider bundled direct mailings where your direct-mail piece is included with a group of complimentary products or services such as packaging or medical services.

DISKETTES AND CD-ROMs

Early-stage broadband cable and phone companies, entrepreneurial independent Internet service providers (ISPs), and software start-ups all mail computer diskettes and compact discs to potential customers. Using diskettes and CD-ROMs as direct-mail pieces represents an excellent way to reach upscale households and businesses and to introduce new products or services. They allow you to create flashy, attention-grabbing designs and text that hold the audience's attention. Diskettes and CDs are seldom thrown away. At some point they will be reviewed and interacted with, often for 15 to 30 minutes, which results in getting the prospect involved and produces high retention rates.

Compact discs allow for more space and viewer interaction, so that ads can include videos, music, animation, and quizzes. People remember 20 percent of what they see, 30 percent of what they see and hear, and 60 percent of what they interact with.

STORE CATALOGS

For consumer products sold through retail outlets, store catalogs offer the early-stage firm or small business an inexpensive means of pre-selling the ultimate user. Most major retailers print numerous specialty catalogs of items that can be purchased by mail, phone, fax, or e-mail, on a Web site, or in the store. Also, buying organizations such as True Value and Federated offer catalogs to member stores. Most major retailers also offer these print catalogs on-line at their Web sites. In December, for example, the store print or on-line catalog might feature toys and computers; in February, linens and housewares; and in May, barbecues and patio furniture. Through such catalogs, your message will reach thousands of affluent customers. Although only a small percentage of those receiving the catalog respond by immediately making a purchase, the rest become aware of the item, possibly the brand, and at a later date may purchase it at any retail outlet, which makes store catalogs especially important for new product introductions. Stores mail catalogs to their charge card customers in addition to people on lists purchased from direct-mail services. Customers can also obtain catalogs in the stores. Of course, anyone can view the on-line catalog and the retailer will try to create on-line traffic through banner ads and links with other appropriate sites.

Retailers confine their direct-mail print catalogs to their store's trading markets. However, with on-line catalogs, multistore, and multiregion retailers, trading markets have expanded beyond city, state, and national boundaries. U.S. consumers shop on-line at Harrods in London, Printemps in Paris, and Ka De We in Berlin.

Generally, stores sell space in their catalogs to vendors, but then place large orders with the advertisers for the goods involved. Immediate sales from the catalogs should pay for your space costs, and so the additional market exposure, the advertising value, costs nothing.

Generally, vendors submit samples or pictures and the store advertising personnel prepare the copy and presentation. Because of excellent print and reproductive quality, visual content can be fully utilized. Consumers read catalogs at leisure in the privacy of their homes and may keep them for months.

Consumers use catalogs as a source of immediate product and price information on which they base buying decisions at the issuing store. Most retail catalogs emphasize product appeal and value. Consumers also use catalogs as a source of general comparative product information on which they base future buying decisions at other stores.

Contact the advertising departments of your retail customers and prospects concerning space in their catalogs. Generally, the reward is well worth the cost.

SPECIALTY CATALOGS

Whether your firm sells a consumer or an industrial product or service, nonretail store specialty catalogs offer an inexpensive means of preselling, especially for new product or service introductions. Specialty catalogs offer a wide variety of products and services, including cigars, Christmas ornaments, chocolates, outdoor apparel and maintenance, material handling, and safety and communication equipment. Through such catalogs, your message can reach thousands of affluent consumers and appropriate corporate decision makers. These catalogs are mailed nationally to previous customers in addition to people and firms on lists purchased from direct-mail agencies, trade associations, and trade publications. The lists classify consumers by income and special interests, such as camping or home ownership, andthey classify firms by industry and size. For consumers, where you live very much affects your buying habits. Target marketing allows mail-order firms to pinpoint prime consumer prospects by their ZIP Codes.

Although only a small percentage of those receiving the catalogs respond by immediately purchasing your product or service, the rest become aware of the item and your brand name. At a later date, some of these people will recognize your product or service at conventional retail outlets or when presented by a field salesperson, and may possibly purchase it.

Some specialty catalogs charge vendors for space, others do not. In the former case, immediate sales from the catalog should pay for your space costs; and in either case, the additional market exposure, the advertising value, costs nothing.

Generally, vendors submit samples or pictures and the catalog advertising personnel prepare the copy and visual presentation. Because of the excellent print and reproductive quality, visual content can be fully utilized.

Consumers and business to business decision makers read these catalogs at leisure in the privacy of their home or office and may keep them until the next issue is received. As with store catalogs, consumers use these specialty catalogs both as a source of immediate product and price information on which they base immediate buying decisions and as a source of general comparative information on which they base future buying decisions. Most consumer specialty catalogs emphasize product appeal and value.

Businesses use business catalogs as a source of general comparative product information that ultimately influences buying decisions. Most specialty catalogs emphasize user benefits and price.

A well-known but small hiking boot manufacturer located in Colorado advertises only in specialty catalogs, even though other retail outlets also sell their shoes. Several small chemical, computer supply, and container firms established brand identification by advertising through specialty catalogs.

Contact specialty catalog publishers who sell to your target customers. Specialty catalogs can produce immediate sales and considerable advertising value.

SALES CATALOGS

Many early-stage firms and small businesses print catalogs that describe their line and list current prices. Such catalogs range from typed pages stapled together to bound versions with color photography to copies of CD-ROMs. Firms mail these in-house catalogs as reference pieces to their customers and prospects, plus salespeople use them as sales aids in their presentations. In the case of consumer retail products, the catalogs go to retail store buyers. In the case of B2B products and services, the catalogs go to the appropriate decision makers, influencers, and gatekeepers at customers and target prospects. The decision maker may be the physician; the influencer, the nurse; and the gatekeeper, the purchasing agent.

Sales catalogs should also be offered on-line. Any sales catalog should contain an easy-to-use order form, with fax and phone numbers, mail and e-mail addresses, and Web site information.

BROCHURES AND REPRINTS

Besides mailing their catalogs to customers and prospects, entrepreneurial firms and small businesses also mail flyers, press releases, reprints of ads and articles, special-interest bulletins, and brochures on specific models or services. Sending reprints of ads and articles concerning your product or service ensures that customers and prospects see them, even though they might have missed the original published version. If they saw the original version, the reprint will reinforce the message. Generally, product or service brochures contain attractive photography, graphics, service or product descriptions, and a list of benefits, along with a return order coupon, fax and phone number, mailing and e-mail address and Web site information. The giftware, software, and copy-machine industries use such product or service brochures extensively. Brochures and flyers prove effective for new product or service introductions and for greater impact can be both mailed and e mailed.

By selecting the correct mailing list, a firm can pinpoint who receives these forms of printed advertising, and it can ensure that the information will be seen by the appropriate decision makers, influencers, and gatekeepers. The sources for these mailing lists would be company records on customers, salespeople's suggestions on prospects, names from trade shows, plus appropriate lists purchased from trade associations, trade publications, and direct-mail companies. Again, you must address in-house sales catalogs, brochures, flyers, reprints, press releases, and bulletins to the specific party you wish to have read them. Don't mail them to a customer or prospect without the name of the decision maker, influencer, or gatekeeper.

Besides mailing product information and promotional material on consumer products to related store buyers, you can also mail them directly to consumers. Such mailings usually require cooperation with local retailers and might involve a statement stuffer. Cooperation would include coupons for rebates at a local store or announcements of special prices. In the case of such products or services as home security systems, insurance, or broadband telephone service, the mailings might include a return coupon or phone number for more information.

STATEMENT STUFFERS

For consumer products or services, especially newly introduced products or services, credit card and retail store statement stuffers allow a small or early-stage business to advertise at minimum cost. American Express, Visa, MasterCard, etc., search out products that might be appropriate for one of their monthly stuffers. Your message can reach millions of affluent people, and will be paid for by the orders received from credit card holders. The same stuffer is seldom sent to all cardholders, but rather to targeted groups who have previously purchased a similar item, live in a certain region of the country, or charge over a certain amount annually. Although only a small percentage of those receiving the stuffer respond by buying the product from the credit card company, the other 98 percent become aware of the item and the brand and may purchase it later through a conventional retail outlet.

Most national credit card concerns subcontract the management of their entire direct-mail programs, including statement stuffers, to specialists. Since the pictures and the text do the selling, these firms design stuffers with a great deal of visual appeal and detailed product information, emphasizing price, value, and benefits. Like newspaper advertising, though, statement stuffers have a short life. Many are not even read.

Retail stores also sell and advertise through statement enclosures, and for the small, early-stage business, these too offer an inexpensive means of advertising. The benefits and mechanics are similar to those of a national credit card stuffer, except you generally reach a smaller regional audience. Although only a small percentage of those receiving the stuffer respond with an immediate purchase, the remainder become aware of the item and your brand and may buy it later at another retail outlet.

Retail store statement stuffers may be designed by either the vendor or the retailer's advertising department. Since the product is also available for inspection and purchase at the store, a less detailed description is required. Generally, the vendor pays the cost of printing the stuffer, and the retailer pays the cost of mailing it with its monthly charge card billing. All statement stuffers should contain an easy-to-use order form and a toll-free phone and fax number to call in orders, plus an e-mail address and Web site location to place orders on-line or view other related products. In this way the entrepreneur and small-business person is leveraging the old and new economies through bricks and clicks.

If you sell a consumer product or service through retail stores, contact the advertising department of customers and prospects concerning statement stuffers. If you sell a consumer product or service that at all lends itself to statement stuffers, contact the major credit card companies. You might also contact a direct-response consultant to assist in this area.

HANDBILLS

For the entrepreneur and small-business person, handbills represent yet another inexpensive form of printed advertising. They can be slipped in mailboxes to advertise a broadband telephone service, placed under windshield wipers in a mall parking lot to advertise a sale or an auto repair service, or handed out to passersby in front of a store or theater to advertise a promotion or special performance. Generally, handbills are simple, don't contain pictures, and have a short life. Handbills allow you to reach a wide variety of consumers in a targeted area or neighborhood. If your business's target customers live in a particular area or pass by a particular street corner each day, handbills can prove an inexpensive means of reaching them.

BILLBOARDS AND SIGNS

Outdoor advertising reaches a large number of potential customers in a defined area. Billboards and signs, including those on public transportation, can prove an effective form of low-cost advertising if your small or early-stage business sells to a well-defined market whose members frequent certain locations.

However, most billboards and signs are not cost-efficient for small businesses because the readership contains too small a percentage of potential customers. Sharing the space with other noncompetitive firms can reduce billboard costs.

When located near a retail store, billboards and signs can serve as a last-minute reminder. Because most people travel the same routes each day or each week, billboards represent an opportunity for multiple impressions. However, the exposure is brief and so the message must be direct. Digital printing has made outdoor advertising more attractive and attention-getting and allowed more variety in the message

YELLOW PAGES AND DIRECTORIES

Many early-stage enterprises and smaller businesses (B2B and B2C) exist from sales generated by their display ads in the yellow pages. An ice-machine rental company runs large display ads under "Ice Machines" and "Ice Delivery." The ads produce 10 leads a week, which result in two sales a week. A solar heat-reflecting window shade company receives good responses from yellow page ads placed under "Shades" and "Air Conditioners."

In addition to the printed yellow pages, you can now list your firm with services that provide this information over the phone and on-line. Customers call for the names and telephone numbers of firms offering certain products or services. Similarly consumers and businesses can go on-line for yellow page classified information by city.

Some industries, for example, gears, die casting, and injection molding, rely on trade directories for critical information. In these industries directories represent an important small-business and early-stage advertising medium for reaching prospects and customers who have already made a purchasing decision but have not decided on a vendor. The directory helps these customers locate the specific product or service they have decided to buy and the vendors that sell these products or services. Directories include telephone books, industrial or trade guides, buyer guides, annuals, catalog files, and yearbooks that list various businesses and the products they sell. Directories can be hard copy, CD-ROMs, or on-line, and are often prepared by trade publications and trade associations. Directories are most often used for products or services involving modified rebuys but are also used for first-time, one-time purchases, new products, and commodities.

Find out which trade directories are read by your target customers and be sure your listing is correct. Consider placing a display ad in the appropriate section. Generally costs are reasonable.

In choosing a directory to advertise in, not only consider who uses it but how often. Do users pay for the directory, or do they receive complimentary copies? Ask for an audited circulation statement.

POINT-OF-PURCHASE DISPLAYS AND FIXTURES

For products sold through retail outlets, point-of-purchase displays get the consumer's attention and outline the item's features. Selling fixtures present the product in an attractive, organized fashion, making it more appealing to the consumer. The customer is in the store; now you want him or her to buy your product.

Point-of-purchase displays can show the item in use, list its benefits, or just announce a sale price. Pictures and copy must be large so they can be read from a distance, and too much information can confuse the reader. Consumers use point-of-purchase displays as a source of immediate comparative product and price information on which they base buying decisions. For this reason, displays are especially important for new products. Point-of-purchase displays can include videotapes, music, and even interactive kiosks.

When a compact disc scratch removal device was first introduced, music retailers used attractive displays to show it in use and outline the benefits. The actual device was contained in a blister pack and hung on an attractive fixture in a high traffic area.

For a manufacturer of consumer products, offering selling fixtures to retail customers represents a useful low-cost advertising aid. Appropriate fixtures help the retailer use space more efficiently. As a manufacturer or distributor, a small business can buy large quantities of retail fixtures for its product and either give them away or resell them at cost, with a saving to the retailer. Good fixtures and displays help your salespeople, your channel partners, and your retail customers to sell more products.

Market research suggests that consumers make over half of all final buying decisions at the point of sale. For small and early-stage consumer goods firms, retail fixtures and displays represent an effective low-cost means for selling the product.

PACKAGING

A firm also communicates product information to users and potential users through packaging. A package must attract attention, arouse interest, create confidence in the purchase decision, and express the product's characteristics, and so packaging proves very important for the introduction of new consumer products. A package should reinforce, not detract from, the product image. For example, a quality product should not have a cheap-looking package. A price- and value-oriented product should not have a luxurious-looking package. The Bombay Sapphire gin bottle exudes status, while the Gordon's gin bottle connotes value.

In businesses that sell through self-service retailers, such as Home Depot, Target, Wal-Mart, Sam's, Costco, drugstores, or supermarkets, the consumer often buys the package, not the product. In many cases, the package must sell the product; it must create an emotional response that says "try me."

Many of these packaging objectives can be accomplished through the correct choice of shape, graphics, pictures, colors, and lettering. For example, bold colors such as red and black express strength and durability, while soft colors such as pastels express femininity and quality. Packaging of generic products is generally simple and plain with bold black letters on a white background reinforcing the value image.

Packaging need not be expensive to be attractive. A well-designed package often costs only a fraction more than a poorly designed one, and sells many more units. Once a year, test your packaging on a group of representative potential consumers. Their responses will indicate whether the packaging communicates the desired information and produces the desired reaction. Before changing a package, be sure to perform a thorough test-marketing procedure similar to a new product introduction.

Many smaller businesses and entrepreneurial ventures offering consumer products are able to establish brand awareness with retailers through trade shows, trade publications, direct mail, and e-mail. These firms then rely on the retailer to help them create brand recognition with consumers through packaging, point-of-purchase displays, statement stuffers, cooperative advertising, and presence in the store. An entrepreneurial start-up or small firm does not have the financial resources to create consumer awareness or brand recognition through national print or broadcast media. However, in conjunction with the right retailers, these firms can create consumer pull-through. A product's presence in the right stores can create brand awareness without the cost of national or regional ads. Consumers often recognize brand names because they see so many units of the product in so many respected stores.

SALES PROMOTION

Sales promotion includes such items as contests, premiums, gifts, rebates, customer entertainment, and special events. Sales promotion reinforces, and is reinforced by, salespeople, channel partners, advertising, e-commerce, packaging, and publicity in communicating product or service information and image to customers and prospects. Many entrepreneurial early-stage ventures give customers small gift items imprinted with the company's name, 800 number, e-mail address, and slogan. These trinkets may be given away at trade shows, seminars, workshops, or on a salesperson's customer visit. Choose items that are unusual, related in nature to the business, and meaningful to customers. For example, a bakery-supply firm gives out paper hats to be worn in the kitchen and hand mixing tools. The same firm has an annual open house for customers and prospects to taste new products.

Sales promotion has many forms. For example, a men's underwear company sent consumers a free brief in exchange for 10 of its labels, and announced this offer in cooperative newspaper advertising. A handkerchief firm offered a seventh "hanky" free if you bought six, and advertised it on their package. Most entrepreneurial ventures and smaller businesses use some form of inexpensive sales promotion, which proves especially effective for the introduction of new products or services.

CONTENT

Entrepreneurs can create an effective advertising message inexpensively by gaining the reader's, viewer's, or listener's attention, inviting interest, arousing needs and desires, and then finally suggesting goals and actions to satisfy those needs. In the message, you use appropriate symbols to represent needs, desires, goals, and products. You demand minimal attitude changes and utilize proven learning techniques. You must also consider the legal restrictions placed on advertising.

Effective advertising does not have to be expensive. I recently saw a three-inch, one-column black-and-white ad for an adult baseball camp that met all the above requirements. The ad showed a baseball with the following copy written on it in large type: "Have your baseball fantasies fulfilled." In smaller type it offered an opportunity to play baseball for a week with a vintage major league team. It told the dates, location, price, and how to call for more information.

Whereas many entrepreneurs and small business managers may feel that they do not have the financial or human resources to create a demand for their products or services, this chapter gave you the tools and knowledge to sell your products or services inexpensively. You can create demand for your products or services inexpensively by effectively using a Web site, e-mail, trade shows, press releases or publicity, trade publications, magazines, newspapers, radio, television, direct mail, diskettes, catalogs, brochures, statement stuffers, directories, fixtures, displays, packaging, and promotion. All these techniques for inexpensively creating demand apply equally to the old and new economies.

ENTREPRENEURS' MAJOR MISTAKES OR WEAKNESSES IN INEXPENSIVELY CREATING A DEMAND FOR PRODUCTS OR SERVICES

- Not fully leveraging available financial and human resources to properly support advertising, promotion, and publicity.
- Not measuring results and evaluating alternative means of advertising, publicity, and promotion.
- Not choosing proper media, e-commerce, e-mail, direct mail, trade shows, or publicity that reach the target customers or decision makers.
- Not using qualified outside professionals to assist in choosing media or preparing copy.
- Not asking suppliers, retailers, and channel partners for advertising allowances.

- Not using appropriate content to gain the receiver's attention, invite interest, and create a desire to purchase.

QUESTIONS AND EXERCISES

1. What is or will be your enterprise's advertising strategy, programs, and budget? How did you arrive at these decisions?
2. How will you measure the results of advertising, promotions, and publicity?
3. What are the alternative media and means for advertising, promotion, and publicity that reaches decision makers in your enterprise's target markets and at your target customers?
4. State your firm's trade show, e-mail, direct mail, and e-commerce marketing plan.
5. What trade shows does your firm plan to exhibit in and why?
6. How will you use symbols, words, pictures, and figures to sell your product or service?

CHAPTER 7

Proper Pricing

Correct pricing represents an important means of financing a start-up. An entrepreneur needs less bank debt and investor equity if the business generates enough cash internally to support growth and working capital needs. Entrepreneurs and small-business managers must price their product or service to maximize dollars of income over time. Few early-stage firms and start-ups fail from overpricing, but many fail from underpricing.

Many entrepreneurs and small-business owners underprice their product or service because they don't understand the pricing model. Because the enterprise is new or small they feel it must price below larger competitors. Often the smaller or newer enterprise excels at product innovation, customer intimacy, or operational excellence and should, therefore, price above competition. It takes courage to realize that price is part of the product or service image. In fact, a low competitive price does not enforce excellence or maximize dollars of margin or profit over time.

Most entrepreneurs and owners of small-businesses use either cost plus or "follow the looser" pricing. First, they estimate the cost of manufacturing their product or providing their service, then they add a fixed dollar amount or percentage to arrive at the price, which tells you the minimum, not the maximum, price. Often the fixed dollar amount or percentage reflects industry tradition or legacy. This cost information should be looked at last once you have determined what the market will bear, not first.

Other entrepreneurs and small-business owners price their products and services the same or below competition. Since competition often does not price correctly and certainly does not exactly replicate the features, benefits, and image of your product or service, this method proves ineffective. We call this "follow the loser," and it represents an entrepreneurial growth buster.

The entrepreneur and small-business owner should price their product or service at what the market will bear, based on the competitive advantage in terms of features, benefits, and image; the type customer; and the type product. This simple model reflects value to the customer and worth in the marketplace. Pricing becomes more complicated when a gatekeeper, middle person, retailer, or channel partner is involved. You might price to these people, but they set prices for the final customer, user, or consumer. Pricing becomes more complicated when you sell the product or service to the final customer but one of these other parties also charges the final customer for add-on services such as installation and training.

An entrepreneur or small-business owner must also understand transactional pricing (net versus list price), the waterfall effect (discounts, terms, and allowances), and how to merchandise the price. Proper pricing involves list prices, discounts or deductions for various activities, and then a net or transactional price. Although dollars of profit or margin are based on the net or transactional price, the gross price and the rationale for moving from gross to net price affects the customer's buying decision.

Another important issue involves who should approve off-price selling: the controller, owner, salesperson, or sales manager? Should off-price selling be part of the merchandising plan for modified rebuy customers? Since these repeat customers purchase the same products or services over and over again, negotiating and transactional pricing are part of the sales process.

UNDERSTANDING THE GOALS OR OBJECTIVES OF PRICING

The entrepreneur or small-business owner must first set the goals or objectives of pricing, which may partially depend on the business's stage of development; early stage, growth, maturity, or latter stage. Since prices are set for each product or service, the goals may also depend on the product's or service's stage of development: introduction, growth, maturity, or decline. Pricing goals will change over time as the business and products or services mature, as new products or services are introduced, and as the competitive landscape changes.

Pricing goals include:

- Maximizing revenues over time
- Building market share
- Maximizing dollars of contribution margin over time
- Maximizing unit sales to minimize unit costs
- Maximizing profits as a percentage of revenues

- Keeping key employees and key suppliers happy
- Protecting licenses, patents, and trademarks
- Combinations of the above

If the entrepreneur's goals involve maximizing revenues or building market share, which is typical of early-stage businesses and new products or services, then a lower penetration price is called for. Often equity investors push this philosophy on start-ups because exit values become based on revenue, not profit growth. Keep in mind that once you start with penetration pricing it is difficult to sell the same customer the same product or service at a higher price. It is much easier to start with skim (higher) pricing and then lower the transactional price with various discounts or deductions.

Pharmaceutical firms and some computer hardware firms like Compaq and Dell let market share gains drive marketing strategy, especially pricing. Telco firms like MCI World Com, Sprint, or Verizon strive to maximize revenues because their costs of transmission are fixed and their excess capacity is high. This changes depending on business conditions.

Entrepreneurial enterprises and smaller firms must realize that they have limited capacity. At some point they run out of the people, equipment, space, funds, or working capital to grow. Most businesses have a clearly defined capacity, a certain number of shots at the marketplace.

These same enterprises and firms must also realize a pricing window or range exists for their products or services, whether for storm windows, consulting services, or bakery products. Most product or services can be priced plus or minus 5 or 10 percent of a certain price point.

Once the entrepreneur accepts these two assumptions, limited capacity and a pricing range, the question becomes realizing capacity constraints: At what price point within the range can you maximize dollars of contribution margin or profit over time? Raising prices this year to harvest a short-term gain at the expense of next year's unit volume does not meet the objective. The entrepreneur must think in terms of several years, not just one.

In industries such as semiconductors or corrugated boxes, with large fixed costs, the pricing goal might reflect maximizing unit sales to minimize unit costs. For example, Intel continually lowers prices to increase unit sales, which drives down unit costs and minimizes competition. Such pricing creates a formidable competitive barrier to entry, but is not practical for a firm without economies of scale.

The goal of some firms that sell luxury consumer goods or specialized business products is to maximize profits as a percentage of revenues, not to maximize dollars of profit. Such firms price high and use skim-pricing techniques.

Distributors often use penetration pricing and give customers rewards for higher volumes because they have contracts with their suppliers that require minimum volumes to keep the distributorship. Also, smaller firms that are dependent on a few key commission sales-people will price very competitively to retain these key people.

When firms have patents expiring and they expect new competi-tors, they create barriers to entry by lowering prices. This might also happen in anticipation of a new technology, a new product or service, or a new competitor from overseas.

As an entrepreneur or small-business manager you must have a valid objective, strategy, or goal for pricing that reinforces your over-all marketing strategy, and you must understand the rationale for using it. Strategy drives tactics and structure.

PRICING AT WHAT THE MARKET WILL BEAR

Let's assume we have decided the pricing objective of our early-stage firm or small-business is to maximize dollars of margin or profit over time. Let's assume we understand our capacity constraints and pricing zones. How do we determine what the market will bear, value to the customer, worth in the market, or our pricing power? Because business is a dynamic process and the future is a moving target, prices must be reviewed each year to reflect new competition and new customers.

Ask yourself at what price point is an increase in dollars of profit totally offset by reduced volume? That is the price you want to be at. A subcontract assembler of printer circuit boards found it could raise prices by 10 percent on a particular job with no effect on unit volume. As prices rose above 10 percent, unit volume decreased, but until prices were raised 25 percent, dollars of profit continued to increase. Once unit prices were raised 25 percent on this particular printed circuit assembly job, the customer had shifted 50 percent of their volume to another supplier.

At $1.00 a board on this job the subcontractor was breaking even and volume was 10,000 units a week. At $1.10 a board the subcon-tractor continued to assemble 10,000 units a week for this customer, creating $11,000 of revenue, but generating a $1000 pretax margin. At $1.15 a board, volume on this job dropped to 8000 units, revenue was $9200, but profits rose to $1200 (15 cents × 8000 units). The company chose to produce fewer units because of labor constraints but make more dollars of profit. At $1.20 a board, volume on this job dropped to 7000 units, with $8400 of revenue, but profit rose again to $1400 (20 cents × 7000 units). However, because of fixed costs, fewer units were starting to increase the cost per unit. At $1.25 a board, volume dropped to 5000 units, with $6250 of revenue, and dollars of profit on this job dropped to $1250.

As you can see, per unit dollars of marginal revenue created by price increases go right to the bottom line, right to profit. An increase in price results in few cost increases, and so the marginal revenues per unit or in total dollars resulting from the price increase flow directly to profits and cash flow, EBIT or EBITDA (earnings before income taxes or earnings before interest, taxes, depreciation, and amortization).

The issue then becomes how sensitive is unit volume to price. If the entrepreneur raises prices by 5 percent, 10 percent, 15 percent, or 25 percent, how much will unit volume decrease, if at all, and at what point does the decrease in volume totally offset the marginal dollars of profit generated by the price increase?

An entrepreneur or small-business owner can estimate buyer response to price increases from focus groups, market research, and test marketing. You might contact a group of customers and prospects asking for their response. You might do a blind telephone survey, or you might charge different prices to different equivalent customers, and monitor results. In each of these situations, the goal is to estimate the probable units purchased as pricing changes.

Entrepreneurial enterprises and small-businesses have limited human and financial resources. They can't afford big mistakes and need models or methodologies to help measure risk versus reward. The reward of a price increase is more dollars of margin. The risk is lower unit volume. What we search for is the pricing and unit mix that maximizes dollars of margin over time. Increasing prices and dollars of margin this year, only to lose the dollars of margin next year, does not meet this objective.

The pricing model or methodology involves running spreadsheets on probable unit and dollar outcomes of various prices. At various price points within our pricing range, what are the dollars of contribution margin resulting from various unit sales levels?

The model or methodology involves estimating unit sales at various price points based on:

- Your product's or service's competitive advantage in features, benefits, and image. What is the customer's value-added? Can you measure it? Can you prove it? What are the customer's alternative costs?
- The type of customer you sell: leader or follower.
- The type product or service you sell: homogeneous or heterogeneous.

COMPETITIVE ADVANTAGE IN TERMS OF FEATURES, BENEFITS, AND IMAGE

To correctly price each product or service, the entrepreneur or small-business owner must understand its competitive advantages in features, benefits, and image. For each product or service is it better, worse, or the same than competition in features, benefits, and image? If a competitive advantage exists, can you prove it to the customer through demonstrating value-added benefits or alternative costs? For a B2B product or service can you quantify in dollars its ability to lower customers' costs, raise revenues, or decrease working capital and capital expenditure requirements? For a B2C product or service can you demonstrate how it saves consumers time, increases their income, or enhances their image?

If you have a competitive advantage in features, benefits, image, alternative costs, and value-added propositions, you should attempt to price at a premium to competitors without these advantages. As you will see later in this chapter, depending on the type of product or service and the type of customer, you may or may not be able to do this. If you do not have a competitive advantage in features, benefits, and image, but are equivalent to competition, attempt to price at a premium to competition but be willing to accept the same price. Entrepreneurs and small-business owners need a premium price mindset from which to benchmark.

If your product or service does not have a competitive advantage, attempt to create one by wrapping an additional service around the present offering. For example, your investment advisory service might issue monthly client statements with graphics, benchmarking the client's portfolio against industry indexes. Your teleconferencing service might offer seminars on how to conduct teleconferences. Your software firm might offer training and installation for users.

If your product or service is inferior to the competition in features, benefits, and image, attempt to price at a level equal to competition, but be willing to accept a lower price, realizing price is part of the image. Many early-stage and smaller firms target lower-priced, lower-quality market segments. As discussed previously, analyze dollars of margin generated at various price points in your pricing zone.

In analyzing competitive advantage revisit the competitive grid discussed in Chapters 4 and 5 under strategic differentiation and sales force training. The grid lists competitors across the top and competitive issues down the side. It illustrates how customers choose among vendors and how competitors compare in terms of features, benefits, and image. Realize that some features and benefits are expected and demanded by customers (table stakes to be seriously considered), but others are differentiators. A city messenger service must deliver within three hours to be seriously considered by clients, but one with a Web site for tracing shipments has a differentiator. A limousine service must pick people up at the appointed time, but the ability to make reservations on-line is a differentiator.

Proper pricing might also involve looking at the total cost (or alternative cost) of the process or system your product or service is part of. The material or ingredient costs of frozen dough to make a loaf of bread exceeds the cost of flour and other basic ingredients to make bread from scratch. But when the baker considers that the frozen dough significantly lowers his labor costs, the total cost of a loaf may be less using the frozen product. This cost savings should be reflected in the frozen product's price.

Alternative costs, such as in the bread-making example, should be considered in setting prices. Another example of alternative costs would be the services offered by an on-line hiring site. Its fees should reflect the time it saves the user, the alternative cost of using a recruiter, and the quality of respondents.

CUSTOMER TYPE

In setting prices, the entrepreneur or small-business owner must next look at whether the customer will pay a premium price for a competitive advantage in features, benefits, and image. This depends on the type of customer buying the product or service and the type of product or service being offered.

Leaders and early adopters, businesses and consumers who want the newest and the best and are willing to pay for it, will pay a premium price for a competitive advantage or for value-added benefits. Generally, these are successful businesses and wealthy individuals. Leaders have arrived and early adopters want to arrive so they mimic the leader's buying habits. Microsoft, Disney, General Electric, Citibank, and IBM might be considered leaders while Adobe, Sycamore, Siebel, and JDS Uniphase might be considered early adopters. An established, older successful businessperson, physician, or attorney might be considered a leader, while a younger, newly successful businessperson, physician, or attorney might be considered an early adopter. These early adopters want to have the leaders' lifestyles as soon as they can afford it.

The entrepreneur and small-business manager must look at their target customers. Are they leaders and early adopters who will pay a premium price for a competitive advantage or are they early majority who look for value, late majority who look for utility, or laggards who only purchase for replacement purposes?

Consumers who are leaders shop at specialty stores, early adopters at department stores, early majority at chain stores, late majority at mass merchants, and laggards at secondhand stores. Early- and late-majority businesses are not willing to pay a premium price for a competitive advantage. Their business model involves buying on price and utility. Many entrepreneurial and early-stage firms sell to more than one type of customer and price accordingly.

A Boston genomics start-up sold similar sequencing and annotation services to university labs and large pharmaceutical firms at very different prices, which only partially reflected the services offered. They priced at what the market would bear, based on customer type, which helped to finance their business.

A Los Angeles neckwear manufacturer offers a slightly better grade tie line at a considerably higher price to a national chain of better specialty stores than it offers to independent menswear retailers in small towns. The national chain of better specialty stores is a leader, while small-town mom-and-pop independents represent early and late majority.

Just as entrepreneurs should search for new ways to differentiate their product or service, add value, and create a competitive advantage, they also should search for ways to target early adopters and leader market segments and customers. All these techniques allow the entrepreneur to charge a premium price. The Boston genomics firm initially sold to university labs but then targeted large pharmaceuticals. The Los Angeles neckwear manufacturer initially sold menswear retailers in smaller towns, but then targeted upscale national clothing chains.

On the other hand, your competitive advantage may be operational efficiency, like Southwest Airlines, which allows you to price below competition, drive unit volume, and spread large fixed costs. In such a situation you target early- and late-majority customers and laggards, who buy on value, utility, and replacement, which your low prices reflect.

TYPE OF PRODUCT OR SERVICE

In setting prices, the entrepreneur and small-business owner must look at whether the customer will pay a premium price for a competitive advantage in features, benefits, and image. This depends on not only the type of customer buying the product (leader, early adopter, early or late majority, or laggard) but the type of product or service being offered. Leaders and early adopters are willing to pay a premium price for a competitive advantage for heterogeneous and specialty, or easy-to-differentiate products or services. Heterogeneous products or services include such categories as furniture, apparel, legal and consulting services, dentists, and fiberoptics. Specialty products or services have limited availability and must be sought out. Some examples are designer shoes, or attorneys specializing in public offerings or environmental issues, and chip sets for M3 cellular phones.

On the other hand, homogeneous products or services, including staples and commodities, do not command a premium price over time for competitive advantages in features, benefits, and image regardless of the type of customer. Airlines and long-distance phone services vary in terms of reliability, features, convenience, and comfort, but the best of class cannot charge a premium price over time because the product is homogeneous. Diecastings and injection molding, both homogeneous products, are sold by the pound, even though some shops do better work than others. Customers perceive homogeneous products or services as difficult to differentiate.

Entrepreneurs who innovate and take advantage of change look for opportunities to move products or services from homogeneous to heterogeneous to create an opportunity to charge a premium price for a competitive advantage. Adding an enhancement to a product or service offers one opportunity; branding, advertising, and licensing offer others.

For example, a North Carolina knitting mill licenses a designer's brand name for its underwear, which creates a competitive advantage in image. The unbranded underwear is sold to chain stores at half the price of the branded designer underwear, which is sold to specialty stores. A total quality management training company adds on-line continual testing for attendees and raises training prices 10 percent. Look for ways to alter homogeneous products and services so that they become more heterogeneous.

Products and services move from one category to another over their life cycle (introduction, growth, maturity, and decline). Personal computers and printers started out as heterogeneous products with pricing power, but within 10 years they had been commoditized and had lost any pricing power.

Many products or services represent combinations of these types. Men's hosiery may be homogeneous (hard to differentiate) as a class, but natural fiber and patterned hose are heterogeneous (easy to differentiate). Daytime pharmacies are homogeneous, but all-night pharmacies are heterogeneous. Genomics sequencing has become commoditized, which makes it very homogeneous, but annotation, analysis, and interpretation of these data have not.

In Raleigh-Durham, a local university mathematics program became the basis for a start-up selling experiential reform mathematics textbooks to grades one through five. Pricing represented an important decision closely tied to targeting and product development. The entrepreneur felt her reform mathematics program was superior to anything on the market, but all her competitors made the same claim. She decided to prove and quantify the competitive advantage using higher student test scores. She decided to target private schools, which are leaders and early adopters. She took her original hardcover textbook, the industry standard, and replaced it with software and soft-cover, disposable workbooks, thus creating a heterogeneous highly dif-ferentiated product. It worked. Revenues increase from $200,000 in year one to $15 million in year eight, and pretax profit runs at 20 per-cent of revenues. In year nine, the reform mathematics textbook firm was purchased by an international publishing firm.

In Chicago, a group of computer or software programmers left a large New York Stock Exchange company to start a computer consult-ing service. They hired full-time and contract programmers to work on a variety of client problems. Many smaller firms wish to farm this type of work out. They carefully recruited their technical staff and looked for people who could work on many platforms. The market for con-tract programming and computer consulting services was growing but the start-up couldn't decide what segment to target, how to harvest a premium price, or how to differentiate themselves. They decided to target midsized and smaller firms because competition is less and the need greater, but these target firms are early or late majority and won't pay a premium price for the start-up's superior services and highly compensated personnel. The start-up had no pricing power with cus-tomers but also had little cost control over expensive programmers providing the services. Customers view programming as a commodity, as a necessary evil. The company reached $2 million of annual rev-enues but stagnated there and generated negative cash flow until it was liquidated.

THE WATERFALL EFFECT: TRANSACTIONAL PRICING

Many entrepreneurs confuse gross or list prices with net prices or transactional prices. When costing products or services and analyz-ing margins, small-business owners often look only at the list price, not the actual transactional price. Most firms, matured or early-stage, will offer payment terms, freight and advertising allowances, and quantity discounts, often based on industry tradition. These items create the waterfall between list and net or transactional prices.

If such allowances, terms, and discounts are expected, then the small-business manager must build them into his or her gross or list price like any other cost. The list price must be increased by 2, 5, or 10 percent to reflect these costs, which we call allowances, terms, and dis-counts. If you do not gross prices up to reflect this, you will significantly decrease dollars of profit margin and underprice the product or service. Your salespeople and/or channel partners must also understand the importance of transactional pricing and the waterfall effect on pocket pricing.

If the entrepreneur or small-business manager offers a product or service that represents a modified rebuy; negotiating discounts, allowance, and terms will probably be part of buyer behavior. The buyer expects to negotiate and receive concessions so build that into the price. If your salespeople call on the same accounts each week, month, or quarter to place new products or services but also get reorders on existing products or services, you are involved in a modified rebuy.

Salespeople and channel partners need to be trained in negotiating prices, terms, allowances, and discounts. They need to understand that different transactional prices can be negotiated for different types of customers, buying different types of products and services with different competitive advantages. In other words, salespeople and channel partners must be trained in the pricing model.

A regional telco start-up resells bulk purchases of long-distance time and multiuser conference calls to small- and medium-sized financial services firms. The product or service is homogeneous, customers are not leaders or early adopters, and the company has few sustainable competitive advantages besides positive relationships with customer decision makers. Direct salespeople and telesales people contact customers and prospects monthly to open new accounts, add services, and renew contracts. Salespeople are given a pricing window based on list prices. Depending on the hours used, length of contract, and mix of services sold, direct and telesales people may discount list price up to 10 percent. Sales training emphasizes negotiating skills and differential pricing that reflects the type of customer or type of product, competitive advantage, and image. Salespeople receive a small base salary plus 30 percent of gross margin on sales they generate. List prices are set 7 percent above expected transactional prices, because in this industry decision makers want to negotiate. The salesperson's job is to satisfy the buyer's need to "get a deal," the customer's need for appropriate economical phone services, his or her need for equitable compensation, and the regional telco's need to make money.

To create happy employees and satisfied customers, salespeople must have the authority to make certain customer-related decisions on the spot concerning customized services and pricing. However, once these decisions move outside certain predetermined parameters they require management approval. This is necessary to control margins and reflect the proper image. Once customers and prospects know salespeople and channel partners can negotiate, they will put pressure on them for concessions. Once customers and prospects know salespeople can negotiate, but only up to a certain point, the pressure mitigates, ranges emerge, and respect for the vendor improves. Larger customers or prospects often perceive start-ups, early-stage and smaller businesses as hungry for their business and willing to give all sorts of concessions. Not tiering control over concessions to various levels of management encourages larger firms to always seek better terms. This destroys the entrepreneur's image and margins.

The regional telco in our example does customize certain services and give discounts in excess of 10 percent to a few large users, but these contracts must be negotiated by a sales manager and approved by a corporate officer. Many larger users know that they can get these discounts but that they must go through the proper channels. For smaller users this process creates a firewall and prevents them from asking for too much.

DIFFERENTIAL PRICING WITHIN A BAND OR RANGE.

The pricing model indicates what price the market will bear; value to the customer, based on the product's or service's competitive advantage in features, benefits, and image; type of customer and type of product. For the entrepreneur, early-stage, or small-business manager this means different prices relative to costs and margins for different products, markets, and even customers. This is necessary to maximize dollars of profit or margin over time.

Airlines perform differential pricing and make prices hard to compare by offering many alternative prices depending on days of week, length of stay, and when a reservation is booked. It costs travelers more to fly on weekdays, not including a weekend stay, from Chicago to Cedar Rapids, Iowa, in March than from Chicago to Paris with a Saturday layover. In June the prices are equal. Similarly, prices for guaranteed overnight package delivery vary depending on whether you drop the package off or have it picked up, whether it arrives next day before 10 a.m., or before 2 p.m., and whether it is second-day or first-day service. These represent examples of differential prices for different market segments, products or services, and customer types.

Consult your attorney for legal issues relating to restraint of trade and price discrimination, but do consider differential pricing. Often differential pricing is rationalized based on volume or activity, so the entrepreneur might give a price discount or rebate based on quantity purchased or will-call versus delivery. For example, a distributor allows a discount for both will-call and prompt payment. However, ultimately entrepreneurs must consider differential pricing based on the customer's willingness to pay and perceived value as illustrated in the airline and overnight delivery service examples.

A firm importing Christmas ornaments and lights takes a smaller markup on light sets sold to chain stores than on hand-painted ornaments sold to department stores. The light sets are homogeneous products sold to early- or late-majority customers and have few competitive advantages. The hand-painted ornaments are heterogeneous products sold to leaders and early adopters and have many competitive advantages.

A small, temporary-help service charges different rates for clericals working in large corporate offices versus smaller organizations. The firm has much higher margins on heterogeneous services such as desktop computer operators and home health care providers than on homogeneous services such as warehouse workers. The firm allows salespeople more leeway in pricing against local competitors than against national or regional competitors.

MAKING PRICE HARD TO COMPARE

Entrepreneurs and small-business managers want to make their prices hard to compare by offering bundling, modules, alternative prices, and possibly charging separately for support services and warranties. For example, you can buy the computer, terminal, printer, and software independently or bundle it in various configurations at various prices. On high-density data storage equipment you can include installation, warranties, training, and service in the price, charge for each service, or charge for some separately. Customers like choices, so offer alternatives. Make pricing difficult to compare without making it difficult to understand.

LOOK AT COSTS AND MARGINS LAST

Entrepreneurs must price at what the market will not bear cost plus. What the market will bear represents the maximum price, the correct price to maximize dollars of contribution margin over time. Cost plus represents the minimum acceptable price to meet your minimum margin requirements.

Once the entrepreneur has run the model and priced at what the market will bear based on competitive advantage, type of customer, and type of product, then it is time to compare this price to appropriate costs and see if minimum margins are being met. Here is an example.

A small, family-owned men's hosiery manufacturer introduced a new nylon-acrylic blend midlength sock that has a color-coded top. This allows consumers to match solid color pairs after washing and find the appropriate dark color (black, brown, navy) in their dresser drawer. Solid brown hose contain a tan top, black a red top, navy a light blue top and so on.

This style hose is clearly heterogeneous and easy to differentiate for the consumer. It contains competitive advantages in ease of use. The hosiery firm decided to offer the color-coded top in their branded line, which is sold to leaders and early adopters through department and specialty stores. The hosiery company had transformed a homogeneous product into a heterogeneous one by adding the color top.

Nylon-acrylic blend solid-color midlength hose, without the color identification feature or benefit sell for $3.50 at retail and $1.75 at wholesale to the department and specialty stores. Because customers are leaders and early adopters and the color-top product is heterogeneous with value-added competitive advantages, the owner decided to price the color identification style at $4.00 retail and $2.00 wholesale.

Next, the owner analyzes the cost of manufacturing this style: material, labor, and factory overhead. To analyze the cost of providing a service, you would primarily calculate the labor involved. The cost of manufacturing this style totals $1.10, creating a gross margin of 90 cents or 45 percent. In order to breakeven, the owner knows each style in the line must produce at least a 30 percent gross margin. To earn a reasonable pretax profit, each style in the line must produce a 35 percent gross margin. The 45 percent gross margin far exceeds this 35 percent threshold, but the $4.00 retail price reflects value in the marketplace and so the owner decides to price the color top style at $4.00 retail and $2.00 wholesale, allowing the retailer a 50 percent markup. Should the hosiery firm's gross margin fall below the 35 percent level on a particular style, the entrepreneur could attempt to sell it at a higher wholesale or retail price, drop the style, or attempt to lower its cost.

If lowering the price would increase unit volume, then that possibility should also be considered. However, will increased unit volume at lower prices actually increase or decrease dollars of gross margin? In industries with high fixed costs and high capacity this may be the case. An empty airplane or theater seat, or an unused telephone line produce no revenue or margin, just fixed costs.

When setting prices for an entire line or just for one item in that line, the entrepreneur must run a spreadsheet on expected unit and dollar results at various pricing levels. For each pricing level, what are the expected best and worst case unit results and how will that impact dollars of gross margin over time. As you can see, it is necessary to run the pricing model first and then run the numbers to check and fine-tune the results.

CORPORATE STRATEGY

Many small and early-stage companies do not generate sufficient profits to provide the necessary working capital or cash flow for growth. To remedy this, management or the entrepreneur may apply the profit-maximizing technique used for pricing each product or service to create a basic corporate strategy. That is, he or she can use these same techniques to evaluate the effect of major changes in pricing strategy and/or cost cutting on overall corporate profits.

Let us say your firm earns a pretax profit of $65,000 on annual sales of $1,750,000. The $65,000 is not sufficient to buy new equipment and seasonally pay off your term loan. However, you require a pretax profit of $165,000 to accomplish these objectives. You need to increase profits by $100,000. You could do so by either increasing unit sales, increasing prices, lowering costs, or some combination of the three.

The firm's present gross margin after labor, materials, and factory overhead expense is $612,500, or 35 percent of net sales; and selling, general, and administrative (SG&A) expense is $547,500, or 31 percent of net sales, leaving a pretax profit of $65,000, or 4 percent of net sales. By applying pricing techniques to this situation, you determine that unit sales would have to increase approximately $300,000, or 17 percent, to generate another $100,000 of profit ($300,000 times the gross margin percentage of 35 percent equals $105,000, minus $5000 for increased SG&A, equals $100,000). On the other hand, assuming no decrease in unit volume, prices would only have to be raised $100,000, or 6 percent, or costs lowered by $100,000, to increase profits to $165,000. Lower costs could be obtained by using less material, by using labor more efficiently, by subcontracting certain work, by lowering factory overhead, or by reducing SG&A expense. Prices could be increased selectively, across the board, discounts and allowances discontinued, or some combination of these.

After considerable study, you decide that pretax profits can best be increased $100,000 by combining a 6 percent general price increase with a $35,000 cost decrease. You estimate that the 6 percent price increase will cause a 6 percent decrease in unit sales volume, but still result in an additional $65,000 of profit. The remaining $35,000 of profit can be generated by reducing travel and entertainment expenses $10,000; advertising, $10,000; eliminating temporary clerical help, $7000; and reducing overtime, $8000. You feel that this plan contains a higher probability of success than trying to increase unit sales.

Highly profitable firms use this same strategy to determine how to maximize company profits. In other words, on a corporate basis, what reasonable combination of overall unit volume, prices, and costs will maximize dollars of profits over time? Your firm, for example, might generate greater profits with higher prices and lower unit volume.

PRICE INCREASES

Most customers dislike price increases, whether the item is industrial fasteners, shirts, testing equipment, or freight rates. Many customers view price increases as a reason to reexamine the product or service relative to competition and to consider a change. Because of this, you must correctly merchandise price increases taking into account appropriate buyer behavior.

For commodities and modified rebuy products or services, announce price increases in advance, and allow customers a limited time to purchase at the old price. This dulls the negative impact of a price increase, shows customers that you care about their well-being, and if they purchase substantial quantities at the old price, it assures that they will continue as customers.

If possible, have field salespeople announce and explain price increases to their customers rather than management sending out an impersonal letter to each account. This personalizes the message. All these suggestions also enhance your human, caring, small-company, early-stage image.

Also, note that increasing prices for the entire line by, say, 10 percent or $20 an item generally draws more attention and creates more customer animosity than increasing prices selectively. Selective item-by-item or model-by-model increases connote a certain sophistication and necessity, and are less noticed. Selective increases suggest that management has analyzed the situation, thought it out, and has found these changes necessary. Across-the-board increases suggest that you decided in a hallway conference that it was time to raise prices again.

LEGAL ASPECTS OF PRICING

This chapter has discussed the many considerations necessary to maximize dollars of profit over time through correct pricing. In order to accomplish this, you must also understand the legal restrictions involved in pricing.

The Sherman Act of 1890 prohibits conspiracies in restraint of trade. The Clayton Act of 1914 prohibits practices that substantially lessen competition. Any concerted action by competitors, or any unfair action by a single company that has the result of limiting competition, is presumed to be an unreasonable restraint on commerce and is thus illegal.

All types of formal or informal agreements among competitors to set prices or to maintain uniform profit margins are illegal. Even informally exchanging price information with competitors at a trade association meeting or over cocktails has been considered a violation. If you find yourself in such a situation, change the conversation or leave.

The Robinson-Patman Act of 1936 prohibits discrimination in price, service, and facilities by a seller in the sale of like grade and quality to two or more buyers. Price discrimination consists of charging different prices to different customers for products or services of like kind and quality. Everything else being equal, which represents the key phrase, the same types of customer should pay the same price for the same product or service.

Although it is illegal to discriminate in price among different purchasers of the same quality goods if such price discrimination injures a competitor, a firm can lower prices to meet competition if this is done without meaning to eliminate a competitor. Price includes terms, rebates, coupons, discounts, promotions, and advertising and freight allowances.

For example, it is illegal to sell at lower prices in one territory than another for the purpose of eliminating a competitor. It is also illegal to sell chain stores or large users at one price and specialty stores or small users at another, unless you can demonstrate a cost saving or a difference. If you offer a 3 percent advertising allowance and 5 percent terms with prepaid freight to Sam's Club, you most likely will have to offer it to smaller accounts, and certainly to comparable accounts such as Costco. If you offer a 20 percent–off promotion on 20 percent of the previous year's unit purchases to Bloomingdale's, you probably must offer the same arrangement to a specialty store, and certainly must offer the same arrangement to Macy's. If you give Standard Oil a 5 percent year-end rebate based on dollar volume, you probably must give the same rebate to smaller customers, and certainly to Mobil.

Larger firms sometimes use their size to coerce smaller firms into giving them preferential prices, terms, rebates, discounts, and allowances. Their action is generally considered illegal, as is yours if you comply. In such situations, you must temper business judgment with legal considerations, and certainly should consult an attorney.

None of these legal considerations eliminate the need for differential pricing discussed earlier in this chapter. But these legal considerations require the entrepreneur to have an attorney who can correctly advise him or her on the legal restrictions involved in industry pricing issues.

Correct pricing represents a key ingredient for entrepreneurial success. Following the model described in this chapter will help you price your product or service to maximize dollars of income over time.

ENTREPRENEURS' MAJOR MISTAKES OR WEAKNESSES IN PROPER PRICING

- Pricing based on cost plus or "follow the competition."
- Not understanding the goals or objectives of pricing for your enterprise.
- Not understanding transactional pricing, the waterfall effect, or the difference between net versus gross prices.
- Not assigning responsibility for off-price selling to the proper person.
- Not pricing based on value to the customer, what the market will bear, or alternative costs.
- Not being able to quantify how your enterprise's products or services increase customers' revenues, reduce customers' costs, or lower working capital and capital expenditure needs.
- Not pricing based on competitive advantage in features, benefits, and image, the type of customer, and the type of product.
- Not pricing to maximize dollars of income over time.
- Not realizing that each product or service has a pricing range and limited capacity.
- Not merchandising the price and any changes in price.
- Not understanding your industry's barriers to entry and customers' switching costs.
- Not reevaluating prices annually.
- Not seeking expert legal advice on differential pricing.

QUESTIONS AND EXERCISES

1. What methodology does or will your new enterprise or small-business use to price products and services?
2. How does your business's products or services compare to the competition's in features, benefits, and image?
3. What type of customer buys your enterprise's products or services: leaders, early adopters, early or late majority, or laggards?

4. What is the contribution margin in dollars and as a percentage of the selling price for each of your firm's products or services?

5. What are your industry's barriers to entry and your customers' switching costs?

6. What discounts, terms, and allowances separate gross from net prices at your firm?

7. What type of product or service does your enterprise sell—heterogeneous, homogeneous, specialty, commodity, or emergency?

8. For each product or service, what is its pricing range or zone?

PART THREE

BUSINESS
DEVELOPMENT

CHAPTER 8

Buying an Existing Business

In Chapter 1 we said three basic ways exist for you to become an entrepreneur:

1. Buy an existing business, manage it, build it, and possibly someday sell it.
2. Start a new business by developing and introducing a new product or service.
3. Franchise someone else's idea or clone a successful business model.

Each of these three alternatives has different advantages and disadvantages, different merits, rewards, and risks. This chapter deals with buying an existing business and Chapter 9 deals with the development and introduction of new products. Each year, more than 500,000 companies are sold and 90 percent of those have values less than $5 million. The average sale price of these companies is less than $200,000, which most entrepreneurs can afford.

REWARDS AND RISKS OF BUYING AN EXISTING BUSINESS

The entrepreneur who starts a business spends considerable time, money, and effort building an organization and developing an effective operation. The buyer of an existing business will have an operation in place (suppliers, employees, equipment) and thus can avoid some of a new venture's risks and challenges. The team, operations, and customers already exist. In some ways, it proves easier to make changes to existing operations than to start firms from scratch. With a start-up, it typically takes two or three years to reach the break-even or cash neutral point, and another two to three years to become stable and successful. With an existing business, the entrepreneur typically starts with some profits and positive cash flow. Sixty percent of all new ventures fail within the first two years of their existence.

Generally, you can more accurately and more easily assess the risks of buying an existing business than you can of starting a new enterprise. A buyer has more and better information on both the operating characteristics of a going concern and its established market than the entrepreneur would have with a start-up enterprise. Market speculation and uncertainty in sales projections are reduced because the business already has a track record. Also, the condition of the plant and equipment, if any, is known.

Another compelling reason for buying an existing business lies in available financing and trade credit. Since existing businesses have assets and lines of credit, and since sellers often will take payment over time, less total equity investment is required. Bankers, other lenders, and new outside investors feel more comfortable lending to or investing in an established business with a track record.

Also, when buying an existing business, the entrepreneur can immediately start drawing a salary, often equal to that earned by the previous owner. In a start-up, the entrepreneur will earn far less, if anything, for the first several years.

To reduce the risk of failure and increase the probability of success, the buyer of an existing business, or for that matter the founder of a start-up, should have many years of experience working in that industry. Small-business and start-up experience also proves helpful. However, in a buyout the entrepreneur will also receive training from the seller, especially if a portion of the purchase price is performance-based or paid over time. The previous owner brings valuable experience to the enterprise, and valuable strategic and tactical knowledge to the new owner.

Lastly, fixed assets can be purchased for less in a buyout than they can in a start-up. For a start-up, machinery and equipment will probably be purchased new, but in a buyout they will be purchased at their depreciated or economic value. This requires less of the entrepreneur's capital.

Disadvantages of buying an existing business could include an inflated purchase price reflecting unwarranted goodwill or a faulty business model for producing long-term profits or positive cash flow. Disadvantages might also involve buying someone else's problem. Possibly the market has peaked: for cyclical businesses perhaps a downswing will begin shortly, a new competitor has emerged, or the technology is changing. Possibly the previous owner may have created ill will. The business may look great on the surface, but customers, suppliers, creditors, or employees may have extremely negative feelings about it.

Another disadvantage may reflect trying to change present employees' bad habits. Some workers may have a difficult time adapting to the new owner's management style and vision for the company. Often it is easier to plan for change than to implement it. Previous managers may have kept marginal employees because they were close friends.

These disadvantages can be avoided by using the evaluation methodology described in this chapter. Remember, the buyer purchases the future, the seller sells the past, unless you can get a lower purchase price by reversing the two.

A final disadvantage reflects the risk of the purchase not occurring. After you have invested considerable funds and time in due diligence, the seller backs out. He or she decides not to sell the business after all or to sell it to a family member. Signing letters of intent and buy-sell agreements can mitigate this risk.

Buying a business involves four steps:

1. Planning your approach and targeting the type business you wish to purchase.
2. Finding available businesses to purchase through appropriate sources.
3. Using an appropriate filter or methodology to evaluate whether you want to buy that business.
4. Negotiating the terms and price for the purchase.

PLANNING YOUR APPROACH AND TARGETING

Based on your skills, knowledge, experience, and contacts, what value can you add to a business you might purchase? Do you bring knowledge of sales or finance, industry experience, or contacts for debt and equity funding? What types of businesses can most benefit from your skills, knowledge, experience, and contacts? Start your search by targeting these industries.

Then decide where you would like to live: Reno or Richmond, Atlanta or Albuquerque, Mississippi or Minneapolis? Contact industry trade publications and associations for lists of appropriate target businesses in these areas. Also contact the state, region, county, and city chambers of commerce for similar industry lists.

After reviewing the list, eliminate the larger well-known publicly owned businesses and obtain credit reports and general business information on the remainder. The credit report which may be hard copy, on-line, or on a CD ROM, will tell you approximate annual revenues, management names and ages, owner's names, type of business, and payment records. Information on individual firms can also be found on-line at OneSource Information Services, Inc. (www.onesource.com) and Zapodata (www.zapodata.com). These sources provide general business descriptions, annual revenues, location, key executives, contact information, and other data buyers can use to screen candidates. From this information decide which firms seem most appealing and contact them (if possible, through a referral).

Planning also involves locating potential equity investors and working capital financing. Any legitimate seller will want information on the entrepreneur's ability to finance a purchase. Refer to Chapter 2 on financing for details.

Talk to equity investors with experience in that target industry and/or in buyouts. This will save time and provide you with valuable information. Determine their interest and potential dollar commitment. Remember they are investing in you.

Determine what funds you will invest in the buyout and what percentage ownership you desire. Outside investors, banks, and the seller will expect the entrepreneur to have substantial capital at risk. The entrepreneur might want a controlling interest or a minority position in the buyout. It is unrealistic to consider buying a business without a substantial personal investment.

At the same time, talk with banks and other lending institutions with experience in the target industry and/or buyouts. What percentages of account receivables, inventory, and fixed assets might they loan and at what rates? Determine their interest and potential dollar commitment. What dollar cap might they place on such a loan?

Next, set some standards as to the size business you would like to buy in terms of annual revenues, pretax profits, number of employees, or assets. Set both minimum and maximum standards.

Finally, determine the minimum acceptable return on investment. Based on the risks involved do you want a 25 percent or a 45 percent annual return on investment? Do you want to exit in five years with three times or five times your original investment?

Knowing your strengths and weaknesses, where you want to live, what you bring to the business, financing sources, type firm you seek, and required return on investment will save you time and money in the search and increase your probability of success in the purchase. Preparing a list of possible sources for finding a business to buy and a list of criteria for evaluating that business will save you time and money in the search and due diligence process, as well as increase your probability of success in the purchase.

Finally, combine all these data into an acquisition profile, a detailed description of the type of company you would like to buy, how you plan to find it, and how you plan to finance it. The acquisition profile would include specific investment criteria including: specific industry focus, target company size, geographic location, and profitability requirements. Again, this helps with the selection process and creates credibility with sellers, bankers, and investors.

Be patient and do the necessary homework. You may find a business to purchase in a month but it more likely will take six months to a year. Once you identify an interested prospect, expect to spend 90 days performing due diligence and another 30 days closing.

WHERE TO LOOK FOR A BUSINESS TO BUY

The more appropriate sources you contact for finding a business, the greater your probability for success. Sources include banks; professionals such as accountants, lawyers, and consultants; venture capitalists, investment bankers, and brokerage houses; advertising in trade publications or newspapers; networking with business associates, and industry contacts, trade association, and business brokers; and searching the World Wide Web.

Most banks have a list of smaller and midsized businesses that are for sale. They provide this as a service for their customers. The list contains a description of the business, but not the name. Should you be interested, the banker contacts his customer for permission to give you the company name and make the introduction. The bank customer will want to know about your background, experience, and financing capabilities. The trick is finding the department and person in the bank responsible for the list. Some of the companies on the lists have troubled loans; others represent successful privately owned firms looking to moneterize their investment. Ask the banker probing questions to determine this.

Accountants, lawyers, and consultants who deal with small and midsized firms as clients also represent an excellent source of candidates. Through due diligence find the key partners' names at these firms and contact them. Certain partners will specialize in smaller enterprises, and helping those interested clients find a buyer represents an important service plus an important source of fees. Reach the key partner by telephone, fax, or e-mail and make an appointment. At the meeting clearly define what you are looking for and your ability to finance a transaction. Using a credible third party for an introduction to any of the sources mentioned in this section proves helpful.

Venture capitalists, investment bankers, and private equity investors, or "angels," also represent excellent sources for locating a business to buy. Often these organizations or individuals have invest-ments in, or knowledge of, larger, more matured businesses that have a smaller division for sale. They invested in the larger entity but one piece has become a bad fit, which represents a candidate for divesti-ture. This division or department lends itself to an owner-manager, not an outside investor. Also, these investment professionals and organiza-tions might have received but turned down opportunities inappropri-ate for them but perfect for you. Contact the appropriate investment professionals and organizations by telephone, fax, or e-mail to make an appointment. At the appointment let them know your interests and capabilities. This involves selling yourself. See if they have an appro-priate candidate. Follow-up is important because it shows seriousness and also keeps your quest in the forefront of bankers and investors.

Advertising in and reading the business opportunity section of appropriate trade publications and newspapers can also produce qualified investment candidates. If you have targeted software or neckwear as your area of interest, advertise in their trade publications and read the business opportunity ads. Do the same for the Sunday newspaper in the cities that interest you, possibly Chicago and Omaha. In your ad state the areas of your interest and expertise. Tell why you would be a good buyer and the benefits of selling to you. Clearly state how the seller should contact you.

Let your friends, business associates, and professional service providers know you are looking. Use faxes, telephone calls, e-mail, and personal visits to accomplish this. Provide them with your acquisition profile, the specifics of what you seek, and how you will pay for it.

Do a search of your college's or graduate school's alumni data-base to find people in your target industry. Contact these alumni and send them your acquisition profile. They might know of an available firm or just provide you with valuable industry knowledge.

Cast the net wide by networking with target industry media peo-ple, suppliers, customers, and salespeople. Talk with editors and writ-ers at industry publications and the managers of industry associations. Advertising salespeople for industry publications can provide valuable leads. Also, some industry associations will assist members in selling or buying a business through confidential listings or open exchanges.

Reputable business brokers can often save you time and help you find hard-to-reach acquisition candidates. Select a broker who special-izes in your industry or location of interest. You need a proven pro-fessional with good industry contacts and an accurate database. Ask for industry references, companies he or she has brought or sold for clients. Ask to contact a client who was not satisfied.

You should be aware though that business brokers earn their liv-ing by doing transactions between buyers and sellers not necessarily by providing the best fit or value or most accurate information. Traditionally, the broker receives 100 percent performance pay from the seller; therefore your best interests may not be theirs.

Some entrepreneurs have paid brokers a fixed fee plus a small commission to represent them as a buyer. A business broker who has good industry contacts and knowledge can help you with the search and possibly with due diligence. However, watch out for unqualified members of this unregulated industry. Business brokers list themselves on the Web, in the yellow pages, and at industry associations. Industry networking probably represents the best source for reputable brokers.

The Worldwide Web with its broad reach has become an excellent source for purchase candidates. Many Internet sites post businesses for sale, most of which are mom-and-pop shops and franchises. Three of the best sites to find midsized businesses for sale are U.S. Business Exchange (www.usbx.com), Merger Network (www.mergernetwork. Com), and Emergers (www.emergers.com). These sites typically provide an anonymous business overview, company location, and some historical financial information. Business brokers and other intermediaries represent most of the buyers and sellers listed on these sites. You can search these sites for appropriate candidates or list your acquisition profile on these sites. The Internet also has sites listing business brokers including International Business Brokers Association (www.ibba.com); Midwest Business Brokers (www.mbbi.com), and Sunbelt Business Brokers (www.sunbeltnetwork.com).

However, a direct approach as described earlier allows you to bypass the banks, accountants, lawyers, consultants, venture capitalists, investment bankers, and networking. Based on the acquisition profile, you screen candidates from industry lists by location using company data available from credit and on-line reports. Then you contact those candidates who most clearly meet the acquisition profile.

Tactfully introduce yourself as someone interested in the industry with the knowledge, experience, and funds to buy a company. Tell them you know their company is not for sale but you would like to meet them. You must sell yourself and the appointment, using flattery where possible. You want to meet with an owner who may also be a member of management.

At the meeting you establish rapport, build curiosity, talk about the industry, and mention the benefits of a sale. Use this same procedure at the first meeting, even when you have been introduced by a third-party source. Most private businesses are for sale under certain circumstances and at a particular price. We will deal with this issue of availability in the section on valuation and negotiation. Most quality small- and medium-sized companies that are purchased were not

originally for sale. Finding a good fit in the hidden market can produce excellent results.

EVALUATING A BUSINESS YOU MIGHT BUY

Evaluating a business involves looking for synergies, areas where the
entrepreneur can add value, where he or she can take advantage of
changes or create change. Entrepreneurs don't buy businesses to maintain the status quo, but rather to add value and perhaps some day sell
them. If you do a good job of evaluating a business for purchase, this
evaluation becomes your business or strategic plan for running that
firm. For that reason, the topics in a business or strategic plan, discussed
in Chapter 1, are the same topics to be evaluated in buying a business.
Also, buying a business has similarities to an entrepreneur seeking
financing. However, in buying a business, the entrepreneur becomes the
investor. For that reason, in buying a business the entrepreneur must
use the investor techniques, filters, models, and methodologies discussed in Chapter 2.

Just as business plans act as a filter for start-ups, the evaluation
process for buying a business acts as a filter or methodology that lowers your risk of failure and increases your probability of success. If the
business candidate can successfully make it through the evaluation
process you probably have a winner. Also, by evaluating these various
topics you will become an expert in the industry.

In buying a business you must evaluate:

- Management
- Customers
- Markets
- Competitors
- Products and services
- Operations
- Distribution channels
- Sales organization
- Marketing
- Human resources
- Information technology
- Financial statements and forecasts
- Critical risks and contingency plans

Before the seller discloses this confidential information so that
you can properly evaluate all these items, he or she will want verifi-
cation of your seriousness and your financial resources to purchase

the business. The seller will also ask you to sign a nondisclosure or confidentiality agreement. Before signing, have this agreement reviewed by your attorney, so you don't limit your ability to compete in an industry or open yourself to litigation.

Management

You will find some small businesses undermanaged and some comparable firms in the same industry overmanaged. The entrepreneur might find a software or neckwear firm with only two managing partners: Mr. or Ms. inside and Mr. or Ms. outside. One partner looks after operations and development, the other looks after sales and marketing. If you were to buy such an undermanaged firm, you must consider hiring more management members and budget that cost into your forecasts.

On the other hand, you might find another comparable software or neckwear firm, each with seven managers: the president/owner, a production or operations manager, a merchandising or development manager, a controller, an information technology manager, a marketing manager, and a sales manager. If you were to buy such an overmanaged firm, you might consider consolidating certain management positions, which would reduce future expenses.

The entrepreneur must also consider who will stay, who will leave, and who will teach him or her the business. If the owner or manager who has the key relationships with the key customers wants to retire or the person who writes the software code will leave, you should be very concerned no matter how much you know about databases. One advantage of purchasing an existing business in a niche market is having the previous owners transfer their knowledge to you.

Should key people leave as described in the preceding paragraph, do successors exist in the organization? Have successors been trained for moving up the organization ladder? For management members or owners who continue in the business, how will they be motivated after the buyout? This depends on a variety of factors, including their age, personal characteristics, and future economic incentives.

Analyze management's skills, duties, knowledge, and experience; what are their strengths and weaknesses? Do these strengths and weaknesses represent a good fit with yours? Management has strong industry or domain experience but needs help in sales or finance. Can you personally provide that help or must you hire someone?

In many small, privately owned firms management consists of family members who have never worked outside that company. Is that good or bad? Investigate whether existing employees must be replaced or added to create a competent balanced team that can accomplish your goals. What is the cost and time frame?

For management members who stay, especially if they continue to have ownership, do their long- and short-term goals coincide with yours? For instance, let's say you plan to emphasize growth in revenues for the first two years, then growth in dollars of profit, and in year five find a strategic buyer. Does continuing management want to concentrate on dollars of profits, not revenue growth, resulting in higher personal compensation? Do they want to exit the business in year five?

In many small, privately owned firms, promises have been made to younger management and younger family members about eventually buying the firm or receiving equity. If you buy the business, those promises will be broken. Can you include them in the buying group or just forget the promises? (Any key managers who continue should have ownership or options for ownership in the new firm).

Especially in family-owned and managed firms, it would be wise to investigate who likes and dislikes other employees or management members. Will these internal relationships or conflicts interfere with change, good management, and good communication? Can the people in this company work together and accept your necessary changes? Be careful of company cultures that resist any change and are only comfortable with a deteriorating status quo.

What does the buyer, the entrepreneur, bring to the business besides personal management skills, and is there a good fit? The company has a proven formula for success that only requires substantial working capital for growth. You have excellent relationships with the banks and should be able to provide that. The company has an excellent product or service that meets a need in the marketplace and only requires introductions to high-level key account decision makers for growth. You can provide those introductions.

As a potential buyer, the entrepreneur also must analyze management compensation. Certain managers-owners receive excessive compensation that reflects not only salary but a pretax return on investment. Should you purchase the company and should they stay, their compensation would be reduced. Other management members, who are long-time employees, may be underpaid but critical to success. How will you deal with this and what impact will it have on future profits and cash flow?

The seller's lawyer and accountant reflect on management's capabilities and judgment. The accountant and lawyer must be people you can work with, trust, and respect. Meet them as early in the process as possible since they have a great deal of the information you need. Do they support the business sale or are they concerned about losing a client? Are they respected professionals or are they family members?

Reasons for Selling

Owners of small and medium-sized businesses have good and not-so-good reasons for selling. Good reasons would include: succession, age, estates, health, burnout, or infighting. Not-so-good reasons would include: peaking business, poor performance, or changing landscape. However, every problem represents an opportunity.

Many successful small and medium-sized businesses are for sale because the owner is older, might be in poor health, has no family member interested in the business, or for estate reasons wants to monetize or cash out his or her largest asset. These represent legitimate reasons for selling a private firm.

Sometimes the firm consists of two partners, who did not get along 20 years ago when they started the business and hate each other now. Going to work becomes an emotional chore and the solution is selling the firm. If one partner stays, make sure he or she is the most desirable.

Also entrepreneurs like anyone, can get burned out. After 5 or 10 years of managing the same business they crave a new challenge. This might represent a great opportunity for you.

Poor performance represents both a problem and an opportunity in buying a business. There is nothing the matter with buying a problem or distressed firm if you purchase it at the right price and have a good plan for turning it around. The challenge is to determine what is causing this firm's problems and whether you can fix the problem. You can provide working capital to grow or replace poor management. However, you cannot correct a declining market.

Be cautious of firms where the business has peaked, new competitors have entered the market, technology has changed, product life has become shorter, and/or the sales cycles longer.

Customers and Prospects

In evaluating a business for possible purchase the entrepreneur, like any other investor, must look at past, present, and future customers. Should you acquire the firm, such an evaluation will become part of your business or strategic plan. Refer to the discussion of customers and prospects in Chapter 1, and also consider the following additional comments.

Entrepreneurs are agents of change and so the question becomes, what would you change relative to customers to add value to this acquisition candidate? How can this firm better serve customers under your management? Can you wrap a service around the product or use customer relationship management software? Can the order or delivery cycle be reduced using e-mail and electronic data interchange? The entrepreneur can also add value by finding new or different markets and uses for a product or service.

For example, can the medical device be sold not only to hospitals but to doctors? Can it be used in a different procedure? Possibly Fortune 500 firms are not the proper target accounts for this consulting business but rather midsized industry specific firms. Possibly the medical software cannot only be used for tracking patient costs but submitting paperwork to insurance firms. Currently, a supply chain management firm calls on purchasing agents and manufacturing managers. Since the supply chain management programs save users large sums of money, maybe their salespeople should start calling on CFOs.

As a potential buyer the entrepreneur is not interested in only past and present customers but potential customers. In addition to a list of the top accounts and the number of total active accounts, you will need a list of inactive accounts. Should you discover that total inactive accounts exceed active ones, find out the reason why. Generally, this imbalance reflects poor quality or poor customer credit or poor delivery on the part of the business, none of which is good.

Similarly, what present major accounts are in jeopardy of being lost and why? We are buying the future and want to avoid surprises. As due diligence progresses, you will want to talk with major accounts to better understand their needs and determine whether these needs are being met. The customer information you seek can be accessed on the Internet, and from credit reports, trade associations, publications, and shows. However, the acquisition candidate's management, channel partners, and salespeople remain the first and primary source of customer information.

Markets

As a potential acquirer, just like a potential investor, the entrepreneur must understand market and market segment size, growth, and drivers. You want to avoid declining or peaking markets so due diligence proves most important in this area. Using available on-line and hardcopy reference data, accumulate important information. Review annual reports of public competitors, brokerage house industry research and private consulting company reports. Hire a college student to assist you. As you progress toward an agreement to buy don't hesitate to use a market research professional. Ten thousand dollars spent on market research can prevent $1 million of mistakes. If you can't afford $10,000, you should not consider buying a business. Again, refer to the Business Plan discussion in Chapter 1 for details.

Consider adding value by finding strategic partners who can help with sales or operations. Consider selling the product or service in the export market or just a different or additional domestic market.

Competition

The entrepreneur does not want to acquire a firm that is facing new domestic or foreign competition. Just like an equity investor, due diligence requires creating the competitive grid mentioned in previous chapters. Who are, have been, and will be the competitors, and how does this firm compare to competitors in features, benefits, and image. Consider both smaller start-ups and established firms. To answer these questions, perform due diligence by questioning company personnel, talking to customers, reading reference material, and using outside consultants.

Who are the market leaders and why? What does it take to become a market leader? How can you add value by creating more differentiation for the product or service?

As part of the competitive analysis, the entrepreneur must analyze the firm's pricing policy and actual prices. Can prices be raised without losing substantial unit volume? If so, you have found a quick, and possibly easy, means to create more dollars of profit and value.

Ask management how they arrived at the price for each product or service. For small, privately owned businesses this is most often cost plus. Generally, cost plus offers you an opportunity to selectively raise prices without significant effect on volume, thus increasing total dollars of profit or margin over time. Which products or services have a competitive advantage in features, benefits, or image? Which products or services are bought by leaders, early adopters, early and late majority, or laggards? Are the products or services homogeneous or heterogeneous, a specialty item, or a commodity? Based on the pricing model, which products or services are underpriced and which are overpriced?

Products or Services Offered

Next, the entrepreneur, just like an equity investor, evaluates the acquisition candidate's products or services. Where do opportunities exist to add value through change? What are the obvious and not so obvious critical risks?

Rank the top products or services from past years by dollars of revenue and dollars of income. What has changed and why? Can the features of the product or service be altered to better serve the customer? Can products or services be altered to meet unfilled needs in specialized markets? How technical are the products and is technology changing? Does the candidate or any of its competitors have patents, copyrights, or trademarks? How is product or service quality defined and can that be changed?

As an agent of change, look for other ways to differentiate the product or better serve the customer. For example, an entrepreneur who buys a tile and carpet retail store might add an installation and remodeling service to differentiate the business. An entrepreneur who buys a belt manufacturer might differentiate the product by licensing a designer name. An entrepreneur who buys an aluminum die-casting firm might expand into zinc die casting and anodizing finished components to better serve customers.

Channels of Distribution, the Sales Force, and Marketing

Channels of distribution, the sales force, and marketing represent the major problem areas for most small to midsized firms. These areas also represent the greatest opportunity for adding value and for creating change in a buyout. Obtain information about these areas by interviewing salespeople and other employees, entering into a dialogue with management, meeting channel partners, and networking in the marketplace.

You will find that legacy issues or industry tradition drive strategy, structure, and tactics in distribution, sales force management, and marketing. Can you make the sales organization more effective by switching from distributors to your own sales force or a hybrid organization? Would telesales or e-commerce help?

What critical risks exist in the sales force and what opportunities for change? Which salespeople will leave and which salespeople will stay? If a lead salesperson with excellent key national account relationships will retire or leave, the entrepreneur should be very concerned. Which 20 percent of the sales organization produces 80 percent of the revenues and income? Who functions as sales manager or do we need to hire one?

An entrepreneur bought a struggling Hispanic food distributor in Houston with seven full-time salespeople but no sales manager. She changed the compensation from 100 percent salary to 50 percent salary and 50 percent performance pay, rode with salespeople a day a week, and instituted a formal training program along with quarterly performance evaluations. Two of the seven salespeople were replaced, and this struggling Hispanic food distributor started growing revenues at 20 percent a year.

She also received cooperative advertising money from both the food producers and the retailers, which paid for appropriate branded newspaper ads and radio and television ads. Depending on what the market would bear, prices on some proprietary products were raised; prices on certain commodities lowered. Racks and displays were offered to grocery stores and certain packaging was altered. Seven years later she sold out at seven times the purchase price to a national Hispanic food distributor located in Atlanta.

Operations, Human Resources, and Information Technology

Before buying a business, the entrepreneur, just like any equity investor, must understand the risks, problems, and opportunities involved in operations.

As in other areas, you may want to hire professionals to help in analyzing operations, human resources, and information technology. The entrepreneur must have a clear understanding of the business's capacity, cost per unit, efficiency, supplier power, labor force, manufacturing or operating process, and quality control. What can you change to add value?

Before you buy a business, make sure you understand the capacity constraints of equipment, facilities, labor, and working capital. Let's say that by instituting changes in the product or service, management, sales force, target markets, and marketing you are projecting 25 percent annual unit growth for five years. However, in year three you no longer have the capacity for growth. You have exhausted available equipment, people, and bank financing for working capital. Can you contract out manufacturing or labor, buy more equipment, add more facilities, or raise more equity capital? How will these alternatives affect operating costs, long-term loans, and your equity investment? The time to analyze capacity issues is before you buy the business, not afterward.

Also, the entrepreneur must understand the cost per unit of operations or manufacturing and how that compares to industry norms. Would newer equipment, better methodologies, a shorter production cycle, importing, or subcontracting lower those costs per unit?

Critical risks might be hidden in pension plans, leases, government regulations, or union contracts. In all four cases, what are the company's rights, duties, and restrictions? Is the pension plan overfunded, offering an opportunity for internal financing of growth? Will the union contract which comes up for renegotiation next year increase payroll costs? Does the company need to invest in pollution control equipment?

Contact key suppliers to discuss availability of materials or key services. Do suppliers have a great deal of pricing power because of scarcities? Analyze a list of suppliers and their competitors. Were present suppliers chosen or inherited? What types of controls are used for inventory and accounts receivables? Are there opportunities to reduce inventory through just-in-time delivery and economic order quantities?

For example, an entrepreneur bought an injection-molding firm in upstate New York without performing this due diligence. Within two years he found out the equipment was below industry standards and an aging union labor force was difficult to replace. These constraints prevented growth until the plant was moved to another location, an expensive alternative.

What information technology and communication systems does the firm use and what hardware and software must be added to remain competitive? Who in the organization is responsible for information technology and are they capable?

The entrepreneur, like any equity investor, must consider which departments are overstaffed and which understaffed? Are people at this firm willing to learn and change or do silos exist? How do the present owners hire, train, compensate, organize, motivate, and evaluate employees and how do you plan to conduct these tasks? In talking with any employee of the acquisition candidate, be sensitive to their fears and concerns about a change in the company's ownership or management.

Profit and Loss Statements, Cash Flow, Balance Sheets, and Forecasts

Like any equity investor, at some point in your due diligence you want to review actual historical profit-and-loss statements, cash flows, and balance sheets for the last five years plus any future projections prepared by management. As discussed in Chapter 1, you should hire an accountant to assist you with this analysis.

Restructure these statements to reflect changes you will make to the business. For instance, payroll will be reduced because certain management members will leave, but on the other hand your salary must be added in. Fringe benefits will increase dramatically, reflecting a new medical insurance plan. Manufacturing or operation costs will change because you plan to subcontract certain functions. Sales force compensation will be lower, reflecting more performance pay. Capital expenditures for equipment and computers will greatly impact on cash flow. Liabilities will reflect a short-term working capital loan. Based on these changes, how will the financial statements look?

For the five years of actual and revised financial statements, the entrepreneur must analyze what trends have occurred in revenues, margins, profits, line-item expenses, receipts, expenditures, inventories, accounts receivable, fixed assets, accounts payable, loans, capital and intangible assets. What trends have occurred in actual dollars and dollars as a percentage of revenues? How do these numbers compare to industry standards? Where do opportunities exist for lowering costs? Determine and analyze the business's key control points, as discussed in Chapter 3.

In addition, for the balance sheet analyze key ratios such as current assets to current liabilities or debt to equity. Be sure to investigate hidden unfunded liabilities such as customer agreements, guarantees, warranties, and leases.

For each additional dollar of sales the entrepreneur must analyze how many additional dollars of accounts receivable and inventory are necessary. Has the growth been internally funded through cash flow or by working capital bank loans? Can you finance future growth through bank debt, equity, or internally generated cash flow?

Some businesses you look at will have audited financial statements, some will not be audited but will have detail on line-item expenses and margins, and others will only have annual tax returns. Start with the tax returns and tie any schedules and more detailed information into that. Have your accountant look at general ledger summaries to obtain missing information.

Next, using historical information and changes you plan to institute to create growth, project the revenues, expenses, margins, profit and loss, cash flow, and balance sheet statements for the next five years. State the assumptions that reflect how the projections were arrived at. Based on best, worst, and most probably scenarios, create three different sets of projections or pro formas, as discussed in Chapter 2. Attach a probability of success to each one. This sensitivity analysis acts as a reality check. Should you buy this candidate the numbers will become your forecast and budget against which to compare actual results.

Imagine that you are projecting 20 percent annual revenue growth based on new products and services, opening certain key accounts, the demise of a competitor, and creating a hybrid sales organization. Accounts receivable growth will be funded by a working capital bank loan and new equipment by a term loan. A building will be sold and leased back, a quality control manager hired, the inventory valuation changed and payroll functions farmed out. All these changes plus more impact the financial statements.

For the five-year projections or pro formas, the entrepreneur must analyze what trends evolve in revenues, margins, profit, line-item expenses, receipts, expenditures, inventories, accounts receivable, fixed assets, accounts payable, loans, capital, and intangible assets. What trends have occurred in actual dollars and dollars as a percentage of revenues?

At this point you might ask why the seller would provide all this information, how long will it take, and how much will it cost? In the beginning, the seller reluctantly provides this information, but soon you bond, common interests are found, and trust develops. Soon the seller starts to learn more about the business and becomes fascinated by the process. Also, much of the due diligence is provided by customers, competitors, employees, consultants, outside experts, and market research. Gathering this information requires buyers and sellers working together.

The cost and time frame depends on how much you know about the industry, competitors, customers, and the company when you start. If you work in the industry or have looked at competitors as possible acquisitions, the due diligence time frame might be 30 to 60 days and the cost $10,000 net of accountant and legal fees. If this company represents your first serious exposure to the industry, the due diligence time frame might be 90 to 120 days and the cost $50,000 net of accounting and legal fees.

Critical Risks and Contingencies

Lastly, in evaluating a business you want to buy, consider known and possible critical risks and contingency plans. What could go wrong and what will you do about it? It proves helpful to plan for what could go wrong because it usually does.

If your largest customer goes on credit watch or is bought, what will you do? If a key employee leaves, what is the succession plan? Should a potential large European competitor enter the U.S. market do you have a strategy? Should the new, faster microchip change the technology for your firm's instrumentation, do you have a backup plan? What if a large competitor lowers prices or a major supplier raises costs? What if government industry regulations change?

Rank the critical risks from most to least probable, and list five action points you will take under each. Assign a cost to each action point.

PUTTING A VALUE ON THE BUSINESS YOU MAY BUY

By using proper sources and a good methodology for evaluating whether you wish to buy the business, you have decided on an appropriate candidate. Now you must negotiate an acceptable price. During your due diligence with management and ownership you have explored some metrics for pricing and discussed a range. Establishing a value for the business you wish to buy is similar to establishing a value for the business you have started and for which you now seek outside financing.

You have decided to purchase a regional commercial trash removal service from the founding family. Look for comparables to establish a value. You discover several similar firms have been sold in the last year. Now you investigate how value was arrived at for these purchases?

Make a list of possible metrics for valuation with the thought that they will define a range. Liquidation value represents one possibility. If you bought the business, and had to liquidate it, what would be left for the shareholders? The 20 trucks and 2000 dumpsters could be sold for $700,000, less accounts payable and long-term debt, plus accounts receivable. Netting out some other minor assets and liabilities, the liquidation value appears to be $850,000.

The recent purchase of several other comparable trash removal services by publicly owned firms has been done at a price of $3000 for each customer, which would amount to $6 million for the company you are considering. However, the $6 million was paid in the stock of the acquiring firm, which is not acceptable to our candidate. The $6 million equals 0.6 times sales.

Publicly owned regional refuse removal firms sell for 8 to 12 times after-tax earnings, depending on revenue and earnings growth rates and quality of earnings. After adjusting our candidate's actual earnings upward for excessive noneconomic family salaries, which will not exist after the purchase, and adjusting them downward for several other items and using a 10 times after-tax multiple discounted for a private firm, this produces a valuation of $3 million. Using the same methodology on an appropriate multiple of EBITDA (earnings before interest, taxes, depreciation, and amortization) the valuation again equals $3 million.

You then take your various five-year projections of revenues, expenses, and cash flow, adjust them for probability of success and discount the most probable cash flow back to its present value. Do this for different discount rates and terminal values. This analysis indicates a net present value between $3 million and $4 million.

Similarly, look at the possible future exit value and discount that value back to a present purchase price. Using your five-year projection of after-tax profits and EBITDA and present market valuation multiples, the trash removal company should be worth $10 million in year five. To balance risks and rewards you wish a 25 percent return on your investment, which results in a current valuation, or a current purchase price, of $3,300,000.

Before buying a firm, establish a time frame for implementing necessary changes and executing an exit. Will the exit be a financial or strategic buyer, a sale to employees, or a public stock offering? If a buyout, who might be the purchaser? How long will it take to make necessary changes in products, services, distribution, operations, the sales force, target accounts, and financial restructuring? Use your evaluation of the firm to create a business or strategic plan. Then put each step of the business or strategic plan into a time frame. When will these changes reflect themselves in increased revenues, margins, profits, and net worth? What might you expect to sell or exit the company for, in which years, and what return on investment will that create for you? Is the return on investment worth the risk? Perform this exercise before you buy the business, not after.

Establish ground rules as to what constitutes your investment and what constitutes return. Does your investment include personally guaranteed loans? Does your return include a portion of your compensation?

The valuation placed on a business you wish to buy will also depend on the method of purchase. If you purchase the trash removal firm for all cash, paid at the closing, and if the sellers have few contingent liabilities, warranties, and guarantees, you might pay less than if payments are made over time and partially based on performance.

If you buy assets net of liabilities or just purchase assets, you might pay a higher purchase price than if you bought a company's stock. When you buy stock, the buyer accepts all the seller's assets and liabilities. When you buy assets, the seller keeps the stock and must pay off the liabilities. What you buy and how you buy it has many legal and tax consequences. You must hire competent lawyers and accountants to assist you with this. You might decide to purchase the trash removal service for a $2 million payment at closing and the rest in a variety of deferred payments. The remaining $1 million to $2 million might be a personal note guaranteed by your stock in the trash removal firm or a note from the trash removal firm itself. These remaining payments might be tied to the company's performance. If present owners or managers continue after the buyout you will want to structure payments so they have some down risk and some opportunity for gain.

You might pay the entire purchase price at closing but borrow part of it back from a bank using the trash removal firm's fixed assets (trucks and bins) and possibly account receivables as collateral. Notes to the bank and to the previous owners will require personal guarantees. In buying a firm consider whether unencumbered fixed assets can be used as collateral to finance part or all of the purchase price. You must also consider whether the firm has sufficient cash flow to cover annual debt service and eventually pay off the loan.

Deferred payments might be made to the previous owners as corporate pretax items such as consulting fees, noncompete agreements, employment contracts, and salaries in excess of their economic value. These are tax deductible for the corporation but are taxed as ordinary income rather than capital gains for the sellers.

You also may choose to buy controlling interest in the company, but leave operating management, who were the previous owners, with a lesser, say 33 percent, stake. This guarantees their continuing motivation and requires less capital on your part. As you can see, the method of payment will affect the total purchase price and the complexity requires competent legal and accounting advice.

NEGOTIATING THE PRICE

What you end up paying for the trash removal firm depends on how badly the owners want to sell, how badly you want to buy, and what other alternatives both parties have. The previously discussed metrics established a range. Based on sales of comparable firms, liquidation value, multiples of earnings, cash flow, and revenues, number of customers, net present value, discounted cash flow, exit value, and return on investment; a broad $850,000 to $6 million range emerges. On further analysis the range realistically narrows to $3 to $4 million.

If, for estate purposes, the trash removal firm must sell for all cash up front within 90 days and you are the only buyer, you will get a better price than if they have little reason to sell and there are many potential buyers. Similarly, if you have many trash removal firms to choose from, you will negotiate a better price than if only one is for sale.

In negotiating price, consider the seller's present total compensation, reimbursed expenses, and dividends versus the potential income from the proceeds of a buyout. Presently, the seller "takes out" $500,000 annually from the trash removal business. A 10 percent return on a purchase price of $3,300,000 is only $330,000. However, if the owner continues on as an employee at $170,000, then the dynamics change.

In negotiating price, prepare a list of the seller's and buyer's motivators. As mentioned, the seller may have estate issues, employee issues, health, or market issues as motivators. There might be time limits. On the other hand, there may be few motivators because ownership is very satisfied.

Your motivators as a buyer might be a limited number of sellers, changes in market conditions, timing on available funds, your plans for adding value, or purchasing a market leader. On the other hand, many sellers may exist, multiples and valuations are declining, and you have a day job that supports your family.

Then list each party's "must haves," and "want to haves." You, as buyer, must have the trash firm owners guarantee the payment of all account receivables, warrant the accuracy of financial statements, and continue to manage the firm for a year. The sellers, the trash firm owners, must have half their purchase price in cash at the time of closing, two-year employment contracts, and no liability for the union pension plan. Both parties also discuss what they want to have: vacations, duties, employment for certain personnel, and compensation.

Based on each party's motivators, those things they must have and those they want to have, and with expert input from the lawyer and the accountant, the entrepreneur prepares a list of alternative purchase terms. Each alternative has a different cash-down payment and then different deferred payments, compensation, warranties, and conditions. Each alternative has a different economic value to the buyer and seller. The alternatives become the basis for a discussion of the final terms.

As the entrepreneur performs due diligence, arrives at a valuation, and negotiates a purchase price, he or she must be prepared to "walk away" from the deal. As you invest more time and money in the process of due diligence and negotiation, you become more committed to a purchase. As you invest more time and money in these processes and filters, you also uncover negative information that can be deal breakers. As you move from introduction to closing, continually reevaluate whether the risks are worth the rewards.

Once the entrepreneur negotiates a general agreement with the seller, both parties sign a letter of intent. The buyer's attorney drafts this document, which indicates a serious mutual intent to move forward and commits to writing the major terms of a sale, including price, form of payment, purchase of what items, employee agreements, noncompetes, and nondisclosures. It also lists remaining due diligence that requires completion before a purchase agreement can be signed. It is similar to the term sheet an entrepreneur would sign with an investor.

Then your final offer takes the form of a purchase agreement prepared by the buyer's attorney. Once the buyer and seller sign the purchase agreement, neither party can change the terms without the other's consent. Besides codifying the purchase price, timing and form of payment, and what is being purchased, the agreement gives the buyer certain rights to offset the purchase price for undisclosed liabilities and warranty violations. The agreement makes the sale conditional on transferring certain off–balance-sheet items such as leases and license agreements. Additional closing documents might include: a settlement sheet, escrow, bill of sale, promissory notes, security agreements, financing statement, noncompete covenants, employment agreements, bulk transfer notice, security interests, tax releases, holdbacks, escrow, closing procedures, and conditions to be met for closing by a certain date.

The model or methodology described in this chapter for buying a business acts as a filter for lowering your risks of failure and increasing your probability of success. The filter eliminates the poor candidate and promotes the good ones. A typical entrepreneur will look at 30 to 50 candidates before buying the appropriate one. This requires time, money, and patience.

Even after this exhaustive process, you will find negative surprises after the purchase and sometimes make a bad acquisition. This methodology does not guarantee success, but not using it greatly increases the probability of failure.

ENTREPRENEURS' MAJOR MISTAKES AND WEAKNESSES IN BUYING AN EXISTING BUSINESS

- Not targeting the industry and characteristics or the type of company you wish to purchase.
- Not preparing an acquisition profile.
- Not arranging for financing before you start the search.
- Not using a wide enough variety of sources to look for a business.
- Not doing enough research on the acquisition candidate's markets, customers, products, competition, human resources, and financial resources.
- Not analyzing the business's exit value, what synergies your presence will create, the total necessary investment, and the final return on investment.
- Not understanding why the business is for sale and what value you can add.
- Not realistically analyzing critical risks and contingency plans.
- Not walking away from opportunities when risks exceed rewards.
- Not understanding how the method of payment may influence the total price or value of the business purchased.
- Not understanding how to negotiate the price, terms, and financial structure.
- Not obtaining expert outside advice from lawyers, accountants, consultants, and industry experts.

QUESTIONS AND EXERCISES

1. What are the advantages and disadvantages of buying an existing business versus starting a new business?
2. Based on your skills, knowledge, experience, and contacts, what industries will you target for buying a business?

3. Prepare an acquisition profile for the business you wish to purchase.
4. What sources will you use to look for a business to purchase?
5. What methodology will you use to place a value on the business you will consider purchasing?
6. Prepare a list of what a business buyer must analyze to properly evaluate an enterprise.

CHAPTER 9

Developing and Introducing New Products and Services

To become an entrepreneur, as we have indicated previously in this book, you can choose one of these three basic alternatives:

1. Start a new business by developing and introducing a new product or service.
2. Buy an existing business, manage it, build it, and possibly someday sell it.
3. Franchise someone else's idea or clone a successful business model.

Each of these three alternatives has different advantages and disadvantages as well as different merits, rewards, and risks. These three alternatives not only represent means for becoming an entrepreneur but for expanding existing growth-stage and small businesses. New enterprises and small businesses grow through acquisitions and the development of new products and services.

RISKS VERSUS REWARDS OF NEW PRODUCT OR SERVICE DEVELOPMENT

Sixty percent of all new businesses fail within the first two years of their existence, 80 percent within the first five years. In addition, 80 percent of all new products and services fail, whether developed by large or small enterprises.

Small businesses have limited human and financial resources, which creates a high cost for failure. A bad lease or poor location, a poor hire, bad debts, and unsuccessful new products or services can produce financial distress. This raises the question, of whether entrepreneurs involved in start-ups, early-stage firms, or smaller businesses should engage in new product or service development.

However, small businesses, start-ups, early-, or growth-stage firms can make faster decisions than larger organizations and can get new products or services to market sooner. Whether your new offer is B2B or B2C, whether it involves technology or is fashion-based, speed to market is extremely important for the development and introduction of new products and services. The entrepreneur often overlooks this advantage.

On the other hand, small businesses, start-ups, and early-stage firms suffer from dependence on one or two products or services and from a limited number of customers in one market or industry. Should that product or service encounter new competition or should the market demand shrink or a major customer leave, the company faces financial distress.

This situation creates a strategic dilemma for entrepreneurs who need to develop new products or services but cannot tolerate the risk. The solution often lies in lowering the risk by licensing products or services from larger firms, forming strategic alliances with them, or living off the product fallout of industry leaders. Hundreds of smaller companies have thrived as strategic partners of Microsoft, AOL, Calvin Klein, and Dell. Similarly, as these larger, seminal firms develop new products or services, smaller firms benefit from the increased and diversified resulting demand.

These risks, dilemmas, and experiences encourage entrepreneurs to be followers and discourage them from being new product leaders. They complain, "Being first may be good, but being big often is better."

An entrepreneurial early- or growth-stage firm faces two major risks in addition to those mentioned. First, the product or service may not sell. It may not satisfy a large enough market demand, resulting in write-offs of inventory and development costs plus customer and employee ill will. Like a bad debt this becomes an unrecoverable cost, lowering gross margin as a percentage of sales and lowering dollars of profit.

Second, if successful, the new product or service will most likely be copied by larger competitors with existing customers, brands, salespeople, and greater resources for promotion. These larger competitors will capture the major market share even though the smaller firm took the major risks. The entrepreneur thinks, "Heads you lose, tails you don't win; why take these risks?"

However, new products and services still represent the fastest means for an entrepreneur or small-business owner to increase sales, market share, earnings before income taxes, exit value, net present value, and return on investment. Entrepreneurs are agents of change, manage change, and change people's behavior. Of course, many new enterprises start from the development and introduction of a new product or service.

The successful introduction of new products or services also enhances the company's image with customers and improves employee morale. Customers and employees enjoy association with a leader.

For the entrepreneur and small-business owner the risks and rewards of new product or service development and introduction are high. Start-ups and early-stage firms must grow through the development and introduction of new products and services. This chapter describes a model, methodology, or filter for increasing the probability of new product or service success and reducing the risk of failure.

The model we present here involves identifying market needs and competitive weaknesses; creating a selection criteria and plan; seeking smaller markets that would be unprofitable for larger firms; innovating rather than inventing; determining return on investment; using market research and test marketing to estimate demand; and inexpensively pre-selling through low-cost publicity, advertising, and promotion.

IDENTIFYING MARKET NEEDS, COMPETITIVE WEAKNESSES, AND LEGACY ISSUES

New products or services fail most often because they do not reflect a need in the marketplace, a competitive weakness, or a legacy issue, but rather the ego of the originator. Even a great idea, a highly differentiated product or service, succeeds commercially only if a need exists: that is, if it satisfies a customer want or a competitive weakness. "Will the dog eat the dog food?"

Sources for new product ideas include customers, employees, trade publications, trade shows, conferences, overseas markets, suppliers, competitors, channel partners, research reports, and focus groups. New product and service ideas that reflect personal needs may not be representative for a larger market.

Approach your customers, employees (especially salespeople and engineers) and channel partners for new product ideas, because they are most aware of unmet needs in the marketplace, of competitive weaknesses, and of legacy issues. During field trips, ask major customers and prospects for their ideas. They will be flattered and more receptive to doing business together. This type of closeness to customers represents a competitive advantage of smaller businesses over larger firms. Devote some time at sales meetings and during field visits to discussing new product or service ideas with the sales force and channel partners.

Assign one person responsibility for collecting and processing new product or service ideas from all employees. Offer an employee bonus for successful ideas. For the entrepreneur looking for a new product or service idea on which to found a start-up, go to the marketplace and talk to potential customers, competitors, and suppliers, plus salespeople, channel partners, and engineers or designers in markets you have selected. To increase the probability of success choose markets in which you not only have an interest but experience, knowledge, and expertise.

When you attend industry trade shows or conferences, and when you read industry publications or research reports, search for unfilled customer needs or competitive weaknesses. Talk to target customers and prospects at trade shows and conferences they attend. Visit competitor booths. Papers presented at conferences often contain ideas or concepts that can be developed into new products or services.

An entrepreneur interested in distance learning visited potential customers at consulting firms, multinational companies, and universities. He discovered a need for programs involving industry-specific cases in strategy. He then contacted well-known professors to provide content and strategic partners to produce and distribute the material. The entrepreneur thus introduced the first product or service for his new enterprise.

Research reports by consulting firms can provide the genesis for successful new products or services. An employee of a major telephone company read a telco industry research report that indicated a need for accurate market share data on cellular phone use. He created the method and the metrics to measure market share and started a multimillion dollar business.

Last but not least, look for new product or service ideas that reflect competitive weaknesses based on legacy issues. As mentioned, many larger firms cannot take advantage of new product or service opportunities because they have large investments in their present products or services. The entrepreneur or small-business manager may have a last-mover advantage here.

On-line and discount brokerage houses succeeded initially because established conventional firms had large investments in human capital and were therefore locked into the status quo. Double-edged stainless steel razor blades were finally introduced to the American market by an English firm, Wilkinson, because Gillette had a high investment in what was then the conventional blade. Eventually, Gillette introduced a competitive product that captured the major market share, because of Gillette's brand name and established distribution.

CREATING A SELECTION CRITERIA

In selecting new products or services to pursue the entrepreneur must also consider issues discussed in previous chapters. The entrepreneur should prepare a selection criteria or plan and consider the following:

1. Does this product or service have a clearly defined, easy-to-reach target market? If applicable, can this target market be reached through the present sales force, channel partners, and advertising techniques?

2. What are the costs for a potential customer to switch to the new product or service and, once chosen, what are the switching costs to chose another?

3. What are the barriers for the entrepreneur to enter this new product or service market and for other competitors to follow? Do established relationships with urologists or department store merchandise managers create barriers to entry? Are large investments in development costs, working capital, or equipment necessary?

4. Does the new product or service leverage the entrepreneur's skills, knowledge, and relationships or the small-business's core competencies? If your skills lie in engineering commercial products, you might not want to start a business by introducing a consumer service. Similarly, if a smaller business's core competencies lie in sales and distribution, it may not want to introduce a new product that requires internal manufacturing.

5. Can the new product or service be clearly differentiated from present and future competitors? Does long-term differentiation lie in the product design or the marketing approach? Can differentiation and competitive advantages be quantified in dollars? Products that cannot be clearly differentiated will be more expensive and difficult to introduce.

6. Does the product or service have a long or short life? Smaller businesses and entrepreneurial start-ups should avoid products with short lives and seek those with longer lives. Smaller concerns do not have the resources to continually replace new products or services, and they are therefore at a competitive disadvantage to larger firms.

7. Entrepreneurs and smaller-business managers should seek new products or services with shorter sales cycles. Larger

firms with greater resources have a competitive advantage over products or services with longer sales cycles and many steps between search and purchase. The new enterprise or smaller business does not have the resources to spend six months or a year involved in analyzing customer needs; doing betas, tests, and trials; selling multilevel committees; and preparing numerous feasibility reports and bids.

8. Have similar products or services failed or succeeded, and why? This requires you to do an on-line database search and interview industry competitors, customers, and suppliers.

Remember the importance of timing in introducing new products or services. An idea that failed three years ago might succeed today and an idea that succeeded three years ago might fail today. Business is a dynamic process with markets, needs, and competition continually changing.

Add other appropriate items to your selection criteria and plan. Quantify all selection criteria in terms of dollars, units, and time. Certainly include criteria on potential market size and market growth, revenues, profits, and return on investment, which are discussed later in this chapter.

LIMITING COMPETITION

Once the entrepreneur has developed a successful new product or service, how does he or she prevent larger competitors with greater resources from capitalizing on the idea? Once you have spent the development and marketing funds to launch a successful new product or service, how do you keep both gorillas and ants from stealing it?

The entrepreneur and small-business owner should investigate the possibility and costs of patents, copyrights, and trademarks. Use an experienced intellectual property attorney with knowledge of your industry.

Many entrepreneurs introduce new products and services that are patent or copyright eligible but the cost of defending that patent or copyright would be unrealistic. Patent infringement litigation can strain an entrepreneurial firm's limited resources. However, as mentioned in a previous chapter, equity investors do value intellectual property for financing purposes. Therefore, you may wish to file a patent or register a copyright or trademark for investor value, knowing it has little value in defending you from competitors.

A patent is a grant from the Federal Government's Patent and Trademark Office (PTO) to the inventor of a product or service, giving exclusive rights to make, use, or sell the invention in the United States for 20 years from the date of filing the patent application. After 20 years, the patent expires and cannot be renewed. Inventors who make new, original, and ornamental changes in the design of existing products that enhance their sales can receive 14-year design patents.

Copyrights are an exclusive right that protects the creator of original works of authorship such as software, videos, games, books, plays, songs, and works of art. A copyright protects only the form in which an idea is expressed, not the idea itself. Just as with a trademark, obtaining basic copyright protection does not require registering the creative work with the U.S. Copyright Office, only first and continual use, but registering does give the creator greater protection. A valid copyright lasts for the life of the creator plus 50 years.

There are 1.5 million trademarks registered in the United States, 900,000 of which are in actual use. Federal law permits an organization or person to register a trademark, which prevents other companies from employing a similar mark to identify their goods or services. The first party who uses a trademark in commerce or files an application with the Patent and Trademark Office has the ultimate right to register that trademark. Unlike patents and copyrights, which are issued for limited amounts of time, trademarks last indefinitely as long as the holder continues to use it.

You should name and trademark any new and all existing products or services. New product names can become brands, which give your firm an inexpensive competitive advantage. As an example, a new bakery product, such as frozen bagel dough, which is not patentable, can be trademarked to protect the name. Again, consult a qualified attorney on these issues.

In developing new products or services, the entrepreneur needs a strategy for creating barriers to entry from larger and smaller concerns. When the equity markets have funds for new ventures, early and growth-stage investing, competition from smaller firms represents a serious threat to new products or services, whether developed by an entrepreneur or by a large organization.

An early-stage, start-up, or smaller business, like a larger one, should use size to its advantage. Because of larger overhead, greater start-up expenses, and economies resulting from higher unit volume, larger businesses often cannot operate as profitably in smaller markets as in larger markets.

As previously discussed, today's markets are very complex and segmented. When developing a new product or service, entrepreneurs and small-business managers should look for needs and competitive weaknesses in a market segment where their size business can operate profitably but a larger one cannot. In this way, you reduce the risk of competitors with greater resources and better distribution, capitalizing on your idea. Smaller businesses and entrepreneurs succeed by specializing, not by being all things to all people.

In the early 1990s an entrepreneur with a background in textiles and some experience in sporting goods, decided to enter the men's hosiery business. In 1992 the hosiery industry had annual sales at wholesale of $3 billion, a market large enough to interest any corporate giant. However, specialized equipment and distribution divided this huge market into hundreds of smaller submarkets or market segments. These specialized submarkets sometimes amounted to total annual sales of only $20 million, appropriate for and populated by small-businesses. For example, pantyhose accounted for half of the market, ladies' casuals 20 percent, and infant hose 10 percent. This meant the total wholesale market for men's hose approximated $600 million, which could be further divided into 80 percent unbranded merchandise for mass merchants and 20 percent branded goods for specialty and department stores. The $120 million branded men's hosiery business consisted of 20 percent designer labels and 80 percent national brands, broken down into 30 percent casual hose, 30 percent athletic hose, 30 percent dress hose, and 10 percent patterns. The casual, athletic, dress, and patterned goods could be further divided between synthetics and natural fibers.

The entrepreneur, using focus groups and market research, decided there was a need for a branded cotton athletic hose with a padded foot and Spandex-reinforced leg. He trademarked the name, located knitters with the appropriate equipment, and started selling the hose to sporting goods shops, athletic clubs, and to a lesser extent department and specialty stores. Over the next five years this start-up became a highly profitable business with annual sales of $5 million. This represented too small a market to interest the larger competitors, and exclusive supply agreements, excellent customer relationships, a trademarked brand name and a first-mover advantage has kept smaller competitors out of this market. As you can see, smaller companies that can subcontract manufacturing or excel in short production runs could make money in these submarkets, whereas a larger concern could not.

As discussed in previous chapters, you can obtain the type of statistical market data you will need to make such an analysis from trade associations, trade publications, chambers of commerce, and government agencies. For every significant economic activity, there is an association that represents it, a government agency that monitors it, and a magazine that covers it.

Also, strategic alliances represent a means of converting large and small potential competitors into partners, suppliers, and customers for your new product or service. When developing the new product or service, list potential present and future competitors, large and small. Does the opportunity exist for them to benefit from becoming your strategic partners, suppliers, or customers?

A small-business Web portal used larger potential competitors such as software giants, other megaportals, banks, credit card companies, and small-business associations as revenue-sharing channel partners to refer customers. Smaller potential competitors such as credit services, recruiters, and public relations firms received fees as service providers for customers. Consider making your competitors your partners.

To prevent start-ups like your own from stealing customer business through low-ball pricing, differentiate your product, create value-added switching costs, and sign long-term contracts with customers and suppliers. If a new product or service has a clearly definable, quantifiable competitive advantage, price becomes less important.

The small-business Web portal created switching costs by providing certain free services and discounted prices for regular repeat customers. They differentiated themselves through the variety of paid-for services and ease of using their site. The prostate cancer seed implant firm limited competition through long-term contracts with its radioactive iodine supplier, major distributors, and hospital chains.

INNOVATING RATHER THAN INVENTING

The risks associated with introducing new products or services can be further limited by innovating rather than inventing. Innovations require less capital than inventions, but barriers to entry, switching costs, and differentiation are also less. Most entrepreneurs, new ventures, and smaller businesses do not have the resources to develop and introduce new-to-the-world products or services, but they do have the resources to develop and introduce new-to-the-company products or services or line extensions and improvements. As you move from new-to-the-world to line extensions and improvements, potential returns drop, but so do risks.

An entrepreneur, new venture, or small-business generally does not possess the resources for inventing an electric car, new material for semiconductors, or a worldwide satellite cellular phone system. An entrepreneur, new venture, or small company does have the human and financial resources to innovate, to alter an existing product so that it meets an unfilled need in a specialized market. You can achieve these innovations in many ways including:

- Different packing and packaging
- Color identification
- Unusual sizing
- Unusual guarantees

- Adding or subtracting features from an existing product or service
- Use of private labeling and licensing
- Adapting from a related market
- Adapting from an overseas market
- Reviving an old idea
- New markets and uses for existing products or services

Different Packing and Packaging

Innovative packing and packaging can alter existing products to satisfy unfilled needs in the marketplace. Different packing and packaging can be the basis for new products, new enterprises, and line extensions.

As an example, an entrepreneur established a new product and a new company by repackaging dog food in smaller, reusable containers using colorful graphics. Many pet owners who were older could not lift the larger bags and many specialty pet shops did not have space to store them. Larger competitors were not interested in this market because they chose to concentrate on mass merchants and supermarkets.

A small financial services company was started by an entrepreneur who specialized in life planning. She differentiated her firm by reducing the minimum investment from the industry standard of $100,000 to $50,000. She started with the smaller accounts in which the larger competitors had no interest but grew them into $100,000 plus customers.

A Hispanic entrepreneur starts a new business based on packing commercial products in boxes with instructions in Spanish. An Indian entrepreneur creates lunch boxes with Indian motifs for high-tech transplants in Silicon Valley. Both these entrepreneurs altered existing products to meet unfilled needs in specialized markets.

As an entrepreneur, look for new product ideas related to altering the size, configuration, and use of packaging. Some of these ideas were also discussed in Chapter 4 on differentiation and targeting. Examine the information written on packages and containers, both for consumer and business products. Is there an opportunity to create a new enterprise or new product or service by altering this information? Also, whether you sell an industrial or consumer product, consider developing a competitive edge or a new product through reusable packaging.

Color Identification

Color identification represents another inexpensive means of innovating to satisfy unfilled needs in the marketplace or to create brand identification. The most successful company in the branded men's hosiery business went from start-up to over $30 million of annual sales by knitting a gold toe into every sock. The company created a brand, "Gold Toe," which could be identified by the consumer after the sock had been worn and washed. The name was trademarked and the process for knitting color into the toe patented.

Examine potential products to determine if color identification could benefit users in some way or could establish brand identification. The cost of adding color is usually nominal. For example, when you think of John Deere tractors, you think of green; when you think of United Parcel Service, you think of brown; and when you think of Caterpillar tractor construction equipment, you think of yellow.

Unusual Sizing

Unusual sizing that meets a need in the marketplace represents another inexpensive means of innovation for the introduction of new products or the creation of a new enterprise. Many electrical and electronic component manufacturers have been started based on making relays, connectors, or semiconductors smaller or larger depending on the end use. Technology did not change, just the size. Many apparel manufacturers and retailers were started to sell king- or queen-size clothing. A Virginia entrepreneur started a successful firm which designs, manufactures, and sells extra-large stretch denim jeans for truck drivers.

At the same time new enterprises were being formed to design and distribute pocket-size calculators, other entrepreneurs were developing and introducing models for seniors with extra-large keys and displays. Laptop computers and Palm Pilots downsize their larger counterparts.

Examine products or services in markets of interest or at your existing small-business to determine if larger or smaller versions would satisfy unfilled needs in the marketplace. This strategy will lead you into submarkets, which may prove profitable for a smaller concern but unattractive for a larger competitor.

Unusual Guarantees

Offering unusual guarantees with a product or service represents yet another inexpensive innovation on which to create a new venture and/or a new product.

Federal Express and Midas Muffler represent new ventures with a new service based on an unusual guarantee. Overnight package delivery and replacement of auto exhaust systems were not new or unusual, but the guarantees were. The guarantees transformed a homogeneous service into a heterogeneous service and allowed the entrepreneurs to start new premium-priced businesses. Financial institutions that guarantee municipal bonds created a new industry. Mail-order houses and retailers also differentiate themselves with guarantees.

Examine products or services in markets of interest or at your existing small-business to determine if unusual guarantees would satisfy unfilled needs in the marketplace. This represents an inexpensive way to create a new product or service or business. Be sure to search for data on comparable companies, products, or services. Has this been tried? If not, why not? Did previous similar ventures fail or succeed? Why or why not? The guarantee may drive expenses more than sales.

Adding or Subtracting Features

Taking something out of or adding something to an existing product or service can often inexpensively create a totally new product or service that will satisfy an unfilled need in the marketplace. Palm Pilots, clock radios, dinner theaters, cash management accounts, universal and variable life insurance, and the next generation of cellular phones all represent new products created by adding something to or combining existing products. New cellular phones combine voice, data, Web browsers, pagers, text messaging, and a 400-number telephone book. Unleaded gasoline, cordless telephones, jogging strollers (three rather than four wheels), and Internet appliances represent new products with an ingredient or part removed. Entrepreneurial early-stage firms introduced many of these concepts.

In December of 2000 the Heely was introduced by a Dallas entrepreneur. This thick-soled sneaker has a wheel embedded in each heel that allows wearers to switch from walking to skating simply by shifting their weight. The shoes made their debut at the Action Sports Retailer Trade Expo in San Diego. Heeling Sports, the developer, focused initial sales on early-adopter skate and surf shops and mall chains, not late-majority mass merchants. The company put up an edgy Web site, sent the shoes to top talk show hosts, and sent press releases to top newspapers and magazines. The company expected to ship one million pairs in 2001. Heelys represent a combination of two products, sneakers and a skateboard. The company successfully used all the low-cost marketing techniques described in Chapter 6 to launch this product.

Examine products or services in your proposed or present markets to determine whether adding something to them, combining two of them, or taking something away from them would satisfy an unfilled need in the marketplace. To facilitate this, review their features, parts, ingredients, and components.

Private Labels and Licenses

Offering branded products or services under private store labels, and unbranded products or services using licensed brand recognized names, represents yet another inexpensive innovation that can satisfy a market need, create new product images, expand existing sales, or allow you to start a new enterprise. Many apparel firms started by manufacturing private store-label merchandise for Neiman Marcus, Bloomingdale's, and Saks Fifth Avenue. Many appliance firms started by manufacturing private store-label products for Sears, Home Depot, and other mass merchants. Similarly, many existing firms found supplying private store-label merchandise a lucrative means to expand their existing businesses.

Large computer firms have created an industry to manufacture monitors, printers, and accessories under their labels. Branded cellular phone manufacturers use contractors to make and assemble their entire product lines.

Also, many start-ups and early-stage firms have inexpensively developed proprietary brands by licensing recognized names from Izod, Polo, Calvin Klein, the New York Yankees, and the Chicago Symphony Orchestra. Licensing is also available in B2B products such as semiconductors, computers, and telephone services.

By 2000, retail sales of licensed goods had grown to $30 billion, with manufacturers paying about $1.5 billion in royalties. Think about recognized designers, brands, companies, personalities, athletic teams, movies, and institutions whose names would appeal to your customers and prospects. See if they are available for licensing. Licensing a brand name can transform a homogeneous product into a heterogeneous one, increasing unit sales and pricing power.

In addition to licensing names, you can license entire products. Often an individual firm, university, or government agency has developed a worthwhile product that they do not have the resources or inclination to produce or sell. Sometimes larger firms have developed proprietary products with markets too small or inappropriate for their organization. Sometimes overseas firms wish to license an American business to manufacture and sell their proprietary products in the U.S. market. To learn of these opportunities, contact Clark Boardman Company Ltd. in New York City, your local office of the U.S. Commerce Department, or the U.S. Chamber of Commerce in Washington. Clark Boardman publishes licensing, trademark, and patent periodicals, and the other two organizations maintain some lists of available product licenses.

Many products in the telecommunications, machine tool, computer, chemical, copying machine, photographic, textile, drug, and fragrance fields are made and sold under licenses from other firms. For example, many pharmaceutical start-ups—e.g., Elan Corp, plc; Medicis Pharmaceutical Corp.; or Forrest Laboratories, Inc.—resulted from the licensing of medications from other drug firms.

Adapting from a Related Market and from Overseas Markets

Often inexpensive new product or service ideas can be obtained from related or overseas markets. Women's tailored clothing came from the men's market. Men's fashion underwear came from the women's market; personal computers grew out of powerful industrial computers. In 2001 on-line banks created customized sites for university students and members of certain organizations. This idea was adapted from a related market, "affinity" credit cards.

See if markets related to those of interest to you offer products or services that, with appropriate changes, could satisfy an unfilled need in your market. Start by identifying previous new products or services that have been successfully adopted from other related markets. Often new product or service ideas can be inexpensively obtained from overseas markets. An American golf enthusiast noticed that English golfers wore shoes with rubber rather than metal spikes. The rubber spiked shoes were lighter weight than the metal, more comfortable, and did not make holes in the turf. The American golf enthusiast contracted to have a similar shoe produced in the United States, and then successfully sold this product to golf shops.

Keep abreast of overseas markets through trade journals and trips abroad. Look for new products or services offered overseas, which could satisfy unfilled needs in your domestic markets. For example, an Indian MBA student in Philadelphia started a tutoring service in New Delhi to help students pass their GMAT exams.

Reviving an Old Idea

Often products or services no longer in use provide the basis for a successful contemporary revival. In the 1950s and again in the 1980s miniskirts were revived from the twenties. In Chicago, a small concern called Western Onion successfully revived Western Union's singing telegram. Some computer adventure games revive and update the plots of classic children's adventure books. Multiplex movie theaters revived an idea from the late thirties. Consider which products or services no longer in use might provide appropriate new ideas for an item that could meet a need in today's market.

DETERMINING RETURN ON INVESTMENT

An entrepreneur can limit the risks associated with the development and introduction of new products or services by estimating return on investment. Before you commit dollars to developing and selling a new product or service, estimate the required investment and profit potential. If this is a start-up involve your accountant. If this is an early- or growth-stage business, involve your entire team: the sales manager, salespeople, channel partners, accountant or controller, and operations manager. If manufacturing or service is contracted out, include the appropriate strategic partners.

Return on investment should be estimated by product or service, but as the enterprise matures, the entrepreneur should perform a historical analysis of the actual results for all new products or services introduced. This might be called the *return on innovation*. Success ratios and survival rates must be measured and benchmarked over time along with the lifetime value of these new products or services. What can the entrepreneur learn from each new product's or service's success or failure to assist in the future? What can you learn from looking at new product or service launches as a group? As a group, was the risk worth the reward?

The new product or service investment includes:

- Labor, material, and services involved in product design, prototype, and product development
- Purchase of additional tooling and equipment for development and manufacturing
- Research, including market research, and concept testing
- Initial commercialization and prelaunch costs, including market testing, advertising, promotional, and selling expenses
- Increased investments in working capital, inventories, and accounts receivable

The profit dollars and margins for your new product or service are calculated by estimating the direct labor, material, and overhead costs required to produce or provide each unit, plus allocations for selling, administrative, and general expenses. You subtract the total of these unit costs from the unit selling price to arrive at a profit margin. Be sure you have included all appropriate costs, such as cost of capital, but have not double-counted by including them in both the investment and unit calculation. Chapter 7 on proper pricing contains more detailed information on calculating costs and profit margins.

Estimating the return on investment for a new service versus a new product contains the same elements but different weightings. A new service will most likely not require much tooling or equipment.

Similarly, profit margins for a new service will be more impacted by labor costs than by material costs.

Because so many unknowns exist in estimating new product or service margins and investments, run several scenarios with different assumptions. Run scenarios at various prices, labor, and material costs, and necessary investment in development and promotion. Weight each scenario based on probability of accuracy and choose a most likely outcome.

Once the entrepreneur or small-business manger has used these techniques to estimate required dollar investment and resulting unit profit dollars and margins, he or she forecasts unit sales for the next five years. These projected unit sales will produce certain dollars of profit margin, which can be measured as a percentage return on investment and show a unit sale break-even point for the new product or service and the time period required to recoup your original investment.

In projecting unit sales use all your available resources. Talk to prospective customers, present or prospective salespeople, and channel partners. Prepare three unit sales and resulting profit estimates using different assumptions for unit sales (best, worst, and most probable). Assign each a probability of success and create a most likely scenario. Unit sales assumptions might include competitive response, number of initial accounts, and reorder rates.

By using this type of financial analysis, you eliminate those great ideas in which the probable return does not justify the risk, development costs exceed any probable return, or unacceptable profit margins exist. By using this type of analysis, you can compare return on investment, profit margins, and payback periods between several potential new products or services.

This analysis allows you to set realistic goals for the new product or service against which to measure actual future results. It allows the entrepreneur to set hurdle rates that any new product or service must exceed. It allows you to eliminate products or services which meet a need in the marketplace but which no one has exploited because costs are too high, price too low, and margin dollars nonexistent.

For instance, the handheld compact disc scratch removal device firm mentioned earlier in the book used this analysis for its new product. The entrepreneur contacted designers, lawyers, accountants, toolmakers, subcontractors, prospective customers, sales representative organizations, and marketing consultants. Based on their input he determined the new product would require an investment of $1 million, including tools, dies, patents, designs, prototype and testing, market research, the promotion or advertising launch, and the initial inventory. Injection molding and assembling was contracted out, and independent sales representatives would sell the product to major music retailers.

The entrepreneur estimated the retail price at $40 with a $20 price to the retailers. The company's dollar pretax profit per unit was $4. These numbers all represented the most probable scenario, although others were presented.

The entrepreneur projected first-year sales of 100,000 units, second-year sales of 250,000, third year at 500,000, fourth year at 750,000, and fifth year at one million. This resulted in a five-year lifetime value of 2,600,000 units times a $4 pretax profit per unit, or a $10,400,000 lifetime pretax profit on an initial $1 million investment. In the second year at a unit volume of 250,000 the investment breaks even.

Consult your accountant for advice on calculating actual return on investment percentages. There are many different ground rules and alternatives for allocating fixed expenses, capital costs, and handling cash flow issues.

MARKET RESEARCH

The entrepreneur and small-business owner can reduce the risks associated with introducing new products or services by using simple, inexpensive market research. Just because you have a great idea which meets a need in the marketplace and produces an excellent potential return on investment does not guarantee that it will sell. Market research can help you determine a consumer or business product's or service's salability, and it can also produce important suggestions for improving it.

First, determine your objectives. What additional information do you require concerning salability of the new product or service, and what questions do you want answered to obtain that information? For example, do you require additional information on pricing, ingredients, advertising, features, and benefits, or after-sale service? Before you actually begin gathering data, you should read all related studies. They provide an excellent source of free material and can save you hours of work.

Next, decide whether on-line, mail, phone, or personal interviews are most appropriate for your market research project. Identify whom specifically you wish to interview: buyer, merchandise manager, CEO, men or women under 49, husbands or wives over 45, or high school students. Now you must correctly design a questionnaire to obtain the reliable information that you desire. Finally, you select a representative sample from the group you've identified for interviews, and you collect and interpret the data.

The entrepreneur or small-business owner can manage and perform the market research himself or herself, contract out part or all of it, or use a hybrid combination. I recommend you start by contacting some market research professionals with experience in the industry under consideration. Call their satisfied and not so satisfied clients for references. Market research is too important for on-the-job training. Eventually you will be able to manage these projects yourself. In any case, do some sample interviewing yourself to capture a sense of the market, but use professionals for most of the interviewing. Also, you can use experienced college and graduate students to do interviewing and assist in managing the project. The cost of market research represents an important part of the development budget. If you cannot afford the market research or market testing, do not engage in new product or service development, because you will have removed an important filter for success.

TEST MARKETING

Test marketing, like market research, can reduce the risks involved in introducing new products or services, since actual experience can best indicate both acceptance of the new item and possible problems. Once you have developed a new product or service which meets a need in the marketplace and which meets your internal standards for return on investment, pick limited representative markets to test customer response. Pick particular regions, states, cities, neighborhoods, industries, or customer groups for the tests. Your test markets should be free from unique or atypical conditions, such as a nonrepresentative climate, unusual income distribution, low freight charges, or domination by one company.

Resources and time permitting, it pays to perform both market research and market testing. Market research tells you what customers think about your new product or service; market testing tells you what they do about it. Potential customers' responses to market research can help you refine the product and strategy for market testing. If you must choose between market research and market testing, the latter is generally more critical.

Test marketing involves asking potential customers to try the new product or service; then, based on their response, altering features and/or marketing strategy. If the response is consistently negative, you abandon the project. If the response is positive, you incrementally increase distribution. Test marketing techniques are different for industrial or commercial products and consumer products.

For test marketing industrial or commercial new products or services the entrepreneur or small-business manager prepares a prototype or audiovisual presentation to show key accounts. The presentation might include PowerPoint, videotapes, or computer-simulated designs, which can be altered at the prospect's request. Your prospects may have ideas for improvement, they may reject the idea, or they may give you an order. If they reject the idea, move on to another test market. If this second test market also rejects the idea, consider changes which might make it acceptable, but also consider abandoning the project. You also may wish to test different prices or different product or service features to see which produce the best response.

If the new product or service is accepted, and you start writing orders, move on to several other test markets and repeat the process. If the response continues positive, offer it to the entire market. Keep inventories at cautious levels until demand becomes more established, and even then build inventories carefully. The cost of late deliveries is considerably less than the cost of unsold inventories. Initially, maintaining minimum inventories further reduces the risks of new product development. For a new service, utilize existing personnel until a positive sales trend develops, and then carefully add to your staff.

Several months after introducing the new product or service, call customers who have purchased it. If possible, question the person who bought the product, the purchasing agent, or doctor; and those who actually use the product, the quality engineer, manufacturing engineer, or secretary, concerning its actual performance. Were they satisfied? Did it live up to expectations? Could they suggest any improvements? In this way you can further refine the new item's benefits and quickly correct problems. Such follow-up after test marketing represents a continuation of the market research process.

Many prospects or customers, especially early adopters, leaders, and visionaries, will purchase and try new products or services. The key factors are were they satisfied and will they repurchase the product or service.

Test marketing of both industrial or commercial products and services and consumer products or service can be performed by the entrepreneur in a start-up, or the entrepreneur plus salespeople and channel partners in an early-stage firm, or contracted out to professionals. Whether you primarily use internal or external resources, do seek expert advice on the process and analysis from industry experts.

For consumer products, you generally test market through stores or direct mail. With samples, audiovisual presentations, and market research results, the entrepreneur visits key stores in the test markets. Try to select stores with sales personnel, display space, and advertising funds capable of emphasizing a new product. The stores may have ideas for improving the product, they may reject it, or they may agree to participate in the test and give you an order. A store may ask for return privileges if the new product does not sell, and you may have to accept this condition. If all the stores you approach in the test market reject the idea, move on to another test market. If all the stores you approach in the new test market also reject the idea, consider changes that might make the product acceptable, but also consider abandoning the project.

Let us assume that several stores agree to buy and test market the new product. You ship them the new product; advertise, promote, and merchandise it; and analyze the sell-through. What percentage, and how many units, of the new product were sold? If the consumer response is weak, you consider changes in product, features, packaging, and price which might increase the sell-through. You test market the product in different stores in different regions to see if the sell-through results remain consistent. You might try different prices, packaging, promotion, merchandising, advertising, and product features in different regions and compare sell-through results. If test marketing in different stores in different regions with variations in price, packaging, promotion, merchandising, advertising, and product features consistently results in weak sell-through, drop the new product.

This approach allows you to better control the risk of high inventories, and to measure sell-through on reorders. Remember, keep inventories at cautious levels until demand becomes more established, and then build inventories carefully. Sometimes consumers will try a new product but not reorder it. Sometimes consumers will buy any potential gift item in December, but not repurchase it the rest of the year. Sometimes nonrecurring factors over which you have no control, such as a snowstorm or a strike, will influence initial sell-through.

If possible, pack a postage-paid, return-addressed card with the new product. Ask the purchaser to return it in exchange for something of value, such as a small rebate. On the card, request information concerning the purchaser's name, address, age, sex, occupation, media exposure, store of purchase, reason for purchase, advertising response, product satisfaction, use, and suggestions for improvement. Such information proves helpful in further refining the new product, advertising, distribution, and marketing strategy. This technique represents a blending of market research with test marketing.

Some new consumer products and services can be inexpensively test marketed through direct-response advertising. For example, the entrepreneur might place an ad for a new home security system or maid service in a regional edition of the monthly AARP magazine, for new travel products or travel Web sites in the regional issue of the American Automobile Association magazine. Such ads include return coupons, Web site URLs, e-mail addresses, and telephone numbers for ordering. You can measure the salability by the number of orders or replies. A month after the product has been shipped, you can interview the purchaser concerning satisfaction, price, product features, appeal, problems, reorders, advertising media, and type of retail stores. Such an approach represents a hybrid between test marketing and market research.

Test marketing cannot be used in situations where competitors are likely to quickly duplicate your new products or service. In these situations, timing proves critical and test marketing would forewarn competitors, allowing them an opportunity to enter the market. By developing new products or services for niche markets, you reduce this risk, because smaller markets have less appeal for larger competitors, but you still face the risk of smaller competitors stealing your idea.

INEXPENSIVELY CREATING DEMAND

While it is always helpful if the customer or prospective customer has heard of an existing product or service and knows its selling points, for a new product or service to be successful, it is absolutely essential to presell it. The very essence of a new product or service means it is relatively unknown (unsought), and dictates the necessity for creating a demand. Many worthwhile new products which meet specific needs in the marketplace, which offer good return on investment possibilities, and which test market well, still fail for lack of preselling.

The entrepreneur or small-business owner who wishes to reduce the cost or risk of introducing a new product because of limited resources has a special set of problems. However, by selectively using and expanding on the techniques discussed in Chapter 6 , an entrepreneur, early- or growth-stage enterprise can inexpensively create substantial demand for new products or services. As explained in Chapter 6, you can inexpensively presell a new product or service through press releases and publicity, trade shows, permission e-mails, and so on, plus sharing the cost of trade and cooperative consumer advertising with suppliers and retailers.

PRODUCT OR SERVICE LIFE

The entrepreneur should keep in mind that new products or services, like living things, pass through stages: introduction, growth, maturity, saturation, and decline. Each stage requires a different marketing strategy and preparation for its successor stage.

Usually only one firm offers a new product or service in the introductory stage. Sales volume rises slowly, distribution is limited, and production costs and prices are high.

In the growth stage, competition begins to enter the market. Sales increase rapidly, distribution expands, and production costs and prices decline.

During the maturity stage, many competitors enter the market. Sales continue to increase, but not as rapidly as in the growth stage. Spare parts and service requirements become more critical. Due to increased competition prices decline dramatically and distribution expands further.

By the saturation stage, the most efficient producers have eliminated some of the competition. This now becomes a replacement business.

In the decline stage, total sales drop, because other substitute products or services have been developed. Prices and the number of firms decline further, and only the most efficient remain. Survivors tend to specialize in basic areas where prices have stabilized, and as a result, distribution contracts.

In developing, marketing, and evaluating new products or services, the entrepreneur must consider their lifetime value. We calculated this under return on investment. How much marginal revenue, pretax profit, and cash flow will a new product or service create over its lifetime from introduction to decline. Will it generate new customers or just replace present ones or cannibalize present products or services? The entrepreneur must set goals, measure actual results, and benchmark one product or service against another. The development and introduction of new products represents a continuous process.

ENTREPRENEURS' MAJOR MISTAKES OR WEAKNESSES IN DEVELOPING AND INTRODUCING NEW PRODUCTS AND SERVICES

- Developing new products or services that reflect the originator's ego rather than a need in the marketplace, a competitive weakness, or a legacy issue.
- Introducing new products or services with long sales cycles, short product lives, or no quantifiable differentiating features and benefits.
- Inventing new products or services rather than innovating by altering an existing product or service to meet an unfilled need in a specialized niche market.
- Not properly researching, estimating, and testing the proposed market.
- Not asking industry experts and consultants for advice.
- Not determining the return on investment before proceeding with the new product or service development.

- Overestimating the market size and underestimating the competitive response.

QUESTIONS AND EXERCISES

1. What are the advantages and disadvantages, risks versus rewards of new product or service development?
2. What are the best sources for new product or service ideas?
3. What are the barriers to entry into the market for your new product or service and what are the customer switching costs?
4. How will your firm keep larger competitors from capitalizing on a successful new product or service idea?
5. How will you create a demand for your new product or service?
6. Why do 80 percent of all new products or services fail? How can the entrepreneur reduce the risk of failure and improve the probability of success?
7. Prepare the selection criteria or plan for developing new products or services.

INDEX

ABOUT THE AUTHOR

Robert J. Calvin is President of Management Dimensions, Inc., an international consulting firm whose clients range from the Fortune 500 to the Inc. 100. As an Adjunct Professor of Entrepreneurship and Marketing at the University of Chicago Graduate School of Business, he teaches M.B.A. courses in New Enterprise and Small Business Management, and M.B.A. courses in Sales Force Management. Specializing both in buying old economy firms that were losing money then managing them back to profitability, and in starting successful new economy firms, he has applied his proven step-by-step formula for success to many businesses. As a teacher, consultant, entrepreneur, and executive, he combines strategy and theory with tactics and implementation. Over the past twenty years he has written numerous books, including *Managing Sales for Business Growth*, *Profitable Sales Management*, and *Marketing for Growing Businesses*. He is also the author of the McGraw-Hill Executive MBA Series mainstay *Sales Management*, winner of the Soundview Award as one of the thirty best business books of 2000. He holds a B.A. from Wesleyan University and an M.B.A. from Columbia University. He sits on the advisory boards and is a director of numerous start-ups and established small businesses.